D1881295

Status of Indian Women

STATUS OF INDIAN WOMEN

Dr. Saraswati Mishra

GYAN PUBLISHING HOUSE
New Delhi-110002

STATUS OF INDIAN WOMEN
[*Women*]

Rs. 690

ISBN: 81-212-0789-4

© SARASWATI MISHRA

All rights reserved. No part of this book may be reproduced in any manner without written permission.

Published in 2002 in India by
Gyan Publishing House
5, Ansari Road
New Delhi 110 002
Phones: 3261060, 3282060, Fax: 3285914
e-mail: gyanbook@del2.vsnl.net.in
visit our website at: http://www.gyanbooks.com

Laser Typeset at Alphabet, Delhi
Printed at Chawla Offset Printers, Delhi 110 052

Contents

PART II: VARIOUS DIMENSIONS OF STATUS OF INDIAN WOMEN IN MODERN PERIOD

Preface

In Indian society, women's status has always remained high theoretically. Powers of God have been described in women's forms as Laxmi, Saraswati, Durga, etc. Thus, Woman has been considered a symbol of wealth, knowledge and strength. Wife has been called 'Ardhangini' (half part of body) and motherhood has also been given a great respect. Mother is the symbol of Nationality also, which gives us impression of women's status, higher than men's status. But the point of grief is this that, in spite of all this, women's status in India has always remained lower than men's status. Practically, although during various periods certain ups and downs in it were visible. From the archaeological remnants and Vedic literature we get indications of women's status in comparison to men's status being higher and same, respectively during pre-Vedic and Vedic periods. But from post-Vedic period its downward flow of gradual deterioration started and continued till the end of medieval period and the women quietly suffered throughout.

During the British regime in 19th and 20th Centuries, owing to the contacts with modern society, intellectual class of Indian society intensively realized the inhuman and injust fact of discrimination with women. Through social reform movements and social legislations, efforts were made to improve the status of women. Along with women's participation in freedom movement, women's movement also got started and consequently the condition changed. In independent India for more improvement of women's status, welfare policy was formulated and various programmes were chalked out. Indian Constitution guarantees full equality between the men and women. Government is very active in all the main directions, i.e., health, education, occupation, welfare, etc. and for achieving targets plenty of money and human energy are being spent. Owing to all these efforts, women's status has improved to some extent, this fact can not be denied. But even after passing such a long period since independence, due to various reasons expected targets could not be achieved.

United Nations Organizations first declared 1975 as International Women's Year and later on declared the period, 1975-1985, as women's decade, during which in the whole world welfare of women was discussed, policies were changed, new programmes were adopted and women study centres were established.

In India also, along with more efforts in the direction of women's welfare, the need was felt that for the knowledge of various realities regarding women's present status, on the one hand, the research work should be encouraged, while on the other, for giving information about the facts to the whole society as well as for preparing good workers to improve women's status in future, at each level of education, somewhere in the course, more or less, subjects regarding women's status, should be included. It was thought that awakening of consciousness and creation of awareness in younger generation through education, will certainly have its positive impact on women's status. Apart from this, teachers contact with the active social workers and other people of the field, was also considered desirable so that they have correct knowledge about the state of affairs and the gap between the theory and practice could be bridged. For the fulfillment of all these objects, in education policy, by drafting the courses regarding women's status, in short form at lower level and in detailed form at higher level, scheme was prepared to impart knowledge to the students. University Grant Commission encouraged various universities to establish women study centres' by giving special grant for the purpose, and for those centres three dimensional activities, that is, teaching, research and field work on women's issues, were determined. Due to liberal financial assistance to the research work regarding women by the institutions like Indian Council of Social Science Research and University Grant Commission, lot of research work on this issue has been done after

1975 and it got published also. This fact is also manifested from the bibliography given in the end of present book. But for the study of subject at different levels of education, acute shortage of books has always been felt. Due to this reason in spite of having independent paper on the subject at postgraduate level as well as the interest of teachers and students, both the sections want to escape from the trouble of searching reading material here and there. Therefore, introduction as well as the selection of this paper is avoided in the educational institutions. Consequently the Government's objective of imparting knowledge to the students could not be achieved properly, while it is very much needed in the interest of women particularly and in the interest of whole society generally.

Since long, interested and connected teachers and students have been asking, rather insisting the author to write a book on this subject. She herself is associated with the teaching and research on this subject while working in the department of sociology, Rani Durgavati Vishwavidyalaya, Jabalpur, M.P., and she has also faced the problem of shortage of general books on the subject. This need only motivated her to write a book and in spite of some limitations, she has tried her best to do justice with her writing work as more as possible.

Although the subject matter of this book has been prepared mainly on the basis of the course of the paper entitled, 'Status of Indian Women', included in the syllabus of M.A. Previous in Sociology, in Rani Durgawati Vishwavidyalaya, it also covers the course of one unit from M.A. Final Paper named 'Indian Society and Culture' and one unit from M.Phil Paper called 'Indian Society: Structure, Problems and Change: At Graduate level also this book is useful for the course on this subject. Effort has been made to write the book in a very simple English language. Apart from this, some other relevant important issues have also been covered in this book. Special purpose of giving more references in the text of the book as well as the bibliography in the end of the book, is to provide information about other books on the subject to the researchers as well as to the students of graduate and postgraduate levels and thus facilitate them to read more literature. In all the

Indian Universities, this book will be useful for study and research. And due to its utility for cross cultural studies, this book will have its value in the international market. It is expected that this book will be liked by the intellectuals.

Lastly, the author expresses her hearty gratefulness to all those people, connected with the government, non-government, University and personal resources, from which she got assistance and facility in selecting the subject matter and writing work of this book.

Department of Sociology
Rani Durgavati Vishwavidyalaya
Jabalpur - 482001 (M.P.)

Saraswati Mishra

Part I

Status of Indian Women During Various Periods

One

Concept of Status and Introduction

As defined in the report of the National Committee on the Status of Women in India* (1974), status refers to a position in a social system or sub-system which is distinguishable from and at the same time related to other positions through its designated rights and obligations. The knowledge about the status of any section of the society may be obtained through its 'roles' patterns and their importance as well as the consequently achieved privileges and symbols of specific respect (Vohra and Sen, 1985).

The concept of status is relative by nature. It is a comparative idea. Since each status position in a particular structure can be viewed in terms of superiority and inferiority, the notion of status involves comparison and grading. Therefore, in order to identify the status of any section of people, it is compared with the status of another related section of people by considering it as the reference group. Due to this reason only, the knowledge about the low, equal or high status of female section is obtained by its comparison with the status of male section of the population. The valuation of women's status, in one society during different periods, and in different societies in one period, can be done by adopting the comparative method only.

As Kumar (1982) has expressed, the concept of status is a very wide term which includes all the aspects of human life. By considering the following aspects of women's life, related with their status, it's clear, total and multi-dimensional picture can be imagined.

(i) Demographic Status

Under this dimension, the ratio of female population in comparison to male population, birth rate, death rate and the health condition, etc., are included.

---

* For further references, only the words 'National Committee' will be used.

(ii) Educational Status

The number of women in different levels and types of general as well as professional education, and the available opportunities to them, are discussed in this aspect.

(iii) Occupational Status

The number of women in different occupations, their working conditions, levels of work, job opportunities available to them, etc., are considered in this aspect.

(iv) Familial Status

Under this dimension the status of female members of the family is compared with it's male members. Her status is evaluated in terms of importance of her roles as daughter, daughter-in-law, wife, mother and housewife, and serious thought is given to the institution of marriage.

(v) Legal Status

In this aspect, the status, provided by the laws, to the women is discussed. The constitutional, legal and judicial protection, available to them and its usage in practice is considered.

(vi) Political Status

In this section, the women's rights of forming the Government and becoming its part themselves are considered. Available opportunity of franchise and its usage in practice are discussed.

(vii) Social Status

In this dimension, the females' mobility and freedom, outside the house is considered. Opportunities of interaction and interrelationship with outside people, specially the males, and its usage, free outside movements for various reasons, organization of women's association and friends society or group and participation in their activities, etc., are discussed.

(viii) Moral Status

Under this aspect, establishment of different moral standards for males and females, as well as the punishment for violating the bindings and its usage in the practice are described.

(ix) Religious Status

In this perspective, reading and reciting of various religious books, propaganda of religion through lectures and public worships, participation in religious sacrifice and oblation, opportunities of daily worship, prayer, religious singing, fasting and their usage in practice, etc., are discussed.

(x) Economic Status

Under this, women's rights in family properties, thought of women's personal income and wealth, economic freedom, etc., are considered.

(xi) Psychological Status

In this dimension, the women's awareness about their own interests, their thoughts and attitudes, towards various social changes and the degree of traditionality and modernity, etc., are considered and evaluated.

A woman, like any other person, occupies different positions at a point of time, performs different roles and enjoys or suffers to certain degrees due to attached advantages or disadvantages. Here the fact has to be kept in mind, as Desai and Patel (1985) have also expressed, that it is not possible to study the above mentioned aspects of status, by keeping them totally separate from each other, because they are interrelated and interdependent. Therefore, while considering them, the entry into one anothers' field cannot be checked completely.

Further, while considering the status of women in different historical periods, first of all, the status in combined and short form, in ancient medieval and modern period and afterwards separately in detail, all the aspects of status have been observed and evaluated in modern period. Along with this, various measures adopted for the improvement of their status have also been described. In the end, after considering their problems, certain suggestions have also been forwarded for their solutions.

Systematically written Indian History is available only after the 16th Century from the Mughal regime onwards. Before that, upto the period of 2000 BC, the sequence of events is speculated on the basis of events described in the Sanskrit literature of that period; and even before that, i.e., upto the period of 5000 B.C., the origin and growth of civilization and culture are speculated on the basis of Vedic rhymes, especially of Rigveda, to some extent, and to a great extent, on the basis of archaeological excavations of remains of things and ruins of the period of Indus Valley Civilization particularly. As Stowell and Mason (1970) have expressed, the script of that period could not be understood properly even now.

There is a great difference of opinion among the scholars regarding the sequence and period of historical events, therefore, the variety of divisions of time into various periods and their titles, may be observed in the literature. For the study of the status of Indian women, the sequence of events is more important and the certainty of time has the secondary place, as Desai (1977: 10) has also stated while expressing her views on this subject. But still, for the facility of a systematic study, the sequence of events have been adjusted in various periods of time. Significantly related with this subject, last 5000 years have been divided into three main periods, i.e., ancient period, medieval period and modern period. Further, these main periods have been sub-divided according to the requirement.[1]

In the status of Indian women, upward and downward trends of mobility could always be observed on the practical level, although on the theoretical level it has always been claimed that the place and honour of women is just the same, as of men — neither less, nor more. According to Hindu ideals wives are called the 'Ardhangini' (half body) of the husbands. Motherhood is respected so much in the Hindu society, that even the country is called the mother India and thus the feeling of devotion and respect is expressed towards it. The powers of God have been described in the original forms of Goddess Laxmi, Saraswati and Durga : In this manner the woman in our country has been considered as the symbol of nationality, wealth, knowledge and power. But these ideals, in the life of a common Indian Woman, have failed miserably in providing her status equal to man, during every period, as Mukherjee (1983: 408) has also expressed, and we will discuss later on.

Social, economic and political conditions of the society greatly affect the attitudes and behaviours of the people. Therefore, before discussing the status of woman in every period, the prevailing conditions and special characteristics of the social situation, in the society at that time, have been described.

Reference

1. Out of three periods, the ancient period has been sub-divided on the basis of its division done in the book entitled *Cultural Heritage of India*, published by the Institute of Culture, Calcutta.

Two

Status of Women in Ancient Period (B.C. 3000 - 1200 A.D.)

I. Pre-Aryan Period (B.C. 3000 - B.C. 2000)

Contemporary Society

In this period we discuss about the totally mature Indus-valley civilization and the status of women before the arrival of Aryans in India. The obtained remains out of the excavations of 'Harappa' and 'Mohenjodaro' demonstrate the fact that the Indus valley civilization might have originated approximately at the time of 5000 B.C. and it was on the peak of development and progress during 3000 B.C. After the excavations in 1920 only, the archaeologists came to know about the fact that these cities were very rich and developed and they had commercial as well as cultural relationships with other developed countries. After the excavation, the roads fixed with 'Ookhali and Chakki' (devices and appliances used for polishing and grinding of the grains), solid houses made of bricks, jewellery, small sculpture and idols, instruments used in agriculture, utensils made out of clay, bullock carts, etc., have been obtained. In this way, we come to know that, in Indus valley, one ancient civilization got flourished which was developed by its Dravidian residents. This civilization, suddenly vanished approximately around 1500 B.C., this is the fact. Why and how it happened? There is a difference of opinion about it among scholars. Some of them believe that the extension of desert situated in neighbourhood barrened the land of that place whereas others are of the opinion that the regular floods have absorbed the land, while another group among them gives responsibility to the epidemics, earthquakes, erosion of the land and the change of climate, etc., for the destruction of this civilization. Totally different from this natural theory, the belief is, that the Indus-valley civilization was destroyed by the Aryan invaders around 1500 B.C. It is speculated that these Aryans had come to India from Central Asia, beyond the 'Himalayas' through north-west 'Khaiber' pass and in order to utilize Punjab-Sindh area for themselves, they overpowered its original Dravid residents and after being victorious driven them to South India, beyond Vindhyachala mountains. From the rhymes of 'Rig Veda" a detailed picture of the flourished civilization and culture, existing at the time of Aryans fighting with the South Indian black people, in the Indus valley, gets emerged (Mukerjee, 1959: 45-52).

Status of Women

Regarding the status of women in this period nothing can be said with certainty due to the absence of enough literature. But as it has been accepted, that, 'the more the society will civilize and culturize, the higher will be the status of women in it', on the basis of this statement as well as the higher status of south Indian women in comparison to north Indian women, at present, it can be guessed that during the period of prestigious and elevated Indus-valley civilization, the status of women also might have been high. Matriarchal family system, prevalent in Kerala also indicates towards the probability of existence of more or less same System during the period under discussion. Idols of 'mother Goddess' (nature and power) and the Seals or stamps obtained after excavations also demonstrate the higher status of women in that period as Mukerjee (1959) has expressed. The dress and jewellery of the males and females had a great resemblance. It seems that the women of that time were quite fond of decorating and making up their faces and bodies and experts in art of dancing. They used to participate, equally as males, in the social functions and other activities (Kundra, 1990 : 17).

The historical events after this period are guessed on the basis of descriptions available in different epics of Sanskrit literature. It is considered that 'Rig Veda' was written around 1500 B.C. There are 1017 Vedic rhymes (small little poems) in it. After that Sam Veda, Yajur Veda and Atharva Veda were written in due course of time respectively. The Vedas provide the directives regarding the proper lifestyle. Along with the poetic form of Vedic rhymes, the 'Vrihmanases' were added in the form of verses, in which the duties of Brahmins were prescribed. After that the 'Sutras' were added through which the laws and sacraments were specified. After Sutras, the 'Upanishads' were written in which the relationships between the soul and God (Atma and Parmatma) were explained. Then 'Aranyakas' got written in which instructions were given to the renunciators for leading a holy life and after this, the Puranas were written in which the holy traditions were described. Manu Samhita, Yagyavalkya Samhita and Kautilya's Arthashastra, etc., prescribed the codes of conduct and established the social system consequently. After this great epics of *Ramayans* and *Mahabharata* were written and *Geeta* showed the right path of life to the people. Later on, the Sanskrit dramas full of great adventure and romance were written. The citations described in the above mentioned literature provide us the knowledge about the events and characteristics of the Indian society during different periods, as Mishra (1987) has also stated.

II. Vedic Period (B.C. 2000 - B.C. 600)

Contemporary Society

The Rig Veda which was written around 1500 B.C. depicts the vague picture of the early Aryan Society. Through it, we come to know that Aryans had brought the concepts of God—Indra, Varun and Mitra along with them which got established gradually in the Hindu religion and spread all over India. It is thought that the race of Aryans was more civilized and cultured than the Dravidians. They used to tame cows and horses, went to other places in search of grazing fields. In India also later on, they got settled in the plains of river 'Ganga' for agricultural purposes. Therefore, the area from the Himalaya to Vindhyachal was called 'Aryavarta'. In the Vedic society of Aryans the 'Varna' System was existing in which at first three 'Varnas', i.e., Brahmin, Kshatriya and Vaisya were formed out of Aryans and later on the Dravidians were included in the fourth Varna, called Sudras. At this time, there was no stratification and differentiation among the Varnas, and no restriction in marriage, eating, drinking, etc., between any two Varnas, was in practice. So much so, that even the occupations could be changed. The warriors used to be selected. There was a great significance of the institution of family and it was functioning according to the patriarchal system. For the worship of God, there was no practice of constructing the temple, instead the Yagya institution of religious sacrifice and oblation performed in the open air, was in practice.

Status of Women

The Vedic period can be called the Golden Age regarding the status of Indian women, because in this period they enjoyed high status. From the study of Vedic literature, it is revealed, as Kapadia (1947: 82-86) has written, that, although due to the practice of patriarchal family system, the birth of a son was given more importance but still, daughters were given all the facilities equal to sons. There was no discrimination between the son and daughter regarding education. Prior to study of Vedas, girls also used to undergo the thread ceremony meant for purification of the body and soul of a person. Among the writers of rhymes of Rig Veda, there were about 20 women contributors. As Rao and Rao (1985) have also written, Uppla, Ghosha, Vishwavara, Gargi and Atreyi were the learned philosophers of this period only. There used to be one section of women called 'Brahma-Vadini' which used to remain involved in studies throughout the life (Altekar, 1962 : 13). The women were respected very much and they used to enjoy very high status inside as well as outside the home. Generally one man used to marry only one woman at a time, although in the case of kings and warriors, this custom was not being followed in a very strict form. During the early Vedic period specially, the women used to go for participation in conferences, and any religious sacrament, especially, the 'Yagya' could not be performed until and unless the wife accompanied the husband.

During the Vedic period, as Mukerjee (1959) has also pointed out, there was no restriction in the mobility of unmarried girls and their interaction with male members was also not banned. They used to move freely in the society and participate in the fates, festivals and functions. Marriage was considered a sacred bond. Although most of the marriages were arranged by parents, but still the girls were permitted to choose their own groom. There was the custom of 'Swayamwara' in royal families wherein a bride used to choose her husband from a galaxy of suitors. There was no Purdah (Veiling) system and the widows were permitted to marry again. In Atharva Veda, their life after remarriage has been called 'Punarbhu', means rebirth. In order to get a son, 'Niyog' that is, the temporary relationship with a man, was also possible. In the case of Polygamy, all the wives were kept with honour as Mukerjee (1983: 408) has also reported.

Regarding the property, nothing can be said with certainty, but still, citations about the custom of presenting gifts, by the husbands to their wives, are available in the literature in abundance. As Mukerjee (1936 : 73) has written and Desai (1977 : 41) has also quoted, Yaskacharya has confirmed the right of a brotherless daughter in the property of her father. According to Purva - Memansa, husband and wife, both used to be the owner of the property jointly. According to Rig Veda, wife makes the home (Madhavananda and Majumdar, 1953: 126) and according to Mahabharata, wifeless home is like a forest (Mukerjee, 1986 : 409).

In sum, it can be said that during the Vedic period, under the patriarchal social structure, the women's respectful place in the society was secured. Above mentioned Vedic traditions, in their original forms, continued till the time when Buddhism got originated and challenged them (Desai, 1977).

III. The Age of Revolt (B.C. 600 - 300 A.D.)

Contemporary Society

During this period, such a change took place in the society, due to which conditions of upheaval and turmoil got created which ultimately directed the society to move further towards rigidity and stability. In the beginning of this period, Bráhmins established themselves at the highest position in the society. At this time only, he Sudra Varna was kept at the lowest position in the stratification system and the duty of serving the rest of the Varnas of Varna system was determined for Sudras. The usage of the word, 'Anarya' also increased, Kshatriyas were not prepared to accept themselves in the position lower than Brahmins due to which conflicts started between these two Varnas. In this period, class differences increased. Marriages among the different Varnas got stopped, their separate occupations were determined and these systems were observed and controlled very strictly. The knowledge about the household affairs and social life, which is obtained from Griha Sutras; demonstrates the fact that, the higher status of women. of the Vedic period could not remain stabilized for a longer time and gradual downfall in it, kept on taking place in due course of time.

At this time, around 530 B.C. due to protest against Brahmanism, Buddhism and Jainism got originated, in which truth, non-violence and purity of thought, etc., were stressed and various sacraments, rituals and idol worshipping, etc., were opposed. In both the religions, Kshatriyas have been declared greater than Brahmins. At this time political power was in the hands of Kshatriyas and they started giving less respect to the Brahmins. After 200 years of Gautam Buddha, in 326 B.C. 'Alexander the Great' defeated King Pourav in war at the bank of Jhelum. With the victory of foreign power the strength of Kshatriyas got weakened. At this point of time, a Brahmin called Kautilya helped Chandra Gupta Maurya of Sudra Varna, consequently the last ruler of Nanda Vansh called Dhana Nand got killed, and the Maurya dynasty got established. In his Arthashastra Kautilya has forwarded directives in detail, regarding the social system along with the political and economic systems. For some time the respect of Brahmins was, increased but upto the regime of 'Ashok the Great', the grandson of Chandra Gupta Maurya, the discrimination between the Brahmins and Sudras got gradually lessened and in the end, after the Kalinga Victory, Ashok accepted the Buddhism.

After this, last ruler of Maurya dynasty, named Brahadrath got killed by his Brahmin Commander-in-Chief named Pushyamitra Sunga who occupied the throne himself. In this way for the first time in 184 B.C. the Brahmin became the King. He performed the 'Ashwamedh Yagya' and destroyed the Buddhism religion. At this time 'Manav Dharma Shastra', i.e., the *Manusmriti* was written and propagated. Due to its political approval the people accepted its codes of conduct and legislation. This Dharma Shastra goes very far in the favour of Brahmins and males and against the Sudras and females. By this time, the caste system had established which means the Varnas were being sub-divided into various groups. After this Brahmins of Kanva Vansh were the rulers and continued for 157 years as the rulers of North India. Then Andhra Kushan tribes came from Central Asia and ruled the north-west province for some time. But after that the honour of Brahmins enhanced to a great extent in Central India and in South India also Brahmin rulership was going on for quite some time.

Status of Women

As far as the status of women is concerned, during this period it kept on decreasing continuously in the society of the followers of Hindu religion. In Bouddh and Jain religion of course, the doors of religion got opened as Desai and Krishna Raj (1987) have mentioned. They got the right of becoming 'Bouddh Bhikshuni' and 'Jain Sadhvi', but still, their status was considered lower than 'Bouddh Bhikshu' and 'Jain Sadhak' respectively. Therefore, as Desai (1977 : 19) has stated, it can be concluded that, in these religions also, status of women was not equal to men, although it was better than Brahminism.

Kauttilya's *Arthashastra* and *Manav Dharam Shashtra* present detailed accounts of the Social system prevailing at this time. By this time, the Hindu sages had determined the 'sacrament system' under which, the status of other class of people was considered low, and was thus not permitted to perform the sacraments. For women, but for the marriage, recitation of Vedic hymns was prohibited. Due to the absence of thread ceremony they became deprived of the study and knowledge of Vedas. Nowhere in Kautiliya's *Arthashastra* and *Manu Samhita*, the education for women has been cited. In this period, the foundation of women's life long subordination to the men, with the social and legal prescriptives, was prepared. In marriage the custom of daughter's donation (Kanya-daan) to the bridegroom selected by her father came into practice. By giving religious sanction to the marriage, the age of marriage of the girl was fixed before the appearance of physical maturity (12-13 years). In the Manu code, wife's faithfulness to her husband, i.e., 'Pativrata Dharma' was greatly emphasized (Desai, 1977 : 17) and 'widow's marriage' and Niyog custom were permitted only in some specific conditions (Mukerjee, 1985 : 425). Although there is no citation about the 'sati' custom in either Kautilya's *Arthashastra* or *Manusamhita*, but still from some citations of *Ramayana* and *Mahabharata* it is known that this custom had started in this period. Kautilya had also permitted widow for remarriage only in specific conditions whereas the remarriage of a widower was declared compulsory. In this way, the double standard of morality got established in the society in this period.

Regarding the property, Kautilya has mentioned that the women will have the right of 'Stri-dhan' only which she will get from brother, mother, father and husband at the time of marriage as gifts. Pure widow had right on her husband's property in special circumstances but in case of remarriage she had to return the basic amount of wealth along with the interest. In specific conditions only the divorce was permitted (Mukerjee, 1985: 434-35). Their mobility, achieved during the Vedic period was controlled. They were not permitted to go alone out of the house and they were given responsibility of looking after only the household affairs within the four walls of the house. The custom of 'Pardah' came into practice during the period of *Ramayana*. About the character of women it was said that, they are emotional, foolish and impulsive, they want to attract men therefore, exercise of control over them is necessary. It is thus concluded that during this period the status of women lowered down to a great extent in comparison of Vedic period.

IV. The Puranic Age (A.D. 300 A.D. - 1200 A.D.)

Contemporary Society

In the Indian history, Gupta imperialism, flourished during this period, is specifically remarkable. At this time only the form of modern Hindu religion got determined. In order to give recognition to the Brahmins again, the Puranas were written, it is said because Bouddh and Jain religions had given challenge to the Hindu religion (Hazre, 1940: 213). Therefore, the stability came in the social pattern and for its continuity the efforts were made. Therefore, again Varnashram dharam, significance of Vedas and implementation of moral laws were emphasized and due to definite relationship among various castes, the society became rigid. Brahminism became the caste religion in India. After that this religion never accepted any non-Indian impact on it and gradually developed as the prototype of Indian nationality. Chandra Gupta could rule Pataliputra without any hurdles only after he accepted the role of a carrier of the flag of Brahminism and subordination of Brahmins. Because Vedism was unsuccessful in defeating the Buddhism, it was being left behind by and by and new sects got created around various Gods. Due to differences among various sects many new branches of religion got generated and the 'Smritis' became the legislation. At this time *Yagyavalkya Smriti* replaced the *Manu Smriti*. The heroes of great epics, Rama and Krishna were regarded as incarnations of God. In place of only one Param Brahma Parmeshwar, of the Vedic period, the powerful tri-idol of 'Brahma-Vishnu-Mahesh' got established. The significance of Brahmins was excessively propagated and they were given title of God. During the Vardhan regime also they got great respect. Due to the fear of damage caused by their anger and curse they were given too much importance. In eighth century 'Adiguru Shankaracharya' propagated again the Vedism and the Sanathan Dharam and in all the four directions of the country established the four dhams for pilgrimage.

During this time only, the Islam religion entered in India. In 712 A.D. a commander-in-chief named Muhammad-Bin-Kasim who had came from Arab, established his rulership after the Victory on Sindh Province and the conversion of Hindus into Muslims got started. After 300 years of this event, Mahmood Gazni and Muhammad Gori of Turkey attacked India 24 and 17 times respectively. They looted the wealth and took it away to their country.

Status of Women

In this period the feeling of slavery increased in the status of women and, obedience and tolerance were considered the essential virtues of women. A woman achieves the same benefits by serving her husband, considering him as God, which a man achieves by the devotion of God. The religious life of a woman got limited to the observation of some fasts. They could listen to only the Puranas, but not the Vedas. By 1000 A.D., the marriages started taking place even before 10 years of age, therefore, there was no use of asking about their desire, in selection of husband. In Puranas, Grahasthashram was given a great importance and in any situation marriage was considered compulsory for women, and the widow remarriage was banned completely. The custom of Sati came into usage with great speed. In the beginning it was considered as the alternative but later on, among the Kshatriya women Sati and Jauhar became a common custom. By Jauhar through own will and others pressure, both the implementation of this custom of self-sacrifice, deteriorated the status of women to a great extent. A very strict attitude and consequently the keen control was exercised regarding their mobility. About the property, in Yagyavalkya Samhita some rights were given to the women. The gifts, acquired at the time of husbands second marriage, were also declared 'Stridhan' and full rights of spending it were given to the women concerned. In 'Vishnu Puran' also, the pure widow, in the situation of having no son, was declared the first successor of her husband's property. Mishra (1987) has also expressed these type of thoughts.

Three

Status of Women during the Medieval Period (A.D. 1200 - A.D. 1757)

Medieval Period (A.D. 1200 - A.D. 1757)

Contemporary Society

By this time, Muslim invaders had established their rulership in India, in order to propagate their religion as well as for economic benefits. In 1206, with the victory of Shahabuddin Gori over Prithvi Raj Chauhan, the Political power of Kashatriyas got finished. In 14th Century Alauddin Khilji attacked south India and established his rulership and in 16th Century Muslims of Mughal tribe established their rulership which went on for very long time. On the other side, caste system had been established properly in the Hindu society. Due to rituals, sacraments, idol-worship, etc., the Brahmins had established themselves on the highest position again. They declared themselves greatest of all and their misbehaviour with Sudras reached the maximum limit. Being fed up with their atrocity and cruelty, the lower caste people started accepting the Islam religion. In order to save Hindu religion from Islam religion, dependence upon purity based fundamentalism became essential and consequently Hindu contact with Muslims was prohibited by declaring them as 'Mlechchha' and the people having contacts with them were socially discarded. For their self-defence Brahmins had to safeguard the Hindu religion. Consequently, the progress of society got stopped, it became static and got tightened by condemnable customs. At this juncture only in medieval period the 'Bhakti' movement started. For checking the lower class of people from becoming Muslims this was the only remedy that the Hindu society should be made democratic, the authority of Brahmins should be hammered and by declaring the human equality struggle should be initiated. In all over the country, in

12th Century, 'Bhakti' Movement initiated by Ramanujacharya got spread gradually (Shukla: 1986: 76). Many branches of 'Sagun Bhakti' came into existence under the leadership of great religious preachers like Ramanuja, Madhav, Nimbark, Chaitanya, and many saints like Ramananda, Kabir, Nanak, Tulsi, Meera, Narsingh, Aeknath, Gyandev, Namdev, Tukaram, Ravidas, Ramdas, Charandas, etc. Being 'humanism' the characteristic of these Bhakti movements, their impact was more on the lower castes. They adopted the method of 'Bhakti' to achieve the God because the methods of knowledge and 'Karma' were the rights of higher castes called 'Dwiz' varnas. Religious books were written in regional languages because lower Varna had no right to study Sanskrit. The leadership of these movements got emerged mostly from the lower Varna only (Prasad, 1968: 568). Social reform movement started by Guru Nanak in 15th Century could not influence Hindus much, as it got converted into the show of Army power for the wars against Muslim rulers, due to their lack of foresightedness. Due to the long period of Mughal regime, social system prescribed in Muslim religion and the customs and traditions of Muslim society had their impact on Hindus which was inevitable and natural.

Status of Women

In this period, after the establishment of Mughal imperialism, the status of women became much more pitiable. In order to save Hindu religion, maintain purity of blood and protect chastity of women, the Brahmins made the rules regarding the women much more rigid. Education of girls was almost finished, Purdah system got much more encouraged and the age of girl's marriage lowered down upto four years. The number of unseen and unmatched marriages increased. Widow remarriage stopped completely and custom of Sati reached its peak. They were made subordinate under men from birth to death and after snatching all their rights and freedom the 'house hold' was made the only centre of their activities and hopes. She became the maid servant and the thing of consumption for her husband who got the right of exercising atrocities on her. Regarding the property, surely some improvements were made in this period. The widow and brotherless daughter started having some rights of succession respectively on the property of her husband and father. But the woman could only consume it, neither could sell it nor could present it, so that it could be preserved for the next successor.

Bhakti movement of medieval period influenced the status of women also. Ideals of humanity and equality encouraged the women also to adopt the 'Bhakti Marg' for achieving the God, the ultimate object of life, consequently, many women saints also became famous as the religious leaders, out of whom Meera Bai, Jana Bai and Mukta Bai are specifically mentionable. The women of higher classes also started worshipping Rama and Krishna who were considered the incarnations of God. Among them worship and prayer of Shiva and Durga also became quite popular. But due to the influence of polygamy and Purdah customs of Muslim society on the one hand, and owing to the control of ideals of fundamentalism of Hindu society, on the other, many difficulties got created in the social and familial life of Indian women and this period proved to be the darkest period for them. Sati custom got started among Brahmins also and the status of widows got worsened to a great extent. In this way, the little efforts of Bhakti movement for improving the status of women could not leave any permanent impact on it and various social laws, such as patriarchal family, Kulin Vivah, ideal of donating daughter to the bridegroom, marriage in the same caste, importance of son in the worship of ancestors, right of religious study to only sons through thread ceremony, double standard of morality through wife's faithfulness and chastity, i.e., Pativrata Dharm, various restrictions and unattractive attire of widow, custom of sati, etc., were being observed with great rigidity in Hindu society, and the status of Indian women was deteriorating gradually. Ultimately she totally became the slave of man and got imprisoned inside the four walls of the house. This situation continued till the establishment of British regime in India.

Four

Status of Women in Modern Period (After 1757 A.D.)

I. Period of British Rulership: (A.D. 1757 - A.D. 1947)

Contemporary Society

Although Indian Society started coming in contact with western society along with the arrival or Portuguese sailor named Vasco-di-Gama in Calicut in the end of 15th Century, but after Portuguese, Dutch and French people, when Britishers started coming from 17th century, the contact with foreigners increased. By this time the Mughal imperials had been shattered. East India Company had come to India only for trading purposes, but later on by taking the advantage of deteriorating social conditions of the country, established the rulership in the whole country. The Company achieved this target in parts. In 1757, the war of Plassey in Bengal was the beginning of this process and in 1849 after obtaining the rulership in Punjab, full authority on the princely states alos, till 1858, was its end (Stowell and Masson, 1970 : 268-278). Pleasure seeking incapable Muslim rulers did not make any effort for the progress and development of the country and the ancient social and economic structure continued to remain in existence. But during the British Period, economic and cultural powers, attached with it gave a new form to the society. By this time in England industrial and modern society had already established, and in social, economic and political fields, new revolutionary changes were coming quite often which had already decided the direction of development in India. Here also materialism and individualism got encouraged and importance of rights acquired by birth and religion, got lessened. From 1850 in India also the process of urbanization and modernization started along with industrialization. In order to run the new economic system and central administrative technique in a systematic way, on the one hand, means of transportation and communication such as railway, post and telegraph services, telephone system, etc., were developed, extended and used by the Government, and on the other, in order to get the employees, a network of the formal educational institutions was laid down in the whole country (Desai, 1977: 48).

During this time only, in India, Raja Ram Mohun Roy, Dayanand Saraswati, Swami Vivekanand and other learned people started social reform movements, in which mainly religious rituals, idol worshipping, caste discrimination and lower status of women, etc., were opposed. At this time, for preventing atrocities on women, the British Government, inspired by the democratic civilization and culture and the values of equality and liberty, passed the social legislation regarding the custom of "Sati', child marriage, widow remarriage, right on husband's property, etc., and women also got awakened (Ghurye, 1947: 106-107).

Although in 1857 only, the queen of Jhansi, named Laxmi Bai had sacrificed her life for the freedom of Country and Indian soldiers had also attempted the revolution, but in 1885, along with the establishment of Indian National Congress, a movement for removing the British Administration and achieving freedom, was initiated in a systematic way. In 20th century, during the First World War when Gandhiji took over the leadership of movement, he included the women also in it. After this, on one hand the women formed their organizations to safeguard their interests, and on the other, they demanded the right of franchise in the political field. In 1930, the women belonging to higher class of society got limited political rights. In the freedom movement, some liberal and sympathetic Muslim leaders cooperated with the Hindus from time to time in between, but conservative fundamentalist Muslim leaders kept on demanding the separate electorates and when they did not succeed in achieving the object, they started demanding the separate country after visualizing the country's freedom essentially in near future. Gandhiji made every attempt to check the division of country but due to British rulers' sympathy with Muslims, in the end, along with the freedom, the country got divided into two parts named Hindustan and Pakistan.

Status of Women

During the British regime every possible effort was made to enhance the status of women and with the consequence their various bonds got loosened. Due to social reform movement of 19th century, awareness regarding the freedom of women came in the public mind and many organisations were formed. Owing to this awareness only, in 20th century, women, along with taking part in national freedom movement started the women's movement for complete liberty and equality and formed independent organisations. They advanced further in the fields of education and occupation. British Government also passed the Prohibition of Sati Act, 1829: Widow Remarriage Act, 1856; Civil Marriage Act, 1872; Married Wife Property Act, 1874; Child Marriage Restraint Act, 1929 and Indian Government Act, 1935, etc., and thus, the effort was made to raise the status of women through social legislations. As a result of it the women got emancipated from the pain of economic, social familial and political disabilities. In this way, by giving equal opportunities to women in every aspect of life, the process of practicing the basic principle of respecting a woman as human being, got started with a great enthusiasm in this period (Kuppuswami, 1990 : 260).

Education got extended among women and they got the opportunities of earning money. Political movement accelerated the women's movement. From it, such conditions got created, due to which many social bonds and blind faiths got broken and women considered participation in the social activities, as their duty and right. They realized the importance of their lives, evaluated their capabilities, proceeded further, and got involved in the struggle of safeguarding their own interests. By taking education, they look careers for economic independence and gave less importance to marriage. As a result, along with the increasing age of marriage, parents gave importance to the desire of the daughter in the selection of husband for her. Purdah custom lessened, situation of widows improved and wife got right on her husband's property. Processes of industrialization, urbanization and modernization changed the familial structure. Joint families got broken and the nuclear families emerged in which comparatively better status of women became possible.

Therefore, we see that, great change came in the status of women and the progress in all the aspects of their life could be observed during the British period. But, the advantage of all these facilities was taken only by the urban women of upper class, that too in limited quantity. The social, economic, familial and political disabilities of common women, especially in rural areas, could not get lessened even up to independence of the country, in 1947; and the reason behind it was that the thousands years old deep roots of the traditional Indian social system, which can not be shaked easily and over night change in the fundamental form of society cannot be brought (Desai, 1977). But it so happened that by this time the people of the country started thinking of the issues regarding the women with a new perspective, which can be said to be an important achievement in itself.

II. After Independence (After A.D. 1947)

Contemporary Society

Along with the freedom from British Rulership in 1947, India got divided into two countries namely Hindustan and Pakistan. At the time of freedom itself the economic condition of the country had been quite bad which further worsened after its division. Dr. Ambedkar prepared the Constitution, Congress party formed the Government and Pandit Jawaharlal Nehru became the Prime Minister of India. Due to the ill feelings between Hindus and Muslims, lot of communal riots took place at this time. At this time only Gandhiji was murdered which created the environment of disorganization in the country but it was controlled by the leaders very carefully. The problem of national integration got created which was a challenge for the Government. A large number of refugees came from Pakistan and for their rehabilitation the Government had to spend a lot of money. The country was declared as the secular and welfare state. Through Indian Constitution, equal rights were given to every Indian citizen without any discrimination. By the directive principles of state policy, the state was clearly directed to make continuous efforts for the maximum welfare of the maximum number of people, and special efforts for the welfare of the backward and weaker sections of the society (Bhartiya Samvidhan, 1988: 3-15). Therefore, during the decade between 1950-1969, for the improvement of the condition of untouchables, labourers, peasants and women, sufficient legal provisions were made. Under the planned social change — while on the one hand, for raising the national income and standard of living by economic planning, through five-years plans, programmes of production and development were determined in the fields of agriculture and industry; and on the other, the country's specially increasing population, not matching with insufficient resources, was controlled by decreasing the birth rate through family planning measures. In order to raise the status of Scheduled Castes and Scheduled Tribes, under the reservation policy along with education and services, in political fields also the seats were reserved for them. In the field of social welfare, the central and state social welfare boards provided financial assistance and guidance to the voluntary organizations also consequently the situation was being improved to some extent but then due to territorial disputes, the wars, with China in 1962 and with Pakistan in 1965 took place. Again in 1971 India and Pakistan indulged in war. In 1975 the state of Emergency was declared in the country. The decade between 1975 to 1985 was declared as 'Women decade' by United Nations Organization and the women welfare was emphasized in our country also. In 1984 Prime Minister Indira Gandhi and in 1991 Prime Minister Rajeev Gandhi got assassinated. During all these events the problem of National Integration got created which was controlled by the Government carefully. After independence of country continuous efforts of extending educational facilities and providing more opportunities of employment are being made by the Government.

Status of Women

After independence, many efforts have been made to improve the status of women therefore their status in the modern society is quite good in comparison to traditional society. By the amendment of Child Marriage Restraint Act, 1929, in 1989 the girl's age of marriage has been raised to 18 years. From the Dowry Prohibition Act, 1961, although no benefit has been gained in practical form, but still, the custom of directly demanding the dowry is being lessened atleast among the educated and civilized families. In the same way, Hindu Marriage and Divorce Act, 1955 and Special Marriage Act, 1954 have permitted women to marry away from the restrictions of religion, caste and to break the bond of marriage, if required. Now polygamy is illegal and the widow remarriage is legally approved. Through Hindu Succession Act, 1956, Hindu women have got same property rights as men. In practice they have not been benefited much but due to this provision, atleast they can rightfully stay in their father's house. Medical Termination of Pregnancy Act, 1971 has helped them in keeping small family and leading a normal life after getting rid of the unmarried / unwanted motherhood. Owing to these legal provisions, status of women within the family has improved considerably.

In every field and level of education, now the women of middle class are also seen and in every field of occupation they are serving and earning as men for their livelihood. In the political field also their participation in large numbers can be observed. Their participation in social activities is also increasing because now they do not have to face very tight bonds regarding their movements outside the home and interactions with outside males. As a result, in them, social awareness, self-respect and desire to prove their capabilities as men is becoming stronger day by day. Joint families are breaking and their status in nuclear families is improving. 'Purdah' custom is disappearing and they are seen with respect to the society. The impacts of Western culture, industrialization, urbanization, modernization and the progress in means of transportation and communication, have given a great speed to their campaign regarding status. Thus, after the achievement of freedom the status of Indian women has improved sufficiently, as Srinivas (1978) has also concluded.

But, in spite of all this, as Desai (1977) has also stated first fact which cannot be denied is this, that, in most of the rural families and traditional urban families, the status of women has not improved much. In modern urban families also, leaving aside some exceptions, their status has improved undoubtedly, but the goal of achieving the status, equal to men, is very far even now and for the achievement of that goal very long journey has to be covered as Yadav (1985) has also found in her study. Second important and worth remembering fact regarding this issue as

Kuppuswami (1990) has mentioned, is that while considering the status of Hindu women generally we are concerned with the status of the women from upper and middle classes that too mainly of the urban society. The status of women of lower class had always been different from the status of upper and middle class women. Never so many restrictions were there for them in the social, moral, familial, marital and economic fields, and even now their status has not changed much. In the same way, in the rural areas, the women of lower middle class have been always working in their own agricultural fields along with men. Although they have been the victim of some other disabilities, but still, opportunities of going out of the house for various jobs were available to them. After this, the third fact, worth considering is this that while talking about the status of Indian women specifically during the ancient period, we are generally concerned with the Hindu women, due to their large number in the society[1].

Reference

1. According to the census report of 1981, there were 85% Hindu, 9.9% Muslim, 2.3% Christian, 1.7% Sikhs, 0.5% Jains, .05% Bouddh, .03% Parsees, .48% tribals and .03% non-tribals in the Indian population.

Five

Status of Women in Minor Religious Communities

Bouddh, Jain and Sikh

Since in India, the branches of Bouddh, Jain and Sikh religions got generated basically from Hindu religion, the lifestyles of small number of followers of these religions and the legal provisions for them are almost same as in the case of Hindus. The development of all these religions was initiated in protest of Hindu Brahminism, therefore, along with opposing the caste discrimination and religious rituals, established by Brahmins, these religions also provided women, the status higher than Hindu religion. While in Hindu religion various religious restrictions were posed, in Bouddh and Jain religions they got permission of becoming 'Bouddh Bhikhuni' and 'Jain Sadhvi' respectively.

In Sikh religion also all the 'Gurus' gave importance to women. Guru Nanak used to consider her respectable because she is the one who gives birth to men. Guru Govind Singh along with giving the title of 'Singh' to the men, gave women the title of 'Kaur' which means 'Soldier'. They were also given freedom and the call for going out of the houses and exhibiting courage and bravery like men, for struggles with Muslims. But in practice in these religions also, the status of women is not much different than the Hindu religion, and common woman under these faiths also, had been living in the subordination of man and leading her life according to his desires. In modern time due to constitutional provisions and legal legislations and opportunities of education and occupation, their status is certainly changing like Hindu women in the direction of excellence.

Christian

In the Indian Christian society due to the extension of western civilization and culture, working area of women is not limited upto the four walls of the house. Like men, they go out of the house, earn their livelihood and participate in the social activities. In this society there is no custom of 'Purdah' and no rigid wall exists between men and women. But since ancestors of maximum number of Indian Christians had accepted the Christianity by coming out of the lower class of Hindu society they keep on getting influenced even now from the provisions of Hindu traditions and social system. In Christian society normally the marriage of the girl is performed after the age of maturity and even after getting education and acquiring occupation, according to her desire. Getting divorce is also easily possible, although even the Indian Marriage and Divorce Act, 1869, (which is applicable for them) discriminates between the rights of husband and wife regarding it. In the case of bad character of the wife, divorce can be taken by the husband on this ground only but in the case of bad character of husband apart from it, the wife has to prove some other reason also, but after divorce Christian woman also gets the rights of maintenance. Regarding the succession there are a variety of laws applicable to the Christians of Goa, Kerala, Pondicherry and other places, but in all the laws women do not have exactly the same rights as men. Therefore, it can be said that in spite of having status higher than Hindu women, Christian women do not have status equal to men.

Parsee

In Parsee society, under the Parsee Marriage and Divorce Act, 1865, the cases of marriages of boys under 16 years and the girls under 14 years of age cannot be brought in any court for decision, it means such child marriage are not considered as marriages by law. In Parsee Marriage and Divorce Act, 1936, apart from the common bases, the wife can also seek divorce in the situation when her husband wants her to persue the profession of Prostitution. After divorce she has the right of maintenance. Most of the Parsee women do not earn themselves and remain dependent on men. Regarding the succession, Parsee daughters get same amount of mother's property as sons get but in the case of father's property they get less than their brothers. Due to this type of discrimination we can say that the status of Parsee woman also is lower than Parsee man.

Muslim

The Indian Muslim society being the largest minor community, forms a considerable part of the country's population. As far as the status of Muslim women is concerned, under Islam, in the traditional form, they have got quite satisfactory rights in comparison to Hindu women. According to Muslim law, generally the girls marriage should be performed only after the age of 15 years which means child marriage has never been accepted in Muslim society. According to Islam, the contract of 'Nikah' is not complete till the girl does not give her consent. Regarding divorce, Muslim women have got some rights in this sense that 'Khula' and 'Mubarat' are the two such social methods of divorce out of which, in first one, on the basis of wife's desire, and in the second one, on the basis of mutual consent between the husband and wife, divorce is possible. For the marriage of Muslim girl, the offer comes from the boy's side and at the time of marriage the husband gives some monetary amount to the wife in the form of 'Mehar'. In this way, due to absence of the custom of dowry, required to be paid by the parents, girls are not considered as burdens in the Muslim families. Muslim women do not have the right on property equal to men. Although the mother, wife and daughter have the right on the property of son, husband and father but they get half the amount of it in comparison to men. Only upto three months after divorce they have the maintenance right and that too when the wife remains within the approach of husband and obeys him.

As far as the polygamy, custom of veiling, rights of getting education and acquiring occupation and rights of social interaction and relationships are concerned, the status of Hindu women and Muslim women has almost remained the same. In the modern period the status of Hindu women in all the above mentioned fields is changing faster than the status of Muslim women which is changing slowly. Muslim women due to lack of education, excessive 'Purdah' custom, etc., have not been able to use their rights in practical form. The advantages of constitutional securities of free India, has been taken only by women of very few economically well-off-families in the form of exceptions. Normally they are leading the life, imprisoned within four walls of house and due to religious sacraments their status is very low.

In this way we can conclude that in all the religious communities of India the status of women is lower than men in the practical level, although in theoretical level, it has been considered same as Vohra and Sen (1955) have expressed through their statement.

Part II

Various Dimensions of Status of Indian Women in Modern Period

Six

Demographic Status

Some demographic traits of Indian female population as, their ratio in population, death rate, age of marriage, reproductivity, migration, health condition, etc., demonstrate their lower status in the society. As National Committee (1974) has reported, although there are some improvements in few fields, available evidences show that even now inequality between the status of men and women exists in India.

Sex Ratio

From the population perspective, India is the second largest country in the world. But, figures of various census reports while on the one hand show the continuous fast growth in total population, on the other, they clarify continuous downfall in the number of women in comparison to men in the population. The explanation of reasons of decreasing number of women in population lies in the neglection of women. The Patriarchal and classified society of India has challenged the life of women, as Desai and Patel (1985) have also expressed. In the census reports of 1931 itself special attention was paid towards the adverse sex ratio of women. Mitra (1979) has forwarded even warning that if this situation continues then it will create a serious problem for Indian society. Mourya (1988), after observation of various census reports, has found out that from the beginning of 20th Century, the continuously decreasing ratio of women per 1000 men in the population, is also becoming an issue of speculation and research along with the issue of worry. Table 6.1 shows the male-female ratio in the country's population in 20th Century. (1901-1991) .

TABLE 6.1
POPULATION GROWTH AND SEX RATIO (IN MILLIONS) IN INDIA (1901-1991)

Census Year	*Total Population (in millions)*	*Male Population (in millions)*	*Female Population (in millions)*	*Sex Ratio women per 1000 men*
1901	233.40	120.79	117.36	972
1911	252.09	128.37	123.71	964
1921	251.32	128.55	122.77	955
1931	278.98	142.93	135.79	950
1941	318.66	163.69	154.69	945
1951	361.09	185.53	175.56	946
1961	439.23	226.29	212.94	941
1971	548.16	284.05	264.11	930
1981	685.18	254.40	330.79	933
1991	844.32	437.80	406.51	929

Source: Various census reports and Mourya (1985).

As Table 6.1 shows, between 1901 and 1971 women's sex ratio has been continuously falling. Between 1973 and 1981 it did rise little, i.e., from 930 to 933, and this too, as it is said (Desai and Krishna Raj, 1987) has occurred due to different methods of data collection, and not because of improvement of women's health conditions. This fact is proved from the census report of 1991, in which the women's ratio has fallen again, from 933 in 1981 to 929 in 1991. In all the religious groups, urban and rural areas women's sex ratio is adverse. In the prosperous states like Punjab and Haryana it is quite low. According to 1981 census, it is 886 in Punjab and 877 in Haryana. Only Kerala is a state where women's sex ratio is in their favour which was 1032 in 1981 and it has increased to 1040 in 1991. Lowest sex ratio was noted in the Union Territory of Andman - Nicobar in 1981 which was 760 followed by the sex ratio of Union Territory of Chandigarh, 767. The fact regarding the existence of women's adverse sex ratio itself is a very powerful indicator of their lower standard in the society. In spite of continuously increasing public health, specifically women's health facilities during the last decades, women's decreasing sex ratio is really a subject to analysis and attention because to exercise check on this demographic tendency at the earliest is very much required.

Death Rate

Demographers have explained this permanent tendency of higher death rates among women of Indian population by giving its main reason as death during infancy and pregnancy. In 1931 census itself attention was drawn on this issue that the Women's death rate is more in the childhood and reproductive age groups. In 1964 per 1 lakh live births their were 252 deaths of pregnant mothers at the time of delivery in the country and 573 in rural areas. According to the all-India birth death figures of 1968-69, in the age group of 15 to 29 years, death of women, not only in rural areas but in the whole country is more than the other age groups. In 1979, death rate of mothers was 680 per 1 lakh birth in rural areas which came down to 500 in 1982, even that is quite high.

In this way from the beginning of 20th Century the women's death rate had been more than men's death rate and it is increasing continuously from then. Life expectation of women remains quite less till the age of 40 years because between 15 to 35 years women death rate remains maximum. After 50 years of age women's death rate becomes less than men's death rate. In India about 1 lakh women die every year due to abortion and birth of the child. The knowledge that this number is 100 times more than the developed countries, makes this fact much glaring. In 1975, out of total deaths, 1 per cent deaths were connected with the abortion and delivery and this percentage increased to 1.1 in 1979 and 1.2 in 1980. Many scholars have the opinion that speculated death rate is more than the noted death rate because figures are less than the reality. Recently in the researches done in the field of medical science, efforts have been made to find out the reasons of women's death in large numbers emphasizing over the reasons of death during the delivery period. It was found out that out of many reasons, abortion or miscarriage, that is, wastage of foetus is an area where there is no special decrease which has taken place during the many decades continuously. In 1972, the number of wastage of foetus was 30 per cent of the malnutritious pregnant mothers. The number of dead births was 11 per 1000 live births. The reason of death before delivery period is malnutrition of pregnant women and lack of iron and blood in their bodies. As Desai and Patel (1985) have written, other reasons for death of infants and women in confinement are frequent pregnancies and births of children due to which lack of protein causes malnutrition. Upto 20 per cent deaths are owing to the lack of blood caused by malnutrition and 16.44 per cent deaths are due to complexities and diseases of foetus, as Mitra (1979) has reported on the basis of conclusions of various studies.

Among the mothers who are of less than 20 years of age, infant death rate is more. In urban and rural areas both among small children, death rate of girls is higher than the death rate of boys. However, as compared to cities, in villages the death rate of girls increases much more in comparison to death rate of boys among educated/uneducated and rich/poor classes because in these classes advantages of health facilities are not taken for girls owing to their neglection and discrimination. In the undeveloped interior villages the practice of girl infanticide also goes on. Nature has made the woman strong. Nature has made it so unintentionally that the numbers of abortions of male foetus are more than female foetus and at the time of birth also chances of remaining alive are higher among the girls than the boys. This fact has been proved by many scientific studies. But after one month of birth social factors start operating. The culture characterized by the male dominance and priority forces to neglect the female infants and due to discrimination regarding the care, cleanliness, nutrition, medicine, etc., girls start dying more than the boys. In 1971, the number of deaths of male infants was 132 while the number of deaths of female infants was 148, per 1000 births. In 1979, the conditions improved to some extent, boys' death rate came down to 120 while the girls' death rate came down to 131, but again in 1981 the situation got deteriorated the boys death rate went up to 126 and the girls' death rate to 135, but the difference between the death rates of infants of both the sexes remained. In 1981, at the time of birth, life expectation for males was 50.5 while it was 49.0 for females. Forty years earlier, in 1941 life expectation of women was found less than men which was 32.90 for men and 31.37 for women. In 1971, the condition was quite improved, life expectation for males was 47.1 and for females it was 45.6 but the difference between the two continued. In 1981, also life expectation of males was more, i.e., 52.5 and life expectation of females was less, i.e., 52.1. In Kerala life expectation of women is highest and in Uttar Pradesh it is lowest in the country. In Kerala infant death rate is also lowest in the country. Due to late marriage, education and occupation of women. The status of women is highest in Kerala among all the states of India, while in Uttar Pradesh, the percentage of achievement of medical benefits to women is quite less as compared to men. They either take the traditional and free treatment or do not go for treatment at all. They are taken to the hospital in the last stage of disease due to which chances of their deaths increase, as Mitra (1979) has written while describing about the study of Dandekar (1957).

Age at Marriage and Marital Status

Average age of marriage for males which was 20.2 in 1911, increased to 22.2 in 1971. From the comparative point of view these figures are 13.3 and 17.2 for females respectively. In 1971, in rural areas, mean age of marriage for women was 16.7 and in urban areas,it was 19.2 whereas for men it was 21.6 and 24.3 respectively. Detailed analysis shows that the marriages of boys are generally performed after the legally accepted age (21 years) whereas the girls' marriages are generally performed before the legally accepted age (18 years). The reason behind this is, that for boys employment before marriage is compulsory whereas for girls household jobs are considered to be her main duty. In the Hindi speaking states average age of marriage for girls in even below 15 years. In rural areas considerable number of girls marriages are performed even before 10 years of age, as it is observed. In 1971 and 1981 in India the mean of the age of girls' marriage was, 17.75 and 18.66 respectively. Female population in the age group of 0-9 years was 30.33, 29.97 and 26.99 in 1961, 1971 and 1981 respectively which shows the gradual decrease in their proportion. In 1981 out of the total number of women in the age group of 10 to 14 and 15 to 19 years, the proportions of married women were 6.59 per cent and 43.47 per cent respectively which demonstrates the custom of child marriage. In order to maintain the sanctity and subordination of girls child marriage is considered proper. In the year 1989 itself, in Rajasthan 9000 child marriages were performed. The marriage of girls is considered to be quite essential. In comparison to men, the number of such women is more who lead their life alone after getting married once. As National Committee (1974) has reported, in 1971, there were 100 widows per 30 widowers. Man is allowed to marry again after the death of his wife but the women in not allowed to marry again after the death of her husband, according to the social traditions, specially in high and middle caste groups. Apart from widowhood, due to barrenness and husband's doubt of her being characterless also lot of divorces and separations take place. In 1971, per 1000 men, there were 761 spinsters, 1024 married 2772 widow, 1630 divorced or separated women. In 1971, in the age group of 0-4, 5-9, 10-14 and 15-19 there were 969, 935, 887 and 883 women per 1000 men. According to 1981 census report, in the whole country there were 144.6 million males and 147.2 million females were married. Out of 147.2 million married women, 112.3 million women were in the age group of reproduction, that is 15-44 years. The fact worth nothing is this that during the decade 1971-81, the growth rate (23.88 per cent) of married women in this reproductive age group was lower than the growth rate of population in the whole country, as Mourya (1988: 97-117) has reported. Above fact indicates towards the death of young mothers during the pregnancy and maternity periods. In South India the condition is comparatively better.

Fertility/Reproductivity

Due to very high rate of reproduction, the problem of population has taken a brightful form in India and simultaneously the condition of women has also deteriorated. In family planning programme, success, as it was expected, could not be achieved. As Mourya (1988) has reported, in India, in 1981, the total reproduction rate was 3.6 and it was 3.9 in villages and 2.8 in cities. Total married women reproduction rate was 5.78 in 1971 which came down to 4.99 in 1981 due to efforts of family planning. In north India this rate was 6-7 and 5-6 in 1971 and 1981 respectively whereas in south India its rate was 5-6 and 4-5 in 1971 and 1981 respectively. For 15-45 age group of women, according to child woman ratio, in the whole country, the number of children per 10 women, was 655 and 556 in 1971 and 1981 respectively. In north India the number of children in 1971 and 1981 was 728 and 656 respectively whereas in south India this number was 652 and 538 in 1971 and 1981 respectively. Upto 1981-82 also, the deliveries of the birth of third child were 51 per cent in cities upto this time only 23.7 per cent population had adopted family planning. Average couple of the developed countries wants to produce only two children whereas the average couple of aeveloping countries wants children in between 3 to 5. India has left behind other developing countries on this issue as we have seen earlier. Above mentioned figures show the situation of 'babyboom' in the country, and also indicate towards more workload of mothers due to frequent pregnancies, deliveries and child care activities and, consequently their bad health conditions. Only 5 per cent working women can get maternity benefit which in reality is available to only 2.3 per cent working women due to violation of law by the employers. While in India, out of births every year, only 40 per cent births are of the first of second child, in developed countries it happens in the case of more than 70 per cent births. This fact also demonstrates the responsibility of Indian women to perform the role of a woman in confinement and their weak health condition. According to a Government of India paper presented at the 1993 international forum meeting of "Education for all" in Delhi, fertility is adversely linked with education. While the fertility rate (live births) for an illiterate woman was 5.1, but below middle school it was 4.5, for middle school but below matric 4, matric but below graduate 3.1 and graduate 2.1 (*Times of India*, 19th September, 1993).

Migration: Internal

Last few census reports reveal that the number of women is more than men in the case of internal migration (within country only). Average ratio of internal migration is 2310 women per 1000 men. Among women the number of migrants from village to village and from city to village is maximum, whereas among men migrants from village to city and from city to city are in large number. The reason of women's migration only upto short and medium distances additional to their marriage, is, acute under-employment and unemployment. The figures regarding the migrating people show that urban environment, from the economic opportunities view is adverse for women. Other reasons for women's migration are unsuccessful marriage, widowhood, desertion and separation. From the figures regarding migration it can be speculated that due to excess of helplessness and insecurity, the status of women gets affected in India and they are required to change the place. As Mourya (1988) has reported, according to 1981 census, migrants were categorised on the basis of their birth place and the difference of last living place from the present living place during the census year. On the basis of birth place, there were 204.2 million migrants in India out of which 62.0 million were males and 142.2 millions were females. In this way, while male migrants were 18.05 per cent of the total male population, the female migrants were 44.24 per cent of the total female population.

On the basis of last living place, in 1981, in India, there were 207.9 million migrants, out of which 63.2 million were males and 144.7 million were females. Male migrants were 18.38 per cent of total male population whereas female migrants were 45.02 per cent of total female population. In this way, 31.25 per cent of total Indian population was compiled of migrant Indians on the basis of last living place. Such male migrants were 30.41 per cent of total migrants whereas such female migrants were 69.59 per cent of total migrants. In 1981, in India 88.39 per cent of the total internal migrants had migrated within the state only which was more or less same, i.e., 88.19 per cent in 1971 also 81.35 per cent of total male internal migrants had migrated in the same state while 18.65 per cent of them had migrated from one state to another state. Whereas, regarding the women, 91.36 per cent of the total female migrants had migrated in the same state and only 8.64 per cent of them had migrated from one state to another state. Among all the internal migrants 91.36 per cent were female. Migration is the main factor which contributes to increased urbanization in India. Employment is the main reason of migration of men in urban areas (46.14 per cent) whereas among urban women, marriage is the main factor (46.61 per cent). In rural areas main reason among men is the change of family's place (33.44 per cent), whereas among rural women marriage is the main reason (79.45 per cent), in which they have to leave their parents' house and place as well as the people and environment known to them since childhood, and go to the unknown place, house, people and environment for leading rest of their life. They have to adopt the particular lifestyle which people of their husband's families follow. This fact demonstrates their inferior status provided to them by patriarchal tradition.

Health

Health of Indian women is weak in comparison to men. From many surveys it has been found out that Indian women, whatever amount of calories they take daily in their food, that is 100 calories less than that, what they burn daily; whereas men, whatever amount of calories they burn daily, they take 800 calories more than that. Women contribute 53 per cent of manpower required for life but their food is quite less than what they require. From the study conducted by World Health Organization, it has been found out that anaemia prevails maximum in India. More than half women do not take the calories, proteins, calcium, iron and vitamin 'A' required in food. In the report given by Indian Council of Medical Research, it has been stated that 70 per cent of pregnant women suffer from anaemia, due to which for 40 per cent of unborn babies as well as for mothers, the danger of death increases. Most important reason of this is the lack of iron in the body. According to the report of National Institute of Nutrition, 10 to 20 per cent mothers die due to anaemia at the time of delivery. During the study conducted by World Health Organization, in spite of increasing the quantity of iron, folic acid and B 12, 56 per cent Indian women, compared to other countries, could not get rid of anaemia. Regarding this fact the scholars believe that many factors may be responsible for it. Due to worms in the stomach, other diseases like cholera, malaria, dysentery, diseases of intestines, mal-nutritious food and non-mixing of iron with blood, etc., the blood producing drugs do not affect. Dirty drinking water, improper latrines, animals' excreta dirty air, dirty environment, lack of proper space, etc., may be another reason as Mitra (1979) has stated.

During the pregnancy period a woman should take 2500 calories on an average, whereas average women gets only 1400 calories. In place of 55 grams protein she gets only 33 grams protein and in place of 0.4 grams iron she gets only 0.2 grams iron. During the state of breast-feeding, this lack of nutrients is observed much more. Regarding the insufficiency of nutritious elements in their food, though the main reason is poverty but most important reason is discrimination between the man and woman. There are 40 to 80 per cent rural women who contribute in the production of grains and 30 per cent women support the family financially. They are the ones who prepare food and serve it to the family members but they themselves take less nutrients in food and men get more. Owing to the low social and familial status of women, in family they eat in the last and that too the left over food and as it is observed, if tasty and nutritious food has been prepared in limited quantity, it is consumed and finished by the male members before she eats. The woman's virtue and speciality of 'self denial' created by socialization right from the childhood days, checks them to keep the nutritious food aside for themselves and eat it later on, which creates serious problems regarding deterioration of health. Along with this, custom of veiling, lack of exercise in open air, and continuity of same, boring and difficult jobs in adverse and dirty atmosphere, also affects their health.

Health of Indian women is very bad and it is deteriorating continuously, still due to lack of awareness regarding their health, they don't think themselves sick or weak. For preparing food, fetching water, cleaning house, etc., in comparison to other jobs, more energy is needed whereas in the absence of nutrients complaints of anaemia, tiredness and heart diseases get created and even the danger of death occurs in their life. In 1981 there were about 25 per cent in cities and 75 per cent in villages and 2/3 of pregnant women who were the victims of anaemia. From the study of lack of nutritious food among women it is known that the diseases caused by malnutrition are not only prevalent among adult women only but are found more among small girls also because in comparison to boys they are given less nutrients in their food.

Apart from this, as Desai and Krishna Raj (1987) have reported, high blood pressure found among women, is 6-7 per cent in small cities and 15-30 per cent in big cities. Ageing women suffer from diabetes more than man. The young women become victims of leprosy due to long working with water and consequently the body remaining cold. In one survey conducted in Rohtak it was found that 15.2 per cent women were suffering from this disease. Mental diseases are also found more among women than men as it has been reported by World Health Organization. Because they get lesser opportunities to express their sorrows and release tension. Whatever adverse situations arise they have to tolerate in spite of their unwillingness and in the unwanted environment they have to adjust themselves and lead their life quietly, without any complaint against anyone which results in mental deformity. Tuberculosis is also found more among the women and the reasons behind it also are neglecting the health and working in the dirty environment. Pain in joints is also more common among women than men.

Benefits from the Health Services

The surprising fact is that along with the increasing health programmes the women's health condition is deteriorating, as it has been found out from a prospering state like Punjab. The reason of this situation is, that, the women get less benefits of health services due to various factors, as Desai and Patel (1985) have also stated. Records of the hospitals show that, per 3 men only 1 woman is benefited from health services because in families women's health is given less importance. They are also not benefited by the medical system, based on institution because along with expenses, visit to a distant place requires enough time. Due to responsibilities of house work and care of small children, their mobility becomes quite limited. Family members are not easily prepared to tolerate the discomforts and turmoil in the house caused by her hospital visit. Apart from this, lack of women health workers, especially female doctors in rural areas, is also responsible for less benefits of health services to women. In 1971, per 4 male doctors there was only 1 female doctor in India. In the field of specialization, per 17 male doctors there was only one female doctor. In 1975 in postgraduate classes of medical college, per 100 male students there was only 1 female student. Although the number of female doctors is increasing day by day but most of them want to work in urban areas only. In villages mostly all the women's health programmes are implemented under the direct care of nurses. Owing to the low occupational status of nursing profession, the number of nurses is also decreasing. There is only 1 nurse per 2-3 doctors whereas there should be 3 nurses for 1 doctor. As it has been known from the study of rural health services, due to insufficiency of nurses in primary health centres and sub-centres, one nurse gets attached with a very large area. For residential medical facilities started later on they are unable to work properly due to scarcity of transportation and residence, difficulties of night stay, and problems of security. Apart from this, due to influential people's monopoly on their services in the villages the distance between the nurse and group of average women, needing their services more, increases. Moreover, community health workers, being 96 per cent males, women can not get benefited from the health facilities. In urban areas also, middle class women are involving themselves in occupational activities outside their home. Due to double burden of work inside and outside of the house, they get no time for rest and entertainment which badly affects their health but due to lack of time and feeling of neglect towards health, they do not take proper advantages of medical facilities. The indifference towards issues of women's health gets created owing to consideration that they are the health problems connected with motherhood.

In this way, the Indian women lead their life with gradually deteriorating health and various physical ailments. From the studies conducted in developing countries it is revealed that the health problems of women are large number of deaths of infant girls and women in confinement, large number of pregnant women suffering from sickness due to malnutrition, births of weak infants having less expectation of life, dead infants (miscarriages) and abortions, frequent pregnancies, and along with bearing the labour pains, workload of bringing up the children, physical weakness and tiredness, mental tension and depression, mental deformity and some gynaecological diseases, all created by mostly anaemia due to malnutrition. Suicide rates are also more among women which shows their state of helplessness. In the health status of women their physical, mental and social conditions are included. Along with biological and physical problems, existing standards and notions of society about the needs and capabilities of women also effect their health condition. These notions affect the maternity care services as well as provision of preventive and curative health service facilities and their usage. Many studies have proved that the lower the status of women will be, that much lower will be their knowledge about the preventive services and even much lower will be their usage of those services. Cultural factors specially affecting the health of women are : attitude towards marriage, age of marriage, rate of reproductivity, sex of children, structure of family organization, status of women in the family and socially approved expected roles of women. All these factors have great demographic importance as we have discussed earlier. Cultural insistence on marriage at lower age, high reproduction efficiency, idealization of the roles of mother and housewife, etc., affect badly on the physical and mental health of women.

Women Health Programme

As National Committee (1974) has reported, since social customs and traditional pose restrictions on women, they are considered a weaker and exploited section of the society. Therefore, for helping this section, the need of special efforts for them was felt, because without it, in the society having values of inequality, getting benefited out of general programmes is not possible for them. Therefore, Planning Commission has paid special attention in all the plans, on women's health, family planning, maternity and child welfare, nutritious food, etc. Central health and family planning ministry performs an important role in national efforts of keeping the women healthy and happy.

For the implementation of health programmes in rural areas, in every community development block (60 to 70 thousand population), one primary health centre has been established, in which provisions were made for atleast 30 beds, 2 medical officers,

4 midwives and 4 trained nurses. From 1963 onwards due to family planning services, extra provisions were made to keep 1 medical officer, 1 extension doctor and 1 assistant nurse in every centre, and 2 more family workers for supervision in all the four sub-centres (10 to 15 thousand population). In urban areas, in district hospital provisions were made to keep three specialists for medicine, surgery and gynaecology and women diseases, and to organize 75 maternity beds and 50 children beds.

Family Planning/Welfare Programme

This programme is totally voluntary and it is being implemented as a compulsory part of total development polity, in which the health, care of mother and child, family welfare, rights of women and nutritious food are included. From the beginning of first plan in 1952, family planning was adopted as a Government programme, in order to control population and improve family's economic status as well as women's health status. This programme was taken ordinarily in first and second plans and the main emphasis was given on research regarding demography, contacts, physiology, reproduction and incentives, etc. Centres were established in some areas in order to guide people, willing for family planning and provide them medical facilities. In third plan the programme was reorganized. Till now people were going to centres for availing health services. During this plan provisions were made to make available the messages regarding health, services and contraceptives also in places other than medical centres. In 1966, independent family planning department was formed under Central Government and in the programme, achievement of targets was specifically emphasized. Under fourth and fifth plans it was given very high priority among the programmes. In spite of it, between 1966 and 1978 birth rate came down only by 0.8 per cent. According to requirement during this period along with the health care of mother and child, family planning programme was extended and integrated. In order to fulfil the public needs, increased due to independent valuation, important changes were made in the programme and in place of family planning, family welfare was given more importance and the programme was started afresh. Through State Governments these programmes are implemented for which cent per cent central help is given.

At the National level central family welfare council advises the government regarding the family welfare programmes. This programme is extended in rural areas through primary health centres and sub-centres and in urban areas through district hospitals, sub-divisional hospitals and, maternity and child health centres. Health of mother and child and immunization programme is also the part of family welfare programme. From seventh plan under the 'tubectomy bed scheme', for the maintenance of every bed the amount of Rs. 3000/- is given provided 60 operations per bed are done. In rural family welfare centres 1000 rooms' are being converted into operation rooms so that better facility of tubectomy and abortion could be provided. From the beginning of the programme 588 lakh operations were done and 225 lakh loops are fixed till 1987, the rate of which was respectively 74.9 and 28.7 per 1000. Out of 13.26 crore couples in which the age of wife was between 15 to 44 years, 37.4 per cent couples were protected by any one of the approved method of family welfare. As a result of the programme upto 31st March 1987, approximately 854 lakh births were prevented. The programme of abortion in the approved hospitals, decorated with medical appliances, with the help of trained doctors, is the measure of health care only, but in a way, it is the substitute of family welfare also, because on failure of contraceptives, under this programme provision is made to terminate the pregnancy legally. The women going for abortions, later on opt either for tubectomy or any contraceptive method. From 1st April, 1972, Medical Termination of Pregnancy Act, 1971 has been implemented. As Desai (1986) has stated in family planning programme, expected results have not been achieved. Upto 2000 A.D. the target of reducing the birth rate upto 20 per 1000 persons has been fixed. For achievement of this target 60 per cent of the couples in the reproductive age group will have to adopt some or the other contraceptive method. For this 102 million couples will have to go for tubectomy or vasectomy and other 102 million couples will have to adopt any other contraceptive method. How much success in achieving the target, will be achieved, only time will show. However, according to the report of National

Development Committee appointed in April, 1993, National family welfare programme has not achieved the expected results and targets regarding population control. Whatever it is, this is certain that for this purpose also only women will have to come forward, make efforts and take pains. Consequently only they will have to tolerate the negative impacts of tubectomy or contraceptive methods on health.

Apart from this, as Desai and Patel (1985) have stated, due to sonographic examination of the sex of foetus before birth, termination of the female foetus through abortion is also going on speedily in the present time which again indicates towards their secondary status in the society. Owing to this the danger of decline in their number has increased more. Due to this even poor people go for abortions which saves them from the marriage expenditure and life long responsibility of the girl. Educated people, believing in small family norms, allow birth of only one son in spite of their good economic condition. Between 1978 and 1982, 78,000 female foetus were aborted. In this way the danger to the life of girls is increasing. On the name of population control and family planning, this fact is being neglected in the society, which will create serious problems later on, by disturbing the sex balance in the society. Certainly the status of women improves due to family planning because its knowledge helps her to get rid of frequent pregnancies and deliveries and to learn keeping control on one's own life and future. It saves from increased consumption of physical resources and provides time for rest and entertainment. Relationship between husband and wife changes and her capacity to take decisions inside the family develops. But some studies have shown that acceptance of family planning methods is directly influenced by the higher status of women due to increase in the age of marriage, provision of good education, increase in opportunities of employment, improvement of life conditions and advancement in general knowledge. It means that the capability of woman to keep her family limited, can contribute in improving her status. Thus, it can be concluded that family planning has double relationship with the status of women. Due to higher status of women family planning is accepted and later on family planning further enhances the status of women.

Maternity and Child Health Programme

During the first few plans, owing to more emphasis on family planning for population control, other health services could not develop sufficiently. But when even after intensive efforts, birth rate reduced very little than the targets, it was felt that due to the social and psychological barriers, created by poverty, ignorance and high death rate of children in lower classes, it can not be controlled purely from the curative and target oriented perspective. As a result in fifth plan, an integration of family planning programme with the maternity, care of children, nutrition programme and general health services, was perceived. Due to serious criticism of methods of motivation and encouragement, in their place, integrated health services alone were considered as source of encouragement. In the beginning, maternity and child welfare services were started as a part of all programmes regarding health but later it was made a special programme by giving it more importance. Arrangements were made to provide these services through maternity and child health centres. In these programmes, effective prenatal care, secured delivery, sufficient postnatal care encouragement to the mothers to breast feed their children for longer time, timely immunization for protection of people from general communicative diseases, prevention of diarrhoea, attention on physical development and provision of care of basic health, etc., are included. Thus, care of mother and children's health is the main objective of this programme which is very important in family welfare programme.

Therefore, along with the extension of basic health services, for achievement of goals, training centres were opened to train the workers properly. For making the specialized medical care of the children, district hospitals, sub-divisional hospitals and mother-child units were decorated with medical appliances. As it has been described in 'India' (1987), in order to make women and child development programmes more effective, separate department for women and child development has been opened in human resource development ministry in 1985. There are two bureaus in this department: Nutrition and Child development and women welfare development. The State Governments are provided guidance and financial assistance for implementing the mother and child welfare schemes. In 1987-88 Rs. 18 crore were arranged for the programme of immunization to mothers and children to save them from diseases malnutrition and anaemia and for buying the medicines. In 1987-88 only for the prevention of dysentery and diarrhoea (loose motions) through 'rehydration' medical method, Rs. 5 crore were kept and in seventh plan Rs. 25 crores were sanctioned. Post-natal programme is such as programme of family welfare whose objective is to take care of the women in confinement after delivery and this programme has been started in National, State and district level medical institutions in which 104 medical colleges and two postgraduate institutes are also included. Apart from this in order to identify cancer in the uterus in its beginning itself among women adopting family planning methods, in 58 medical colleges, Pap Smear Test facility is available. In sub-divisional hospitals, the object of extension of post-natal programme is to make mother and children services available in the rural and semi-urban areas, so that their health could be improved. Till the end of 7th plan this programme was implemented in 1200 sub-divisional hospitals. In urban areas in order to make available the primary health care, family welfare and better maternity services, one special urban scheme has been started. Instead of opening any new family welfare centre in city, only in present urban centres, more medical appliances and facilities are made available. Health check posts and city family welfare bureaus are being established and the hospitals run by State Government, local institutions and voluntary organizations are being given financial assistance for this purpose.

Under the Integrated Child Development Programme, provisions of supplementary nutrition for the children upto 6 years of age and the women pregnant or in confinement, health education and informal pre-school education for children in balwadis, etc., are included. These schemes are being implemented in selected quite backward blocks of rural, tribal and urban slum areas. In creches, working or sick mothers' children, aged upto 5 years, get advantages of day care, sleeping arrangement, supplementary nutrition, medicines, entertainment and weekly health check-up, etc. In this field, voluntary organizations are also working with the national and international financial assistance, especially in urban areas.

In 1973, health and family welfare ministry had appointed a special committee for examining full utilization of beds available in primary health centres. According to report of this committee, in Bengal and Kerala, they were being utilized 50 per cent, but in other states, the utilization of these beds was only between 5 to 15 per cent. The reasons for this under-utilization of beds were, indifference of workers, difference of status between doctors and the people of low socio-economic class and absence of even one female doctor in many centres. Later on, enough efforts were made to improve the situation and they produced some results also, but even now the condition is not very satisfactory. Regarding this, two factors which obstruct the way of women for getting benefits by the medical facilities are: Class system and patriarchal traditions, due to which their outing from the house and the supply of services to them are quite difficult propositions. For the success of these programmes, attitudes and behaviour of masses especially the women, are required to be changed.

Reasons of Changing Demographic Features of Women

It is true that between the two sections of males and females, the difference regarding demographic tendencies is still there which is due to deep rooted traditions in Indian society differentiating between the two sexes. This fact also cannot be denied that, during the last 100 years, within the section of women themselves, lot of improvement, regarding many demographic tendencies has taken place and it shows the progress in their status. For example, their age of marriage has increased, reproduction rate has decreased, death rate has decreased and life expectation has increased and their health conditions have improved. The credit for all these demographic changes goes to the Government and private efforts, started from the British period itself. Social reform movements, social legislations, propaganda and extension of formal education, end of purdah system, increased opportunities of employment due to industrialization and urbanization, increased awareness due to westernization, women's participation in the National Freedom Movement, Womens' movement, etc., initiated the advancement of women towards the goal of achievement of higher status, equal to man. Great change has occurred in the status of women, owing to the process of modernization, availability and usage of means of transportation and communication. Supply of the audio-visual sources of entertainment and under family welfare programme being implemented by Government of India, family planning and mother and child health services, political rights of women and reservation of seats for them in the political field, changing attitudes and behaviour of men and women, etc., further made a catalytic effect. As consequence of all the above mentioned factors, change in the demographic features regarding women become essential. If this tendency of demographic features, i.e., changing in the positive direction, is maintained in future, a time may come when the features like male-female sex ratio and internal migration may show their existence if not in the favour of women but atleast some positive trend in the direction of decreasing the gap, provided the women themselves become aware of their own interests and become active to safeguard them.

Seven

Educational Status

Education is considered both, an end in itself, and as mean in attainment of certain ends. It develops the personality and wisdom of people, makes them capable of performing certain economic, political and cultural functions and consequently their socio-economic status enhances. Education has been accepted as such an equipment which can be used to forward the process of change and development in he society, in the direction of desired goals. It brings mobility in the society and helps in bringing the equal status among the people coming from different social levels. Education system is the only institution which can uproot the deep roots of inequality between the man and woman; which are settled in the minds of people through the process of socialization. Therefore, in the whole world in order to improve the status of women, education has been considered as an important source. Education not only makes the women more capable comparatively to perform their traditional duties of mother and wife but it also makes them active and more efficient members of the society in the process of social, economic and political development. Womens' education is such an appliance which makes them more capable, for creating a new social system.

Development and Growth of Formal Education for Women

Under formal education there is a strict bond of specific written rules regarding admission in the educational institutions, teaching and examination, which are to be followed essentially. In order to run new administrative and economic system, started during British regime and to fulfill the need of a large number of clerks, schools were opened in different cities, and along with other subjects the students were taught English language also.

Since Indian women did not have to earn their livelihood, there was no requirement of education for them, though it was being considered. In the beginning British Government also did not pay any attention towards it because it did not want to interfere in the Indian religious and social system. But the social reformers raised a voice and prior to Government. Christian missionaries and some learned people made efforts in this direction. As Desai (1977) has informed, first of all in 1824, in Madras, a girls school was opened by missionaries in which very few girls came for study. After this, in Bombay in 1849, Students' Literary and Scientific Society opened few morning schools only for two hours, 7-9 a.m. in different areas of the city. Well established first girls' school was opened in Ahmedabad in 1849 by Gujarat Vernacular Society, but in that also very little number of girls took admission. In the field of higher education, in 1857 universities were opened in Calcutta, Madras and Bombay but their doors were closed for girls, which got opened in 1877, and in 1882 two girls could take graduate degree from Calcutta University. Although the British Government was willing since a long time to make a scheme for educating the girls but different aspects of women education could be considered only in 1882 by the 'Hunter Commission' appointed for this purpose. In 1888 the Commission gave the report that 98 per cent girls of school going age are out of the school and out of 99.7 million girls, 99.5 million girls could not read and write. Due to the custom of veiling, child marriage and household work. many hurdles were coming in the education of girls. It was decided that which ever local institutions want to do this work, they should be permitted. At this time Municipalities opened many girls' schools.

By 1882, 2600 primary schools, 81 secondary schools, 15 training schools and one college had been opened, In 1887-88, in Grand Medical College of Bombay, along with medical classes training classes for nurses were also opened. At this time in Ahmedabad and Pune, Teacher's training colleges were opened. Raja Ram Mohun Roy, Ishwar Chandra Vidyasagar, Anne Besant, Saiyed Ahmed Khan, etc., laid emphasis on women education. At this time special conditions of India were changing very fast. Indian National Congress and Indian National Social Conference, both organizations greatly emphasized the need of women education. In Bombay and Pune, South Education Society, Pandita Rama Bai, Rama Bai Ranade, D.R. Kurve, etc., voluntary organizations and social reformers made efforts and created awareness in this direction. During those days educational institutions for teaching fine arts to the girls were opening because at that time, through national language women education was being emphasized for better performance of their household role.

In 1891-92, more than 3 lakh girls took admission in primary school but out of them only 2 per cent girls studied in the secondary level. During 1901-1902 there were 76 girls in medical college and 166 girls in medical school.

In 1902, Indian University Commission was established. In 1904, Lord Curzon pointed out the lack of education of women and stressed on its requirement. During this time some progress was made but with a slow speed. Between 1907-12 Indian Universities gave admission to the outside students also for appearing in the examination. In 1916, under the leadership of Dr. D.K. Karve, in Bombay S.N.D.T. Indian Women University was established and special subjects were kept for study by girls, on which different types of restrictions were observed. Dr. Karve had already done this type of experiment in Pune. The University ran a college of 30 girls, Medical education and midwife and nurse training was also arranged. In Delhi also Lady Hardings Medical College was opened for providing nurse training along with medical education. In this college a university degree in the field of medicine and full training of nursing was provided. In this way due to awareness of public during the First World War, the field of education got developed. At this time, owing to the extension of education and health services, in the field of women education, teacher and doctor, two professionals got introduced. In 1921, a decision about giving education department to the Indian control, was taken. In 1921-22, 19 colleges, 675 secondary schools and 21,956 primary schools were there for girls. Owing to the increase in the age of marriage, education got encouraged. The increased demand of educated girls by the educated boys for marriage provided more opportunities for the growth of education. In 1922, there were 197 women in medical college, 334 in medical schools, 67 in teacher's training college and 3903 in teachers training school. Due to serious efforts of Gandhiji at this time despite the problems of political conflict and economic scarcity education got developed. Due to active participation of women in the National Freedom Movement, enthusiasm of masses in women education increased more.

Many women took education in the commerce and technical fields also. In 1937, the states got autonomy and the responsibility of education was given to the education minister of state. In 1946-47, 57 arts and science colleges, 2370 secondary schools and 21479 primary schools were there for girls. At this time, while on one hand, girls colleges for their special education (Home Science) were opened, on the other co-education was also started.

Literacy Rate

In 1947, more than half girls were studying with the boys. In 1947, the number of girls who took admission in Primary schools (3,475,165) was 80 per cent of the number of total admissions. In secondary schools 281,000 girls got admitted which was only 7per cent of the total admissions. In higher education their admission (23,000) was less than half of 1 per cent of the total admissions.

As Reddy (1986) has written, after independence in 1948-49, under the chairmanship of Dr. Radha Krishnan, University Education Commission was established which forwarded many suggestions regarding women education. In Constitution the promise of providing equal opportunities of education to men and women without any discrimination was already there.

In the directive principles of state policy also order of providing higher education was there. In 1950-51, in university education there were more than 46,000 women. In higher education the percentages of women's admissions per 100 boys were : 10 per cent in 1948-49, 13 per cent in 55-56, 17 per cent in 60-61 and 21 per cent in 65-66, while in 1950-51 per 100 boys in colleges and universities the girls number was 16 which increased to 27 in 1960-61. In the field of higher education at this time the urban middle and upper class girls came in a large number because the educated boys were demanding educated, at least graduate girls for marriages. The number of girls increased in the school level also but the speed was comparatively slow. In 1950-51, in primary schools, per 100 boys the number of girls was 30 become 44 in 1960-61. In 1958, under the Chairmanship of Mrs Durga Bai Deshmukh, a National Committee was formed for women education. This committee was appointed specially to examine the syllabus connected with women education and it got approved the syllabus for girls different from the boys so that their education does not hinder their family life. After 1960 many committees regarding education were formed. In 1962, Hansa Mehta Committee was formed to consider professional education for women and it suggested that they can be taught any subject. In 1964, Kothari Commission also encouraged the professional syllabus and gave important suggestions. In 1965, under the Chairmanship of Shri M. Bhakta Vatsalam, a committee was appointed to examine the problems of women education. Along with all this education of women was also growing gradually. In primary schools, per 100 boys the number of girls from 12 in 1901 rose to 39 in 1950-51 and reached to 55 in 1965-66. Proposals and decisions of education policy of 1968 also emphasized more on women education. In 1970, UNESCO celebrated the International Education year and encouraged women education. In 1970-71, per 100 boys the number of girls was 60 in primary classes, 43 in middle classes and 37 in secondary classes and 38 in colleges (general education). In 1974, National Committee on Status of Women also studied the educational status of women and reported that urban middle class is more against the co-education than the rural middle class. National Committee suggested about providing equal opportunities to girls and boys both, for the study of all types of courses. In 1973-74, in the primary level 2 crores 44 lakhs, in middle level 45 lakhs, in secondary level 23 lakhs, and in higher education 9 lakh girls were studying. United Nations Organisations celebrated the year 1975, as the 'women year' and later on declared the period upto 1985 as the women decade in which like other countries of the world, in India also programme were chalked out to provide new perspectives to women education. As a result, differences between the girls and boys reduced further. Girls number in Primary schools was 5.4 million in 1950-51, 18 million in 65-66, 24 million in 73-74 and 27.2 million in 1979-80. In 1980-

81, per 100 boys in primary level 65, middle level 52, secondary level 43 and in colleges (general education) 45 girls were studying. In 1984-85, in primary level 48.5 million boys and 34.2 million girls, while in middle level 16.6 million boys and 9.2 million girls were studying. At the end of women's decade, it was noticed, from the primary level to middle level of education among the boys and girls considerable differences still remained. Most of the girls used to leave studies after primary classes and engage themselves in the household affairs.

In the National Education Policy of 1986, provision for free education of the girls upto 14 years of age has been made. In new educational policy also women education has been emphasized. In interior rural and tribal areas also network of schools are being laid down and the girls are being specifically exempted from the education expenditure. In 1990, National Womens' Commission was established incorporating schemes and programmes regarding womens' education. In spite of all these efforts the girls are still lagging behind the boys in the field of education. In 1991, literacy rate among men was 63.86 per cent whereas it was 39.4 per cent among women. The difference between the literacy rates of both the categories, is about 25 per cent. Women literacy rate shows that even now more than 60 per cent women are illiterate. The biggest problem of women education is to leave the studies in between, after taking admission once. Thus, we see that, although enough progress has taken place in the field of womens' education and from the beginning of 20th century, their number is increasing, they are still availing less advantage of educational facilities in comparison of boys. International welfare institutions are also providing great help to the Indian Government in the field of education, through financial assistance and guidance both. Recently during the last decade between 1980-90 University Grant Commission has opened women study centres in many universities in which three dimensional programme of teaching, research and field work on women issues, has to be followed. For conferences, seminars, workshops, etc., at regional, state, national and international level also, arrangement has been made to provide financial assistance.

Administration of Formal Education

Before 1976 whole responsibility of education was on states and centre used to only coordinate and determine the standard, that too of the technical and higher education. After amendment in Constitution in 1976, responsibility of education has come on centre and state Governments both jointly. Apart from educational policy formulation, chalking out the educational scheme with the help of state Government, is also the responsibility of central education department. According to the education policy of 1986, in the management of education at the national level, central education advisory board performs a decisive role in determining the revision of educational development resources, implementation and changes, etc. This board functions through various mechanisms and committees formed to determine the contacts and coordination in different fields of human resource development. The representatives of centre and states education departments are the members of these committees. At the state level also, state education advisory boards are established which function through different state level committees related with human resource development. At district and local levels, district education boards are responsible for management of education upto higher secondary level. Local committees perform an important role in school improvement programme. On the condition of proper management, non-government and voluntary institutions are also encouraged and giving financial assistance. Education upto class 12 in the schools, is the responsibility of state education board. In almost all the states now, 10+2 method has been adopted. Higher education is imparted in the country in 135 universities and various affiliated colleges of arts, science, commerce and professional education. Apart from this 20 research institutes and other institutions are also working. University Grant Commission, established in 1953, does essential work for growth and coordination of higher education by determining the standard regarding teaching, examination and research in universities inquiring and examining their economic needs and giving them sufficient grants, establishing new universities and advising the Government on other issues related to higher education. At state level also State University Grant Commissions have been established, which are responsible for proper development of educational institutions and educational standard at state level. Financial assistance is given to the colleges run by the voluntary organisations also. By considering the importance of the role of the principal of any educational institution, special attention is paid towards his selection and training.

Development and Growth of Informal Education for Women

For taking education under this system there are no rigid bonds or particular written rules regarding admission in educational institutions, teaching and examination. Although from the 19th century itself social reformers and social welfare voluntary organisations have been making some efforts of informal education, but at the National level an extensive programme of informal education was prepared by the Government under National Education Policy 1986 which is being implemented with great enthusiasm. Under this, resolution passed for the children was that till 1990 all the children upto the age of 11 years, and till 1995 all the children upto the age of 14 years, who will remain deprived of the five years' school education of primary level, will be imparted education of the same level through informal method. Through Balwadi/Anganwadi programme, arrangement has also been done to impart pre-school education to the children less than 6 years of age in informal environment. Apart from this Government has prepared a massive programme of adult education named 'National Literacy Mission'. Under literacy comes the capability of reading and writing with understanding. The target of this programme is that 800 lakh illiterate people coming under the age group of 15 to 35 years should be made literate. Out of them 300 lakh till 1990 and 500 lakh till 1995 should be made literate. For this, in various states and union territories at present, 513 literacy schemes are being implemented. In the adult literacy programme voluntary institutions have been included by Government. At present in this field 382 Voluntary Institutions are performing important role.

Apart from this, for informal education of labourers 40 labour 'Vidya Peetha' and 16 State Resource Centres are working to provide technical assistance to the programme, under the public programme of public literacy, started in 1986, under which 4.20 lakh people come. In order to make this programme successful, a more ambitious programme was adopted in 1987 in which assistance of university and college teachers has been taken and resources are made available for research and studies. At the time of chalking out the programme, attention has been paid to the needs and language of the learners. Along with language and mathematics women are imparted knowledge related to the proper care of household affairs, healthcare of children, occupational training and ways of earning livelihood, etc. Under this programme, apart from educating the adults at group level by the trained workers in informal environment, an appeal has been made to every educated person to educate at least one illiterate person, which has been named 'each one teach one' programme. All the books and note books required for literating the illiterates are distributed free of cost.

Apart from this, in order to provide opportunities of higher education to the people and to make education the democratic resource available for the people open university and programme of distant studies or correspondence courses at all levels have also been introduced. The branches of Indira Gandhi Open University established in 1985 have been opened in various universities of the country. Under this education system, for examination to the graduate degree neither it is compulsory to have certificate of passing higher secondary school examination, nor the clearance in any other university examination of lower level is required. In Open University centres, apart from audio-visual resources, essential study material is also made available. Besides, this, any university can make arrangements for imparting education through distant studies or correspondence courses, in which along with sending the study material by post, the students sitting at distant places are contacted and their capability, efficiency and progress in studies is evaluated. All these schemes are specifically useful for women. Those who do not get opportunity of formal education or leave the study in between due to marriage and household work, can respectively go to adult education centres to become literate, and get education by visiting an open university centre. Some times or while sitting at home along with responsibilities one can become educated through distant studies or correspondence courses. National Womens' Conference had passed a resolution in 1984 that by year 2000 illiteracy of women should be 0. In the direction of achieving this target informal education programmes are performing very important roles.

Administration of Informal Education

Provisions of education, open education and correspondence courses, etc., are centrally directed and financed by the University Grants Commission. For implementation of these schemes all over the country, in every state, few universities are selected and different centres for different purposes, are established. The teacher of professor category is appointed as the director and after appointing other required staff under him he is given the responsibility of running these centres. Adult education programme is conducted by running various adult education centres, in the society while the activities of open education and correspondence courses are limited within the premises of University. In order to achieve fixed targets of these programmes, a whole management structure has been created. Time to time, universities have to send report regarding their achievements of targets related with these programmes to the University Grants Commission and they are evaluated.

For administering the management of these programmes properly at all levels and to get correct information one computerized management information system has been established.

In this way, formal and informal education are being used as a means of bringing basic changes in the standard of women. National education system is performing a positive interfering role for making the women capable. New values are being developed through new syllabi and textbooks with the help of educational institutions which is necessary to finish the inequalities and deformities continuing from past. In various syllabi the study regarding status of women is being encouraged. For removing women's illiteracy those obstacles, due to which women can not complete their education even of the primary level are being cleared off. For this purpose special assistance services are being arranged. At different levels participation of women in technical and professional education regarding livelihood is being emphasized. Different programmes are being implemented among women and the policy against discrimination is being practiced with great enthusiasm.

Literacy Rate

In spite of all the above mentioned efforts 60 per cent women are illiterate even now. Seventy per cent girls of school going age are out of the school and engaged in different household and outside jobs. These facts are demonstrated by Tables 7.1 and 7.2 in the following pages.

TABLE 7.1
LITERACY RATE IN INDIAN POPULATION IN DIFFERENT CENSUS YEARS

Census year	*Male*	*Female*	*Total*
1901	9.8	0.6	5.3
1911	10.6	1.1	5.9
1921	12.2	1.8	7.2
1931	15.6	2.9	9.5
1941	24.9	7.3	16.1
1951	24.9	7.9	16.7
1961	34.4	13.0	24.0
1971	39.5	18.7	29.4
1981	46.7	24.9	36.2
1991	63.86	39.42	52.1

Source: Indian Census Report, Paper I, 1991 Provisional population totals, Registrar General and Census Commissioner for India.

Table 7.1 shows the situation regarding literacy among men and women in India, right from the beginning of 20th century to 1991. Under literacy, the capability of reading and writing with understanding is included. The person who can only read but cannot write, cannot be called literate. It is not necessary that a literate person should attain minimum education from a formal institution by appearing in examination. Normally the children before 4 years of age come in the category of illiterates

(Mourya, 1988). As the Table 7.1 reveals, in the beginning of 20th century, not even 1 per cent of women were literate while about 10 per cent of men were literate. It means there was a difference of 9 per cent between the literacy rates of both the groups. In the forthcoming census years literacy rates of both the groups have increased which is natural due to development of education but the fact worth consideration is that the difference between the literacy rates of both the sections has been continuously increasing with every census year, which got increased from 9 per cent in 1901 to 24.44 per cent in 1991. It means advantage of growing educational facilities has been availed by males more than ever before with every census year, while women, opposite to this, have availed less than before every time. Therefore, we see that during this period in spite of increased percentage of literacy in 1991, where only 36.14 per cent males are illiterate, 60.58 per cent females are illiterate. As Chana (1988) has stated, this tendency of widespread illiteracy among women shows their lower status in the society. In rural areas even now educating the girls specifically, is not considered essential because throughout the life they have to perform only the household jobs. Therefore, even in 1981, among the children of school going age but who were out of school, 70 per cent were girls in rural areas. As Sharma (1988) has stated even at this age they are engaged in various household jobs. In comparison to North India, in South India, in general and in Kerala in particular, literacy among women is found more. Career orientation and late marriages are the reasons behind it. In Kottayam district of Kerala, literacy rate is 94 per cent while in Barmar district of Rajasthan it is 17.68 per cent in 1991.

Participation of Women in Various Levels and Types of Education

Education is the first condition of progress and development, and the medium of social change. Therefore, being an inseparable part of development process of the country, education has been given higher priority among the priorities of planning. During the four decades after achievement of freedom, the number of literate has increased four times due to coordinated efforts. In primary schools the number of children has increased more than four times and the number of such schools has also increased to more than double. The number of universities has increased more than five times. Along with increasing the number of educational institutions, improvement in the quality of education is also being emphasized. After considering womens' education as the measure of creating efficiency of solving the problems of life and removing all the evils, it is thus being greatly encouraged with the hope that educated women will help in bringing about a social change. The number of girls in all the levels and types of education has increased during the last decades but in spite of environment being in their favour, rate of progress has grown with a slow speed and it is not same all the time. Table 7.2 shows the number of girls in comparison to boys at different levels of education after independence.

TABLE 7.2

NUMBER OF GIRLS ON ADMISSION OF 100 BOYS AT DIFFERENT LEVELS OF EDUCATION

Year	*Primary level*	*Middle level*	*Higher Secondary level*	*Colleges and Universities (General Education Graduation and Post Graduation)***
1950-51	39	22	16	15
1960-61	48	35	25	27
1970-71	60	43	37	38
1980-81	65	52	43	45

** At this level if Professional and Technical education is included, the number will be much less.

As the Table 7.2 reveals, after independence, the number of girls has increased at each level of education during every decade, but in comparison to boys, their number had always remained less. The difference between the number of boys and girls was quite large in 1950-51, which due to very slow speed of decrease, even now, is a matter of concern. In cities mostly middle class girls after taking education are advancing further in the direction of taking some money earning job. Mainly due to contribution of this class, women education advanced after independence and the number of girls in all the levels of education which was 64 lakh in 1950-51 became 398.64 lakhs in 1980-81. In the same way, the number of girls per 100 boys which was 33 in 1950-51, increased and became 55 in 1980-81. But in lower class, rural and tribal communities, due to lack of understanding the importance of education, between the boys and girls, even now a very wide gap of 45 per cent is existing. According to a Government of India Paper presented at the 1993 International Forum Meeting of Education for all in Delhi, girls still accounted for only 45.7 per cent of the enrolment at the primary level and 37.73 per cent at the middle stage. The dropout rates for girls were also higher with 49.69 per cent at the primary and 68.31 per cent at the middle level compared to 46.74 per cent and 59.38 per cent respectively for boys (*Times of India*, 19th Sept., 1993). In this way, in the field of women education, main issues causing concern are: widespread illiteracy, dropouts after admission, less benefit of educational facilities to girls, rural-urban imbalance, girls admission in limited branches of higher education and their concentration. As Ghadi Ali (1988) has stated, in comparison to boys large number of girls dropouts, is in itself an indicator of their lower status in society.

Women Education in Different Types of Educational Courses

If in higher education we see the percentage of 17-21 years age group of girls, we come across quite a frustrating scene. The women studying in Universities are only 3 per cent of the total female population. But the size of this section of educated women is so large that it can be considered important. Even though at different levels of higher education the admission of girls has increased, still in all the subjects a noticeable difference of the number of girls from the number of boys can be observed. During the last few years also no specific difference has been seen in the girls' admission pattern. Even now they prefer to study the subjects of arts, medicine and education, therefore their concentration can be seen in the faculty of these subjects. Regarding this, whatever little difference which has come, during last few years is that in technical education, industrial training institutes and commerce faculty, some more girls have taken admission. They very rarely study the courses of engineering and polytechnic. Now the number of girls working as managers, accountants and clerks is increasing therefore the number of girls studying commerce is also gradually increasing. In 1971, the number of commerce graduate girls was 72.84 which became 1,02,564 in 1982-83. Due to modernization of our economic system, opportunities of employment are available for the technical trained persons, therefore in spite of many social and cultural barriers, girls are studying in the technical and industrial training courses on the other hand, it is sad that their number in the medical faculty is decreasing. In Table 7.3 the percentages of the number of girls in 1979-80 in different levels and types of education has been shown. More or less the same tendency is observed even now. In this Table the attainment of different subjects, education between both the sexes is clearly demonstrated due to their special interests.

TABLE 7.3
PERCENTAGE OF BOYS AND GIRLS OUT OF TOTAL NUMBER OF STUDENTS IN DIFFERENT LEVELS AND TYPES OF EDUCATION (1979-80)

Levels and Type of Education	*Percentage of Boys out of Total Number of Students*	*Percentage of Girls out of Total Number of Students*
Ph.D/D.Sc/ D.Phil	73.9	26.1
M.A.	62.2	37.8
M.Sc.	68.4	31.6
M.Com.	92.4	7.6
B.A./B.A. (Hons)	64.2	35.8
B.Sc/B.Sc (Hons)	73.2	26.8
B.Ed./B.T.	59.1	40.9
M.B.B.S.	75.7	24.3
B.Com/B.Com (Hons)	86.0	14.00
B.E./B.Sc. Eng./B. Arch /B.Tech	96.5	3.5
Intermediate Junior College	79.0	21.0
Pre-Degree, Pre-University	60.8	39.2
Higher Secondary	75.3	24.7
Teachers Training School	51.2	48.8
Technical and Industrial Training School	80.9	19.1

Source: Selected Educational Statistics, 1980-81, Ministry of Education, Delhi - 1982. Desai and Patel (1985).

The table shows that in all the levels and types of education and number of boys is much more than the girls. In school teachers training courses the number of girls is largest, i.e., about half of the total number of students. After that comes their number in the graduate and postgraduate classes of general education. In the medical education 25 per cent students are girls. Very small and smallest number of girls are in the education of commerce and engineering, which are 7.6 and 3.5 per cent of total students. During the decade between 1980-90, a tendency of increasing admissions of girls in the colleges for study of these subjects is observed, but even now the difference between the number of boys and girls is very wide. Professional courses of business management and chartered accountant have also not remained untouched by the girls. They are advancing in every field but due to social barriers, the speed of their entry and work in new fields is quite slow.

Problems Regarding Women Education

In spite of unprecedented progress in the field of women education after independence, the situation is that even now lot of efforts are to be made in this direction. Out of main problems connected with this situation, the first one is the widespread illiteracy even now. In classes 1 to 5, out of every three girls only two girls go to school. In classes 5 to 8 out of five girls only one girl goes to school and in the higher secondary level out of every eight girls only one girl goes to school. Looking after the younger brother - sister at home, household work, bringing water and firewood from outside, working in others houses to earn livelihood, etc., are done mostly by the girls of lower class families in the villages and cities, therefore they cannot be sent for studies.

Second problem is that the drop out rate, i.e., leaving the school after enrolment in between the studies, is also very high among the girls. They are admitted in the schools with a great enthusiasm, but later on when the family members face difficulties due to obstacles in the jobs inside and outside the home, they are taken out of the schools and their studies get stopped. The girls leaving studies in class I are very soon, again lost in the darkness of illiteracy. Enrolled for admission in class I, out of 100 girls, only about one-third, that is, only 30 girls reach up to class 5.

Going down from the 66 per cent enrolment of the girls at primary level to only 22 per cent enrolment in class 5 to 8, itself shows the fact that, after getting the girls educated only upto primary level, their parents are satisfied with the achievement and their studies are stopped. By the time a girl finishes her 8th class studies, she becomes 14 years old and then due to her insecurity in young age and the preparations of her marriage, her education in higher secondary classes is obstructed. At this level; their education is not considered important, therefore at this level their enrolment remains only 12 per cent of their total number. In urban areas high school education is limited only upto the higher and middle classes even now.

In rural areas also, mainly financially well-off families of middle class take advantage of studies in higher classes. In rural areas in the classes of this level girls form not even one-fifth, that is, 20 per cent of the total number of students. Thus, All India average of dropouts in different levels of education, has remained very high among girls in comparison to boys. At the University level ratio of girls is more at postgraduate level rather than the undergraduate level. The reason of this fact may be that the boys take employment after graduation while the girls keep on studying till their marriages. Since higher education in India is limited upto a very small minor section of people even now, if the total situation is considered, the impact of this tendency on the educational development of women cannot be called quite sufficient.

Thus, out of the students passing school examination per 1000 boys, the growth rate of the number of girls is comparatively slow. At the level of first degree from University the growth rate of this number is comparatively fast. Higher education of women in comparison to other sections is generally limited upto the urban, higher and middle classes.

In the field of women education one more problem is their concentration in the study of certain special subjects. Due to lack of career orientation, and consequently the absence of aptitude, they study mathematics and science less even at school level. In the field of professional education, before independence, for the girls only medical, nursing, education and law courses were available because it was considered that they will be able to perform well only in these professions. After independence, by keeping in mind the principle of equality, opportunities were made available to them for the study of all the subjects. But in spite of the facilities of studying the engineering, industrial, agricultural, commerce, etc., subjects, their interest in the study of these subjects and its usage in the field of profession has not increased even now. Therefore more girls take admissions in teaching, medical and fine arts and lesser in other fields.

National Committee on women education had suggested to arrange separate educational institution for girls in order to finish the prejudice regarding girls education, because most of the parents do not want to educate them along with the boys in the same institution. Therefore, during the period after 1960-61 the number of girls institutions increased very fast and even in 1967-68, out of total institutions, 29 per cent of them were established for girls only which were only 10 per cent in 1947-48. Owing to the distance of educational institutions girls could not go for studies, therefore the programme of laying down the network of schools having only one teacher was started even in small villages. But some adverse symptoms of this fast development could be seen very soon. Most of the schools of interior rural areas, having only one teacher, were closed quite often due to absence of the teacher. Because of this, enthusiasm of many parents to send their daughters to school became weak. In many middle and secondary girls' schools there are no teachers and education facilities (laboratories) and if they are there, their standard is very low. As a result, in these schools selection of subjects becomes very limited for girls. The number of girls' colleges also which was only 81 in 1953-54, increased to 435 in 1971-72. Owing to the fast growth of these institutions, many such institutions have been established out of which, in most of them less than 500 and in many less than 100 girls are studying, which is not practical considering their financial condition; and their standard of education is also very low. This became possible because the government and university have relaxed the conditions of eligibility for approving the girls colleges.

It is essential to be careful regarding the standard of education, otherwise later on in spite of having equal opportunities, they will not get employment due to their inability to get success in competition.

This fact has also been accepted always that for development of women education increasing the number of female teachers is a compulsory condition. In 1947, in the field of teaching in schools only 14.4 per cent were women. In 1973-74, their ratio increased to 26 per cent in primary schools, 37 per cent in middle schools and 30 per cent in higher secondary schools. In universities and colleges their ratio which was 8.5 per cent in 1950-51, increased to 15 per cent in 1970-71. Their highest representation has been in education (23.9 per cent), arts (19.7 per cent), and medicine (19.2 per cent). In universities, their ratio in teachers section was 3.6 per cent in science and 10.8 in law but in other faculties their number was negligible. In rural areas female teachers have to face many difficulties. The teachers coming from outside have to bear the opposition shown by the family members along with the problems of transportation, residence, security, etc. Owing to the lacking means of satisfying essential needs such as education of children and medical facilities, urban women do not like to stay in the villages for teaching work. Women of villages do not take their teaching work seriously therefore cannot perform their role properly. In order to reduce this imbalance between the urban and rural development of education a solution of difficulties and problems of rural areas is essential. In some states due to absence of arrangement of female supervisors also, female teachers have to face some difficulties, due to which in spite of capabilities and unemployment girls are not easily prepared to go to distant areas for doing the teaching job specifically. Therefore, proper arrangement of female supervisors is also necessary.

Change in the Attitudes Towards Women Education

Although in rural areas even now traditional attitudes and behaviour are seen towards female education but the attitudes and behaviour of urban higher and middle class people are changing very fast. By considering education very important to solve the problems of life girls are being given higher education and quite a few of them are allowed to take employment also. Earlier it was thought that girls have less capability and aptitude to study the subjects like mathematics and science, in comparison to boys, but now their grand success in various examinations in comparison to boys, has ruined this concept. In the field of professional education, they are taking admissions in the subjects like engineering, industry, agriculture, commerce, law, research, etc. beside medical and education whereas earlier they used to go for medical and education mostly. Now education is not considered an end only but also the means of earning livelihood. Before independence very few women and that too forced by the conditions of economic hardship, used to go out of the four walls of the house and involve themselves in the money earning occupations and activities. Service of the women used to be considered against the honour of the family and the serving women were also looked down upon. Therefore, girls used to take education in order to get an educated and financially well off husband, and if required, to become financially independent during any emergency in life. But now this attitude is changing and the parents have also started selecting the subjects for education as well as the field of profession also for their daughters as they do for their sons. Specially in the reference of intelligent girls it is a fact that for their education special facilities inside and outside the home are made available. Earlier the service of a girl used to pose an obstruction in her marriage, therefore they had to opt between marriage or a profession for their life, and advance in that direction leaving behind the other one. As a result, most of the girls, active in the field of profession, had to remain unmarried throughout their life. But now it is not so, and by adjusting in both the fields, adopting a balanced lifestyle is possible these days. Now it is considered that a working women is an honour for the family and family members provide assistance and cooperation to her in various ways. Quite a few women take education even after marriage and make its use.

Due to rising prices and ambition of higher standard of life today educated boys of lower middle-class want to marry educated working girls. In spite of having no economic requirement, women of higher class families are becoming active in the field of some profession due to their desires to become financially independent, have their own identity, to achieve higher status and realise self-respect, etc. Higher education is considered as a big achievement and symbol of modernization now. By understanding the difficulties of working wives, educated sensible husbands do not expect an excellent performance of household roles from them and provide them assistance to cope with the double roles they perform.

Owing to the increased age of marriage also, girls are able to get education. In cities free mobility of girls in the society is being approved and the hard bindings of various social restrictions on them are being loosened. In rural areas also, getting the girls of higher middle class family, educated upto school level is considered a very important task of parents. Later on early marriages pose restriction for education of higher level because most of the girls are married before the age of 20 years. For the highly educated girl more highly educated boy is required for marriage for whom lot of dowry is expected. In this way parents have to spend double amount, i.e., on education and marriage of daughter. Due to this reason also girls are not given higher education. In the lower class, urban and rural both, indifferent attitude towards women education is seen even now. Out of this class, some people think of giving no education at all to the girls whereas most of them do not want to give them higher education. In the lower class now, sending wife outside the house to earn money, is being considered against the honour of husband therefore they are unable to understand the utility of education. They feel that the training of household jobs they get right from the childhood days can be used any time in life to earn livelihood whenever required. Due to lack of desire for very high standard of life, without education the life can be maintained, therefore in spite of special facilities provided by Government, lower class people do not take benefits out of them specially in rural areas.

The impact of educational growth can specifically be observed in urban areas. Most of the girls of all the social classes are taking education in schools. Girls of higher and middle classes are advancing towards the adoption of career oriented lifestyle after taking higher education. Quite a few married and unmarried women of these classes are engaged now in the field of profession. In every field women are working shoulder to shoulder with men successfully and they have proved that they are not any less capable than men. The most prominent impact of education is seen in the society in the form of establishment of new values of equality between the men and women due to which change in behaviour is also observed. In the educated families, believing in the values of equality, educated girl is considered to be an asset and not a liability and educated wife also today is not considered the slave of husband but a companion and friend. The process of this change has started only among the urban educated higher and middle class people and its speed is quite slow. But as the education will extend in the rural areas and among lower class people, these impacts will certainly be created. Along with improvement of women's status through education, the process of progress and development of the society has also gained speed, due to their social, economic and political participation. For spreading this fact widely in society fast, well thought, well planned and continuous efforts are being made for necessary reforms in the education system, and hence, their desired consequences will certainly be observed in future.

Eight

Occupational Status

For the development of society it is necessary that all the sections of people fully participate in it and the opportunities of full development of potentialities of women are available. Women remain financially dependent therefore they are exploited. This can be considered as the non-acceptance of human rights and non-availability of social justice for them. Opposite to this, from economic independence, economic base for the freedom of women gets prepared which later on opens the path of social freedom and getting rid of the slavery of men becomes possible for them. As it has been stated in the report of National Committee (1974), distance from home saves them from the bindings of social customs which control and regulate their life all the time. Apart from this, they come into wide social contacts from occupational activities. New thoughts, knowledge of rights and duties in themselves are quite encouraging for the development of their personality. Their social and creative powers are utilized not only for them but for the progress of society also. Therefore, this is the basic principle of United Nations Organization's Declaration that discrimination against women should be finished. Social reformers have also always strongly opposed the discrimination between the roles of men and women. Therefore, they should get opportunities and equal rights of economic participation in the society which is quite necessary for the improvement of their status (Desai, 1977).

Role of Women in Indian Economy

In order to have knowledge about economic participation of women and its evaluation, it is necessary that economic roles should be studied in different forms in different fields because in all these fields due to their social, economic and local characteristics and as a result of their degree of adjustment in the economic process, they are being differentiated. Therefore, by considering the female workers as a homogeneous group, its gross analysis in pure quantitative references, cannot explain the whole situation.

India is an agricultural country. In the traditional agrarian system, working of the women by going out of their homes, has remained a common fact. In agriculture work, craftsmanship and other small petty jobs, women have performed clear and approved roles in the field of production and marketing, and even today wherever the traditional forms of economic system are in practice, they are doing so, specifically the wives of landless farmers or those having very little land have always worked along with their husbands in the fields. According to 1981 census report, more than 80 per cent women are engaged in the agricultural activities (Vohra and Sen, 1985). But as Dak (1988) has mentioned, Indian social system does not permit the higher class women to go out of their houses for working. Therefore, the women of the houses of big farmers and landlords used to remain imprisoned within the four walls of the house. Even now in this class, not permitting the women to go out for working, is considered an honour to the family.

In India the process of industrialization, included development programmes where poor women got opportunities to work in great numbers in factories, mines, plantations and construction works. Due to financial constraints, leaving their villages and going to cities along with the family to earn livelihood was a compulsion for them. In lower class, in front of the problem of satisfying the basic needs, the thought about the status of women as it is, does not have any meaning and among women themselves, in the absence of awareness about their own interests, it gets lost even more. Their act of earning livelihood was being taken as a normal phenomenon and therefore as its consequence no symptoms of progress in their familial status could be observed. Technological changes have adversely affected the economic participation of the women of this class. Due to downfall of rural industries, modernization in the field of agriculture, mechanization in the field of industries, usage of new techniques in the construction work, etc., mainly the males are employed and the females get less opportunities. In this way, the process of development has affected the economic participation of women of lower class negatively.

On the other hand as Kapoor (1970) has also stated, comparatively a new fact has emerged after independence owing to the extension of education among the women of upper and middle class; that is, their engagement in the occupational activities by using their educational achievements for earning money and their realization of freedom by coming out of the four walls was traditionally approved. After independence, in Indian Constitution, women were given right to get equal opportunities in every field, and in practice also the doors of all types of education were opened for them. Social changes in urban areas and on top of it increasing expenditure on maintenance, removed all those restrictions which had great impact on upper and middle-class women earlier and as a result they could enter in those professions in tertiary field which were forbidden for them earlier. Quite a few women become professionally occupied not due to shortage of money but to establish their independent identity in the society and to increase their self-respect. Owing to the changing attitudes of people, working woman is now considered a source of additional honour to the family. Economic participation of these classes is increasing continuously during the last few decades. Its positive impact on their familial and social status has also started among the common women. Specially talented women are leaving the men behind and advancing in every field but they are the exceptions only. In this way we see that not only in education and medicine but also in agriculture, engineering, technology, law, commerce, research, etc., and they are employed in a very large number in different offices in white collar jobs. In rural areas also they are employed in the fields of education, medicine and development.

In this way, as Savara (1986) has also stated while on the one hand, economic participation of lower class female labourers doing manual jobs is decreasing the economic participation of higher and middle class women engaged in intellectual jobs requiring mental capabilities, as Lev, Pentson and Averate (1984) have also stated, is increasing. But in totality, in Indian economy, picture of only deteriorating role of women can be seen. The reduction rate among women is specially higher than the men, although as Table 8.1 demonstrates, in comparison to 1971, in 1991 work participation of women has increased a little while work participation of men has decreased a little.

TABLE 8.1

WORK PARTICIPATION RATES IN INDIA (1911-1981 CENSUS YEAR)

Census year	*Women*	*Men*	*Persons*
1911	33.9	62.0	48.2
1921	32.8	60.6	47.0
1931	28.4	57.9	43.6
1951	23.3	54.3	39.2
1961	28.0	57.1	43.0
1971	11.8	52.5	32.9
1981	14.4	51.2	33.4
1991	22.69	51.52	37.64

Source: Census report 1981, Series 9, Karnataka Paper 2 of 1981, Provisional Population Totals. P. 90 and cited by Rao (1985) Census Report of 1991.

As the Table 8.1 shows, during the 20th Century, total work participation and work participation of males and females separately, all have decreased due to modernization, mechanization and usage of new techniques, etc. But the difference between the work participation of males and females which was near about 30 per cent in 1911, got increased to near about 40 per cent in 1971, which is existing even in 1991 with a very little improvement. This determines the fact that women, quite less in number in comparison to men, go out of the house to work for earning money and the impact of modernization and development has been quite adverse on their jobs. Now less opportunities of work are available to them. This fact is observed in both urban and rural areas. Although in 1991, little improvement can be seen in both the areas but it is negligible. The improvement in the status of women's work participation in 1991 has been possible due to entry of educated girls in different professions. Table 8.2 shows the women's work participation in rural and urban areas. Both the groups of girls belonging to middle class, that is, those residing in rural areas as well as those going to rural areas from urban areas, are active in the offices and service-fields of education, medical and development fields in rural society. This fact has improved their status in 1981. In 1991, although the work participation rate of women has sufficiently increased, the gap between the females' and males' status, regarding, it is quite wide.

TABLE 8.2
WORK PARTICIPATION IN RURAL AND URBAN AREAS IN INDIA (1961-1981)

	1961		*1971*		*1981*	
Area	*Female*	*Male*	*Female*	*Male*	*Female*	*Male*
Rural	31.42	58.30	13.44	53.62	16.49	52.21
Urban	11.16	52.37	6.68	48.82	7.57	48.18
Total	27.93	57.16	12.12	52.61	14.44	51.23

Source: Census of India, 1981, Series 9, Karnataka Paper 2 of 1981 and stated by Rao (1985).

Detailed analysis shows that in total female population, the percentage of working women which was 33.9 in 1911, reduced to 12.12 in 1971. In the same way in total labour power their percentage which was 34.44 in 1911, came down to 17.35 in 1971. In between 1961-1971 both male and female population increased more or less in the same proportion that is, 25 and 24 per cent respectively, but in comparison to this, while the number of male workers got reduced only by 5 per cent the difference between the percentages of female workers in both the census years was of 16 per cent. It means their number got reduced by 16 per cent in 1971, in comparison to 1961. Although in 1981 women's condition has improved in comparison to men but still they are far behind the males and the difference of 37 per cent is existing between the male and female workers regarding work participation. On the whole, the situation demonstrates continuously increasing unemployment (among males less and among females more). As

Savara (1986) has stated, upto 1930, in Bombay cotton textile mills, 25 per cent women were working but their number has reduced to 5 per cent in 1975. Discrimination against them has been increasing continuously.

Women's Participation in Unorganized Sector

In the unorganized sector in which agriculture, industries and other services are included, for workers no security measures and regulative mechanisms exist. Neither Government legal provisions are there for safeguarding their interests, nor as Boston (1980) has stated, labourers are organized. Therefore, they become the victim of exploitation due to their inability of collective bargaining. As National Committee (1974) has reported, most of the labourers are working in this field only. The status of women workers is clear from this fact that, 94 per cent of them are working in the unorganized sector. As Bhoite (1987) has found, in rural areas women workers have to face too many problems. Commercialization of agriculture and modernization, establishment of rural banks and agriculture products' markets (Krishi Upaj Mandi), efforts by the Government to stabilize landownership and maintain minimum wages, etc., have neither helped a bit, in organizing the production relations or in decreasing the amount of exploitation of weaker sections in agriculture and other occupations nor in solving the problems like low productivity, poverty, unemployment and under-employment. In this sectors women have been specifically exploited because as Desai and Patel (1985) have also stated, their wages are less than minimum wages of male workers, and their financial contribution in the family has not been approved. They become victim of both, unemployment and under-employment more. In rural areas 60 per cent and in the whole country 56 per cent of the unemployed people are such women who search for a job and they do not get it, otherwise also the number of women needing the job will be much more. In the same way in both urban and rural areas, the number of underemployed women is more than men.

The basic problems influencing the roles and opportunities of employment among women have been created by forced dependence of women due to lack of proper employment opportunities, limited skills and illiteracy, restricted mobility and lack of autonomous status. Condition of women workers remains very bad due to absence of control on the sources of production and chronic indebtedness created by continuous gap between income and consumption; which deprives them from all the bargaining power and occupational mobility. Main part of this large group, coming in this sector, is composed of unskilled workers, landless farmers, members of families of farmers having non-economical landholdings and women employed in traditional rural and cottage industries, most of whom are leading their life below the poverty line. Specific disabilities which are associated with women's rights and opportunities of economic participations are more powerful in unorganized sector.

According to 1971 census report, 80 per cent women are working in agriculture. This number in rural and urban areas is respectively 87 per cent and 17.5 per cent of the women's working force. In this field in the last many decades opportunities of employment for agricultural female labourers have lessened as stated earlier. In villages their status is associated with the status of either husband or father. Due to continuous deterioration in financial condition of farmers, having non-economical landholdings, after being landless, they themselves become agricultural labourers and their wives are also forced to do so and most of them have to face the problem of either unemployment or underemployment. Low rate of wages is determined for female labourers against which they cannot protest due to ignorance of laws, illiteracy and poverty. Owing to the downfall of rural and cottage industries and consequently the end of skills and substitute occupations, a situation of occupational immobility has been created, which is a disability for women labourers. They want to work only in their villages. Social-psychological factors and bindings of familial obligations restrict their mobility. As the consequence of usage of new technology in agriculture, women are gradually being dislodged from the cultivation work, because agricultural extension officers want to bring quick change by teaching the new methods to only male workers. Need of less labourers do not allow usage of women labour. As Majumdar (1983) has written, process of change in villages is unable to create the desired impact.

In agricultural occupations due to low capital investment, inferior technology, low productivity and insufficient debt facilities, downfall of rural cottage home and small industries had started from the beginning of British time therefore the number of women is gradually decreasing and they are being exploited in these industries. As Khan and Ayesha (1982) have reported, the amount of money which is being spent on the improvement of women's status through development of village has not resulted in a corresponding increase in their status in the same proportion. In the construction industry they are extremely exploited by contractors. Leaving aside their thoughtlessness about the provisions of fair wages, residential facilities, health services and creches, they do not even realize the need of providing any social security in emergency. In Bidi industries, wages of women working in factories and residences, are deducted due to various reasons. No provision of providing maternity benefit has been made by contractors. In Chikan industries, 90 per cent of workers are women, who get quite exploited by middle-men. Self-employed women in the status of producer or retail trader are also exploited by middle-men due to their dependence on them owing to obstacle of illiteracy, lack of resources, ignorance about modern marketing methods and sale increasing techniques. Their real income remains quite low due to earning of very little profit.

Women in Organized Sector

In this sector all those establishments of production in public sector and private sector, beside agriculture, are included in which 10 or more persons get employment. Modern relations of production are considered a special feature of organized sector. This sector is regulated by those labour organizations, alongwith labourers working conditions and security laws, who can bargain collectively. In this, those establishments of services and professions, in public and private sectors are also included which are controlled by various rules and labour ministry keeps on collecting regularly, detailed information about workers. In this sector though in last few decades, the number of women has increased but out of total employment, the ratio of women got stabilized on 11 per cent only. In organized sector, employed women in 1971, were only 6 per cent of total women workers, out of which 2.7 per cent were working in industries and 3.3 per cent were employed in services and professions. The number of women has increased more in public sector and comparatively quite less in private sector. Their ratio has also increased in public sector whereas it has decreased in private sector.

In spite of continuous growth of employment in industries during last decades, women's employment has decreased. Their ratio was 11.43 per cent in 1951 which came down to 9.1 per cent in 1971. In mines their ratio reduced from 27.1 in 1951 to 11.9 in 1971. Their number decreased maximum in the Coal mines, that is from 55,000 in 1951 to only 2,000 in 1971. Plantations of tea, coffee and rubber was the only area, where for special jobs women labourers are needed and therefore during this period, the number of employed women has either remained stable or increased a little. The reasons for downward trends of women's employment in industries and mines are considered the adverse impact of security laws for female labourers (regarding maternity benefits, creches and separate provisions for cleanliness etc.), policy of equal wages, and unification of production methods and structural change in the economy, leading towards modernization. But National Committee (1974) has disapproved the first two concepts. In textile and jute industries and mines, most important factor for their big downfall is the extensions and types of modernization methods. The industries which have adopted such an expensive technology, resulting in labour's retrenchment, they experienced women's retrenchment to be easier than men's retrenchment and they justified it on the basis that, illiterate and unwilling women lack skill of learning new processes, while they are not given opportunities of training even when working. Wherever they got opportunity they have demonstrated their efficiency more than men. The traditional concepts of their dress and interest in special professions have also been proved wrong because women working in new modern industries, are rarely traditional and conservative. But still illiteracy, ignorance about the alternate job opportunities, lack of training opportunities along with increasing rate of general unemployment in country and most of all women's limited mobility also discourages their competitive spirit and they are mostly found suffering from the problem of unemployment or under-employment. Women's participation in non-traditional services and professions has increased rapidly specifically after independence. The reasons for this trend are constitutional promise of not practising discrimination regarding employment and exercising equality of opportunity; development of women education and consequently their entry in those fields of education and occupation, on which men monopolised till now; gradual change in social values regarding gainful employment of women in urban middle class, and extension of tertiary field as a direct result of development after independence.

In the public sector among workers of other affiliated sections like sections of professionals, technical workers and teachers, the number of women workers is continuously increasing since 1960. As administrative executives or organiser and manager the number of women increased from 10,000 in 1960 to 12,000 in 1966 itself. In the section of clerks and other affiliated workers, number of women got greatly increased from 37,000 in 1960 to 79,000 in 1968. During this period number of female workers has remained stable in transport, collection and communication systems, but in services, games and entertainment, their number rose from 5000 to 13,000. At this time only the number of unskilled women working in offices got decreased from 25,000 to 16,000. In the sections of private sector where both increased the number and ratio of working women are seen, they are : clerk and in other alike jobs, services, games and entertainment, and teachers of primary and middle schools. In the beginning in all sections employment of women remained slow but now the situation is improving. Some new industries like advertisement, marketing, research, hotel management and cottage industries are employing women in the category of managers but in traditional industries, women have not been accepted at this level.

Two tendencies of professional pattern of women working in services and industries are clearly seen. First is that, there is a concentration of working women in medical and teaching professions, and second is that in clerical services, few less prestigious jobs are considered suitable for women.

In 1970, there were only 17 per cent women among the workers of professional, technical and other affiliated fields out of whom three-fourth were teachers. As scientists most of them were social scientists because now subjects like research and social work are emerging as new professions suitable for women. In particular professions women's ratio in comparison to men is like this: doctors, 7.1 per cent, advocate, 1.2 per cent, teachers, 30.3 per cent, nursing and other affiliated services, 72.2 per cent: Scientist, 10.9 per cent. In primary schools the number of female teachers is 71 per cent and after this 21 per cent in secondary schools. This concentration of women in teaching profession is the symbol of opportunity and priority both. Considering the prevalent social conditions, professions like engineering and medical for which a long training is required; are within the reach of only a very minor section of women belonging to the higher middle class. Society approves the teaching profession for women because along with teaching they can perform their household duties easily. In the medical field, in 1968, in the group of 1,20,000 doctors, there were 12,000 women doctors. Although according to 1971 census the number of trained female doctors was 25, per 100 male doctors but the number of employed female doctors was 6.1 per cent, per 100 male doctors. This fact shows that they are not being fully utilized in the country and leaving behind their own country they are going abroad for employment. Since their patients are mostly women, most of the female doctors specialize in gynaecology and women diseases, though they have started entering in other fields now. Owing to various reasons female doctors do not want to work in the villages therefore they get concentrated in urban areas. After independence the number of nurses, mid-wives, and female health inspectors has extended too much. Although the number of women advocates is increasing they get negligible opportunities of becoming judges. A new profession of social worker, trained at professional level, has emerged for them after independence, and they are employed in both, public and voluntary social welfare institutions and departments. In 1968, there were 3,153 social work graduates and their number rose to 6,000 in 1971, out of whom 30 per cent were women. In this profession, due to women's personal interest and their specialization in primary social work and community organization mostly, they get employment easily whereas due to men's interest only in labourers and industrial relations less employment opportunities are available for them. In spite of a very large number of women, employed in this profession, very few women are appointed in important posts. Educated women are getting enough opportunities of employment in the posts of clerk, steno, typist and receptionist, etc. In Government offices also, in the group of class III workers concentration of women is maximum. At this level, rather than any other level of services, the number of women has increased quite rapidly. In private sector also, in the clerical cadre, they are concentrated. In the field of management, there are few women in the public sector but in private sector, their number is negligible. Among central services, in the ratio of successful women in Indian administrative service, police service and foreign service, there is improvement in comparison to men; but in other services such as Indian economic service, statistics service, engineering services, their ratio is very small. In rail service also they are appointed only in accounts and medical sections at the level of first class services. The deficiency which is found in the ratio of women at the levels having more responsibilities comparatively, is on the one hand, owing to the prejudices and differentiating recruitment policy, and on the other due tc lack of career orientation and feeling of devotion, for work in women themselves. Although in the tertiary field rapid extension of opportunities for women has taken place due to development process, adopted after independence, but this is certain that, owing to the limitation of resources, along with increasing controls, growth of this unproductive field will also be decreasing gradually in future, due to which there is a possibility of decreasing employment of women also. Till the job opportunities for women are not developed in the productive field, it will not be possible to check the downward tendencies in the employment of women. Table 8.3 clarifies the condition of women workers in comparison to men workers in widespread occupational categories.

Table 8.3 demonstrates two facts mainly, firstly, even now an overwhelming majority, i.e., 82.99 per cent of working women are engaged in the field of agriculture, and secondly except cottage industries, in all other occupational categories, they are employed less than men. There are special problems regarding economic participation of women, due to which working women have to face various difficulties and which prevent the entiy of women willing to work. Owing to the compulsion of performance of roles of housewives and mothers, women require special facilities.

TABLE 8.3
PERCENTAGE OF MEN AND WOMEN WORKERS IN WIDESPREAD OCCUPATIONAL CATEGORIES IN 1981

Occupational Category	*Men*	*Women*	
1. Cultivators	43.66	37.50	Working women in agricultural field 82.29
2. Agricultural labourers	19.83	44.79	
3. Livestock, forestry, fishing, hunting and plantation orchard and allied services	2.37	1.79	
4. Mining and quarrying	0.61	0.27	
5. Manufacturing, processing servicing and repairs			
(a) Household Industry	3.18	4.44	
(b) Other than household industry	8.85	3.14	
6. Constructions	1.81	0.68	
7. Trade and Commerce	7.28	1.75	
8. Transport, storage and communications.	3.29	0.29	
9. Other services	9.12	5.35	

Source: Women in India, A statistical profile, Govt. of India, Department of Social Welfare, New Delhi 1981, stated by Desai and Patel (1985).

In order to remain active in the field of profession, whereas they have to remain deprived even from general facilities. For Indian women, opportunities of occupation are very limited (Desai and Krishna Raj 1987). The reason behind this is the explosive problem of unemployment due to very large population of country, along with limitations of industrialization and professional education. For the getting success through all means in competitions with men and entrance in various professions, is, if not impossible, certainly difficult. Apart from this, in the unorganized private sector, for the jobs given to women general pay scale is also very low. Offering higher pay to men and lower pay to women for same job is very much in practice. The policy of equal pay for equal work is not given any importance in the unorganized sector. In the private sectors owners act according to their own will. At the time of recruitment mostly unmarried women are given preference because married women need more leave and they are forced to leave jobs at the time of deliveries. Regarding the working conditions, this is the fact that in unorganized private sector, even now leave with pay is not given at the time of delivery, there is no guarantee of getting job again in the same place and there is no provision of creches for keeping the children.

On the requirement of retrenchment of labourers, mostly women labourers are removed from the jobs, because otherwise also, they are considered as temporary workers, as they can leave their job any time due to marriage and child birth. In the unorganized sector owing to the absence of their own trade union like male labourers they are unable to enforce demands. In organized sector also, only 7 per cent women labourers are the members of trade unions and they too do not have any importance because they are not holding any important posts. They also do not get opportunities of training in their field of work because owing to the lack of seriousness towards their job they will not be able to give full benefit of that training to the establishment. Due to this reason obstruction gets created in the way of their promotion. Male colleagues get success in occupying the higher posts while they remain on the lower posts only. This situation is very frustrating. The situation is like this, that there is no lack of devotion towards work among women. Double work load of occupational work along with compulsory domestic roles, sometimes forbids them from too much involvement in the professional work, but on the whole, they can produce results, far better than men, if they are given opportunities of advancing further. It is very difficult to get the job for aged women, willing to work because even among youngsters there is too much unemployment. One problem of women's entry in the occupation is that, while working in some other place, away from their own home town, living alone in the rented house is not safe for them. Therefore, they do not go to any other place away from their own city or village for occupation.

Suggestions for Better Employment Conditions Among Women

For the progress of women in the occupational field first of all it is essential to provide them general education. Then after considering their capabilities and aptitude in particular profession, as well as opportunities of promotion in it, they should be provided facility of professional education. After their entry in the profession, they should get opportunities of training for promotion, equal to men. They should get equal pay for equal work and equal opportunities of work along with favourable working conditions. In the industrial establishments, apart from maternity leave with full pay at the time of child birth, according to law, there should be provision of creches for small children. Along with job security, promise of financial assistance at the time of emergency, will keep them carefree and increase their work efficiency. Apart from this, for the women who can not take full time jobs due to familial reasons, provision of part time jobs is essential. For the women, leaving their jobs in between due to familial reasons only, guarantee for facility of re-entry in the same occupation is also very necessary. For the aged women, willing to work, arrangement of special assistance and advice should be made. For women's entry in the occupation age limit should be increased in such a manner so that they can enter after marriage and birth of two children. There will be less chances of obstruction in future in such cases, which will be beneficial for both female workers and employers. In order to solve the problems of residence and safety of the working women positive measures are required. As National Committee (1974) has suggested, service conditions should be improved and considering the conditions of women they should be given special facilities. Specifically, arrangements for transportation and prevention of unnecessary transfers are quite essential. In the organized sector, emphasis on the implementation of laws is essential whereas in unorganized sector also imposition of legal binding on employers is very much required, so that even if desired, they are unable to adopt the policy of differentiation regarding female workers and behave with them in a justified manner.

Effective steps are to the taken for organizing labour unions in unorganized sector and in all labour unions women wings are necessary for solution of womens' problems and their improved participation in union activities, so that they can be saved from exploitation, especially from the difficult situation like retenchment and pay-deduction which bring conditions of poverty and hunger for them. For the self-employment of women, apart from training in particular profession or skill, and along with knowledge about the market system for facing competition, knowledge about arrangement of capital resources, introduction of ways of getting raw material at proper rates, and provision of proper facilities to them is also quite essential. Economic progress of the society will be possible in the long run from their engagement in the field of production, along with their increasing economic participation. Sahay (1985) has suggested that, 25 per cent of the government services should be reserved for women.

As Desai (1977) has stated, if the women get opportunities equal to men, they can work in every field like men. Today, if she lags behind a little it is not her fault, but it is the fault of traditions which have suppressed them since centuries. Owing to this, her own thoughts also hang around only familial life and her nearest environment also do not provide favourable conditions for her devotion in the outside work freely. For changing the situation along with economic growth, social progress is also greatly required.

Nine

Familial Status

The structure, cultural pattern and value system of any society affects the social expectations regarding behaviour of both the sexes — males and females, and upto a certain limit, determine the roles and status of women in the society. In Indian society, the most important institutions are religious traditions, lineage system, familial organization and marriage which provide a moral basis to the rights and duties of men and women (National Committee, 1974). All these institutions have traditionally determined a four layered role and status order for women, i.e., daughter, wife, housewife and mother (Jain, 1988) through which the world of a women got limited to family only and even in family she became subordinate to men and occupied secondary place.

Hindu religious traditions deprive her from worshipping and reciting Vedas, direct her to remain under the man's authority, accept her role as mother and wife only in the form of ideal role, give more importance to son by backing the patrilineal social structure and consider the women inferior to men. In the Hindu religion itself, as a result of protest movements, some branches of it, such as Bouddh, Jain, Vaishnav, Vir Shaiv and Sikh religion, emerged which tried to improve the status of women, especially their status regarding religious and spiritual activities. But in spite of this, in these religions also the woman was being accepted mainly as mother and wife and she got positioned in the category lower to men. Later on religions like Islam, Christianity and Parsi brought along with them a particular attitude regarding women but in due course of time they also got themselves coloured in the Indian colour of practical customs and traditions.

In India, in few south-west and north-west regions, Matrilineal system is practised in which lineage tradition is accepted from the woman's side but in the woman's family, power still remains in the hands of man, specially in the higher caste group where the wife remain engaged inside the house and the husband goes out of the house for work. All overwhelming majority of Indian population follows the patrilineal system of lineage order. Man advances the lineage and work of family. At the time of marriage the daughter leaves the family and lineage of her father and joins the family and lineage of her husband. This affects the status of woman which is related to her legal rights also. Some religious duties of the family can be performed only by son owing to the social cultural compulsion of daughter's marriage, the girl has been considered a burden, specially because the parents spend money on their rearing, education and health, without any expectation of financial assistance of any sort, from her and due to this reason only in these matters and in right of property, differentiation between the man and woman has been practised. This cultural concept that the role of woman is only secondary, i.e., of assistant, is related with this tendency directly and it is the outcome of mainly patrilineal system and wife's living in the husband's residence.

Joint familial organization is combined of those patrilineal male relatives who have equal rights on property and the total expenditure on them comes from the same source, who live in the same house and eat food cooked from the same fire place. It is expected from a woman that after marriage she should mould herself according to her in-laws' household. Owing to the process of socialization starting from the childhood, after some time of marriage she develops the sense of belongingness towards new family and along with passing of time this feeling of oneness or affinity keeps on strengthening. She is kept under strict control as a daughter-in-law. In the decision-taking on any issue, she has either very little or no say and she remains in subordination under her mother-in-law directly. Her status in the family mostly depends upon her husband's contribution in the household economy. In the higher and middle classes her status depends even on the dowry brought by her at the time of marriage as well as the financial benefits got from the parental family from time to time. In the middle class, the mother of grown-up children gets respect and privileges and she gets the right of taking decisions also. Although women perform only marginal role in decision-taking generally privileges of mother, which convert daughter-in-law into a maid servant, get diminished along with the old age and widowhood or due to increased importance of daughter-in-law as the wife of a bread earner for the family and mother of growing-up children. In north India, customs of veiling in front of husband's relatives and touching their feet by the wife are quite prevalent.

In patrilineal society, after marriage a woman gets transferred from her birth lineage to her husband's birth lineage. For girls, marriages arranged at small age are considered most desirable because this concept is connected with the importance of protection of virginity, restriction of marriage in the same lineage and proper adjustment in husband's house, etc. The marriage is fixed by the parents. There are many facts in Hindu marriage which highlight the lower status of women, such as: for fixing marriage showing the girl in front of the boy's side people, donation of daughter at the time of marriage, presents and gifts given by the girl's side to the boys side, at the time of marriage and other occasions, compulsion of higher caste of boy's side and lower caste of girls side, social acceptance of polygamy, hell like life of widows, etc., demonstrate the woman's status of subordination and helplessness only, observation of fasts by the woman for the long life of husband and sons, festivals demonstrating the importance of men, special ornaments and symbols used by women to show their status of wife and mother of sons, etc., only tell the story of her inferiority and dependence on men. Since the woman has to perform the functions of reproduction, nursing and rearing of children her stay at home is essential, thus, she has been imprisoned within the four walls of the house and responsibilities of looking after the needs of all family members of all age groups and providing services to them along with house-keeping have been given to her. Whereas, when the man comes home after the work of earning livelihood and moving around freely outside, he is given special care and treatment, and on priority basis all the facilities and services are provided to him. According to husband's desires only a wife has to lead her life and she has to keep her own desires hidden at her heart. This is the ideal lifestyle predetermined and prescribed for her in the Indian society. But giving more importance to chastity towards husband (Pativrata Dhram), virtues of woman of loyalty to her husband, have been appreciated to a great deal in the religious books. So much so, that in the higher and middle-classes, even after becoming widow, a woman has to lead a life of renunciation by keeping the memory of her husband in the heart and depriving herself from all the joys and happiness. This is her destiny.

Socialization and its Bases

Through the process of socialization starting from childhood itself, a person is converted into a member of the society. He is introduced with his various roles and statuses, and he is made aware, of his rights and duties. In the process of socialization directions of the people of older generation of the family have a very important place and also lots of manners are learned by observation.

Sex Role

In the socialization process of women, socialization of the daughter by her mother is important. As Lott (1981) has expressed a mother trains her daughter for her future roles of housewife and rearing of children very easily by making her own assistant in all the household jobs. Apart from this, through observation of mothers performance of different roles, daughter herself internalizes the ideas regarding expected behaviour and utilizes them in future. Thus, as Channa (1988) has stated, while the girls is made an expert of the household affairs before her marriage, the boy is trained and prepared for earning the livelihood by giving him opportunities of experiencing outside world through getting the outside jobs done by him. In this way, due to sex difference the girls and boys are socialized for different roles mainly by the family, although the process of socialization goes on throughout the life, for accommodation of person according to changed circumstances. But in every situation there is division of labour between the man and woman. The jobs needing more physical strength are done by the boys and the jobs needing less physical strength are given to the girls generally, even inside the house.

During the process of socialization, differentiation between the boy and girl is justified on different bases. First of all on the basis of the different biological structure of the man and woman. Due to particular biological composition only the woman can give birth to the child and maintain the life of newly born infant by breast feeding (Gupta, 1986). Later on also, since for bearing and rearing of the children mother has to suffer a lot, as the mother can bring up her growing children, no man, not even any other woman can bring them up, because fulfillment of not only physical but also the psychological needs, is necessary for the proper development of their personality. Therefore, looking after the children by staying at home should be the main function of woman. Other basis for woman's socialization, different than man, is the anthropological fact that by nature woman is less powerful in comparison to man. Her muscles are not developed and well built like man's muscles, therefore she can not perform the jobs needing more physical strength, hence it is proper that she should only take the responsibility of household affairs, needing less physical strength. Due to her specific biological and anthropological features possibility of the problem of her physical security, specially during night time and at lonely places always exists, therefore it is not considered proper to give her freedom of going out alone specially at odd hours and on odd places and allow her to mix freely with opposite sex specially outside male members. Regarding this, according to modern thinking, if they are trained properly, they can become enough powerful to fight at least for their self defence. One more basis for differentiation is socialization of both the sexes is psychological. Under this, it is considered that they are inferior to men.

In comparison to men they have less intellectual capabilities, logical mind, perception and farsightedness. By nature they are imaginative, emotional, impulsive and cowardly. They get influenced by others very easily and they themselves are unable to think and act rationally. It is thought that they do not have the efficiency to take important decisions, hence the responsibility of functions having long term effects, should not be handed over to them, because they cannot handle it properly. Therefore, the functions needing more mental ability should be performed by men only. If the assistance of women is required it can be taken by men in order to complete the task. Owing to this reason, right from the beginning women are taught to include the virtues of adjustment, obedience, subordination, submissiveness, dedication, etc., in their personalities. They internalize the negative self image originated by socialization (Channa, 1988). Through stories, movies and dramas also such imaginative picture of woman is presented which is considered ideal in the Indian society.

The thought of inferiority of women was prevalent in the whole world throughout the medieval period which got challenged by many scholars. They stated that woman should achieve every characteristics of human being because intellectual and other disabilities or weaknesses, existing among women, are not by birth but they are the result of their inferior social status. Therefore, today, what is called the nature of woman, it is artificial owing to the consequence of their helplessness and suppression in some directions, and the unnatural excitement in some directions. They expressed that till now we were accepting the morality of submissiveness but now we will have to accept the morality of justice. Earlier it was considered that girls do not have efficiency of studying subjects like science and mathematics but now women's better performance in these subjects and their success on responsible posts of service, have proved that they are not less efficient than men.

One more basis for man-woman differentiated socialization is sociological which considers the division of work according to the efficiency of members of society significant in order to maintain continuity and stability of social life. According to it for satisfying various needs of all the members of society, i.e., for proper functioning of society, all types of jobs are required to be done. If those jobs are given to proper people, they will finish them with more efficiency. As far as division of work between man and woman is concerned, nature itself has divided their work by giving them different biological composition. As Gupta (1986) has stated their functions can not be exchanged. Women's objective to perform all types of jobs outside home like man is without any basis and useless because man can not perform all those jobs which woman performs at least not of bearing and nursing of the children. Therefore, two cultural streams should be accepted out of which one flows from woman and other from the man. Since both are required they should be developed fully. Apart from this, for maintaining social organization also it is needed that all the people should perform their roles properly and do not interfere in others work by entering in other fields, otherwise consequences may disturb the social system. Beside this, attempting to do the jobs more than one's physical and psychological potential may result in personal disorganization which ultimately contributes to social disorganization only. Hence, in the interest of society as well as individual it is necessary that they should make efforts to perform their duties given to them by nature. Against this thought also the logic is forwarded that working women can be given maternity leave with full pay at the time of delivery and thus their job can be made easy, and for rearing the children and other household jobs men can work equally or fully if required, so that she does not suffer from double burden of work, does not face role conflict and her physical and mental health remains good. If woman can properly work outside for earning money she should be given opportunities equal to man and all the family members should help her in household chores to make her burden light.

In this way regarding the roles of women one stream of thought directs them to perform household jobs and particular outside jobs different than men, by pointing out their particular biological structure responsible for their specific psychological composition different than men. Havelock Alis Sigmund Freud, Scanfield, etc., represented it. Other stream of thought considers the cultural patterns provided by present social environment, responsible for their different psychological symptoms, and by changing them through social changes permits them to work outside the house like men in all the fields. The propagators of this stream of thought are J.S. Mill, Halen B. Thompson, Margaret Mead, C.C. North, L.B. Pekin, George C. Ward, Joseph Folsom and Wolstone Craft. As Desai (1977) has stated the first stream of thoughts is comparatively older against which the new stream of thoughts, i.e., the later ones got originated.

Economic Evaluation of Household Work

In India woman is considered connected mainly with household. She is expected to look after the household affairs and duty of housewife and mother are considered to be her specific roles. In the cultural perception of people, household affairs like bearing and rearing of children are thought to be related to womanhood. For woman only household jobs are considered compulsory and they are the unpaid worker of the family generally. In the financially well-off families, with the help of domestic servants, they are spared a little from providing household services but they are expected to run the household and rear the children properly. For taking help from the servants in household jobs they are paid but if the same jobs are done by the housewife, in spite of her saving money, her work is not evaluated in terms of her financial contribution in the family. Women from lower middle class spend 18 out of 24 hours in the household jobs but instead of understanding its economic importance, it is taken for granted that it is only the process of performing her duties as housewife and mother. Nowadays by increasing the importance of household jobs it has been made a subject of art. Education of home science was specifically started for girls to make them good housewives. Honour of motherhood is also much more propagated and for good motherhood also provision of training has been made in home science college. From the educated mothers it is expected that they should rear the children well and pay attention towards their education, along with keeping the house clean, beautiful and attractive, cooking variety of rich tasty dishes of food and welcoming and looking after the family friends and relatives. Owing to particular biological symptoms, these jobs are considered quite natural for women. So much so, that even working women are expected to be good mothers and housewives. House work is considered inferior and unproductive therefore its performance by men is considered shameful because they enjoy higher social status. 'A Penny saved is a penny earned', if according to this proverb, house work, rearing of children, etc., are recognized as socially and economically productive jobs, men will also participate in them. If the work of housewife is accepted as the work contributing in national saving and economic stability, instead of her present workload without any respect or recognition, her status will be raised and she will bear its burden happily, By providing facilities through household jobs, the housewife, without earning any money directly, increases money earning efficiency of family's male members hence house work is required to be included in economic activities.

House work is unproductive, difficult and laborious work which is done by every woman. It is insignificant and there is nothing in it which helps the development of woman. Women of lower economic status are forced to do it like slave without which the whole family structure will collapse. In the whole world this is a common problem of women although in cities less time and labour is spent on it in comparison to villages. According to Chatterji (1988) 'Characteristics of house work are that it is essential for the social and economic structure whose basic unit is family, it is insignificant and makes one realize the sense of loneliness, it is continuous, difficult and thankless work in which never ending time is consumed. For it no payment is given and it is done free of charge by the women. Therefore, but for household expenditure, women have very little extra money with them which they can spend wherever they want, that too when they do not have to give account of expenditure to the money earner. Thus, there are no fixed working hours, leave and payment for housework and it is done by only women generally.'

In India, 63 per cent adult women are engaged in housework, out of 50 years average age of women 8 years (working hours) are spent only in Kitchen for cooking food. From the standard of Western countries also house work is considered to be the primary work of women, even if they are going to work outside, outside work is secondary and less significant for them, this has been determined by men (Chatterji, 1988). According to one study, rural and urban women were spending 61 and 81 hours respectively in housework in one week and those going out for work, were spending 40 hours in it. Thus, even if women are not working outside, they work more than the men, in which there is no rest, satisfaction and enjoyment. Owing to the absence of help from joint family, urban women have to spend more time in house work. As Berk (1980) has stated domestic appliances provide some relief from labour but then other jobs get increased and on the whole more time is spent on housework. It is only possible for men to spend more time in earning money because whole responsibility of housework is taken by women, but in his property, wife has no right until and unless husband presents her.

In western countries it is being greatly emphasized that housework should be evaluated economically. If the house is considered an economic place and the time, which is limited like other sources of production, is accepted as basic economic unit, a theory of Investment of human capital regarding the inclusion of housework into economic works can easily be developed. In 1965, Baker kept the foundation of this theory that housework should be regarded as activity of non-marketed economic work. On the basis of importance of time's price, decision of woman may depend that how she should distribute her time between the jobs at house and labour market. The more educated and capable she will be the more income for the time she will get from outside work. The less importance and time she will give to the housework. In such a situation housework will be done either by other members of the family or the servants. In 1974, time of woman's housework and outside work was financially evaluated by an economist. Time given to both types of work depends on the fact that for woman working outside, what is the rate of her pay, how much is the productivity of housework, how much work is needed at home, etc. The higher the education of women will be that much higher will be the price of her remaining away from the labour market (opportunity cost), because from education, productivity of her time in the labour market increases much more in comparison to household work. Studies show that there is a difference between the time spent in the housework by the working women as compared to housewives. They spend per week 34 and 57 hours respectively in it. The housewife does some such jobs which working woman does not. According to the report of International Labour Organization, if the cost of housework is considered equal to cost of services of cook, cleaner, nurse, etc., it will contribute half of the total National Production in many countries.

In 1985, the American women had, demanded that by accepting housework as productive work its payment should also be given to women. There is a difference of opinion regarding this. The capitalist group says that housework is not productive work, because woman in the form of labour, is not the victim of exploitation by capitalists, more than required value is not produced from housework, such things are not produced through which money can be earned and in the situation of excessive production the process of production can be stopped. The communist group states that housework creating labour power is productive. For capitalism and nation it is important because without it, there will be shortage of work efficiency and production will not be done. Berk (1980) has expressed that household should be recognized as the small factory. The raw material which is bought from the market in the form of vegetables, wheat, rice, pulse, etc., consumption goods, food, etc., prepared out of them increase work efficiency of family's male members. Housewife is more connected with second part. By bearing and rearing of the children housewives work to prepare the labourers of second generation also. Lower status of housewife is due to her exploitation; in the form of unemployment from more children, diseases from more eating, familial conflicts from more expenditure, etc. As the consequence of production more than requirement, family disorganization and obstruction in housework is also possible, housewife produces things and services, more than her requirement which mostly male members use and help in maintaining the capitalistic system.

In India, definition of housework is non-work. In 1971, 80 per cent males and 20 per cent females were workers. In non-work, cooking food, collecting wood, bringing water, taking care of house and rearing the children, etc., are included. If only cooking food is taken, average, Indian woman spends 73,000 hours of her life only in kitchen which is harmful for her health. This is only about cooking food in which jobs connected with food, prior or after cooking are not included.

Some learned people think that by giving payment for the housework, women's subordination sense will increase much more. Therefore, objective should be that by understanding its status, helping hand should be given by the men in it. Specially in the case of working women, measures to give them relief from housework should be thought off and facilities should provided (Desai and Krishna Raj, 1987). Women totally engaged in housework should not be considered dependent and their indirect financial contribution in the family should be evaluated. Consequently, if not equal to working women, but certainly better than their present status, will be felt by all and due to increased respect by others their self image will improve. Chatterji (1988) has suggested, woman should use their right of working outside by decreasing the time, labour and interest in housework, and for care of children and food services, good arrangement of creches and canteens should be made in the community so that they can be benefited.

Decision Taking in the Family by Women

In any group, status of its members gets expressed to a great extent by their rights of taking decisions regarding themselves and the whole group. In family various decisions are required to be taken regarding the daily affairs like maintenance of house, lifestyle of members, food and relations with outside people, and regarding particular occasional acts having far-reaching effects such as financial budget of family, purchases of things to be used for a long time, buying and selling of immovable property, education, profession and marriages of children, etc. Generally in a group power of decision-taking depends on person's sex, age, education, income, etc. An aged, experienced, educated and financially sound person gets the leadership of the group automatically. In the traditional Indian family, the oldest male member used to be the head of the family and all the important decisions were taken by him only. Wife of the head of the family used to get right of taking small decisions inside the house, specially regarding the women, automatically. In the family, roles of man and woman respectively are about outside and inside affairs of the house which are the result of division of work based on sex, therefore, decisions regarding the outside and outside affairs should be taken by man and woman respectively (Scanzony, 1980).

Since Indian woman is totally subordinated to man, she takes all type of atrocities on herself with a sense of submission in quite a natural way and as Channa (1988) has stated internalized negative self-image through specific socialization right from childhood, is responsible for her in doing so. Therefore, in the modern nuclear family also, husband tends to keep all the decision power with himself, regarding all the important matters of inside and outside home, utilizes it on the occasion, and his wife being his obedient follower, only helps him in converting his decisions into practice. The logic behind this tendency is that firstly mental efficiencies of women are less than men, and secondly by leading a life limited to house only they do not become worldly wise and efficient enough to take important decisions. Wrong decisions may put the family in difficulties, therefore decisions are to be taken very carefully by understanding their effects and this efficiency could be generated by male members only. For women who go out for working, since they attain only limited knowledge about outer world due to limited activities regarding their profession and office, therefore their advice is taken on the issue only for formalities sake. By chance if the opinions of husband and wife are same, the decision is called a jointly decision taken after discussion and the wife becomes happy. But if they differ, the husband's opinion prevails and decision is taken accordingly, and considering her husband more capable, wife also has no complaint against it.

Many studies have proved that education and economic independence of women have undoubtedly raised their status (Devi, 1980), but in spite of her equality in education and income with the man, equality in her familial status with man, is far away even now, achievement of which will take time. In the lower class where woman has been always earning money, even the non-working and non-earning husband, who drinks, eats and even enjoys his life with other women, by using the wife's earnings, beats his wife if she does not allow him to do so. Old customs and traditions of the Indian society are so deep-rooted that in order to erase their effects and to change the thinking of men and women both, special efforts, are needed to be made by the interested and concerned people themselves. Woman has no right to take decisions, not only connected with the whole family or any other member of the family, but with herself also. Her own likings and dislikings, willingness and unwillingness regarding various issues concerned with her own life have no importance and they don't direct her activities and she has to lead her life according to her husband's wishes and expectations. In the name of her loyalty to husband she has been made a wooden doll dancing according to his whims and fancies. Generally, decisions concerned with household daily affairs are taken by women by keeping in mind the husbands likes and dislikes, but the decisions regarding important issues outside the home are mostly taken by men as Sinha and Jain (1988) have found out. This fact is applicable completely in the case of women belonging to upper and middle classes, but for exceptions. As in the case of the short-tempered and obstinate wives of excessively peace loving, inefficient or submissive husbands who become free to do every work according to their own desires, they take all the decisions and husbands dominated by them.

After becoming mother-in-law some authority can be exercised on daughter-in-law in comparison to man, average position of Indian woman is, that, in the kitchen food is prepared according to the like of husband and she herself dresses up according to the husband's likings. After marriage a wife has to change her interests and mould her habits according to her husband's wishes. Women are trained prior to marriage to make adjustment with their husbands because the question of changing life partner does not arise in the upper and middle classes specially. Therefore, in order to maintain a peaceful atmosphere and good relations in the family she has to sacrifice her desires and ambitions. Since she can get love and appreciation of family members through this way only, willingly she makes continuous efforts to change her original personality according to the husbands likings. This is her destiny and anomaly. In this way a Boudreau, Sennot and Wilson (1986) have expressed, due to particular sex role, they do not have control on their own life and they are prevented from social life participations.

Ten

Legal Status

Social change to come about not only in our country, but in many modern societies needs to have great dependence on enactment of suitable laws to provide the momentum. People are forced to behave according to legal provisions and those violating laws, are punished by authority. Thus, in spite of unwillingness, people have to mould their behaviour according to laws due to fear of punishment. When in India, various social reform movements of 19th century, could not achieve expected success regarding enhancement of women's status, the enactment of social legislation became essential. In British regime only the process of inactment of laws for removing the differentiation and double standards between the man and woman, had started which was completed after independence properly. Apart from equal constitutional provision in the interest of women, separate laws have been enacted regarding are of marriage, widow remarriage, polygamy, divorce, dowry, right on property, adoption and guardianship of children, maintenance expenditure and abortion, etc. In the interest of women labourers also special legal provisions have been made so that they can be saved from exploitation. But as Desai and Krishna Raj (1987) have written, due to lack of emphasis on the implementation of these Acts, women are not benefited much out of them. For understanding the legal status of women, detailed description of various laws is necessary.

Age of Marriage

The destructive effects of child marriages forced social reformers to get them prevented by enactment of law. Therefore, in 1929 Child Marriage Restraint Act, was passed in which for men and women, minimum age of marriage was kept 18 years and 14 years respectively. In 1978, after amendment of this Act, age of marriage has been increased to 21 years for men and 18 years for women. This Act is applicable equally to all communities. Child marriage has been considered a punishable crime for the parents or the performers but the legal acceptance of such marriages has been left untouched due to which total prevention of such marriages could not be possible. The requirement is that, child marriages should not be accepted by law, it means they should be declared null and void legally. In rural areas and specially in lower castes child marriage is very much in practice even now. Rajasthan is quite famous for child marriages specially. Provision of appointment of child marriage restraint officer is essential because in the absence of any complaint, taking any action against it, is impossible.

Abolition of Sati

The Act denouncing Abolition of Sati was passed during the British regime in 1829. According to this Act, due to husband's death, willingly or unwillingly the dying woman and people encouraging or forcing her to die, are declared criminals and punished. The practice of Sati has been reduced to a large extent in India, although it is still existing.

Widow Remarriage

Hindu Widow Remarriage Act was passed during British regime in 1856, so that they can be saved from the hell like life of widowhood. Even after more than one hundred and fifty years, the situation regarding this issue is, that widow remarriages are seen very rarely in the form of exceptions only. Even now, after adopting the modern lifestyle outwardly traditional patterns are existing in the attitudes, thoughts and behaviour of high and middle-class people. No man is ready to marry a widow and young widows also do not take initiatives due to fear of public opinion and criticism. Widow mothers submit their life to their children and by keeping in heart the memory of their husbands lead their whole life with dissatisfaction and sufferings.

Polygamy

Custom of polygamy which was in practice in India since many centuries has been tremendously weakened during the last few decades. But for the Muslim community, on the whole of Indian population, pressure of one marriage at a time is being exercised and people are following it. Under Hindu Marriage Act, 1955, bigamy has been considered a crime for Hindus and second marriage is not accepted by law. But still such marriages have not stopped completely. Approaching the court is difficult for uneducated and financially dependent women and in accusing the husband they do not get their family's support always. Generally due to barrenhood, absence of son, bad looks, illiteracy, etc., woman has to either tolerate the second wife of her husband or lead her lonely life in other's shelter away from her husband.

Divorce

Without right of divorce, a marriage may create difficulties for both the sides. The concept of living together in any condition is weakening gradually because today in all the legal systems, in particular situations, divorce has been included. Hindu Marriage Act, 1955 permits both the sides to seek divorce on the basis of characterlessness, change of religion, madness, infectious disease, absence for more than seven years and renunciation. But keen observation shows some inequalities and ambiguity between male and female in the law. Otherwise also, initiative for divorce is taken very rarely, from the Indian women's side. Mostly men only seek divorce on some or the other basis or it is taken by mutual consent. On upper and middle classes, of Hindus the grip of sacraments and traditions is so light on people's lifestyles that in adverse conditions also husband and wife lead their life together and never think of separation. They do not get family's help for divorce. Therefore, in India even now divorce has not become a common phenomenon. In Muslim community also under 1939 Act, husband and wife both have got the right of getting divorce, but due to acceptance of polygamy, the wife does not require it much and law is also more in favour of man than woman. For the Christian community Indian Divorce Act, 1869, is applicable. Apart from this, in Indian Christian Marriage Act, 1872, also this provision is there. But in this community also there is a differentiation between the rights of husband and wife. For husband the basis of wife's characterlessness is sufficient to seek divorce, whereas for wife, other basis along with husband's characterlessness, is also necessary. In Special Marriage Act, 1954 also which is applicable on all religions equally, there is a provision of divorce. Amendment is required to be done in all the laws in order to remove inequality between the husband and wife regarding bases of divorce.

Dowry

In Indian society requirement of giving dowry (Money, Gold, Clothing, Domestic appliances, etc.) at the time of daughter's marriage is a curse. Consequently some girls have to remain even unmarried whereas others do not get husbands of their own choice. Due to the custom of dowry, many women have sacrificed their lives and still many are forced to lead miserable lives. The fact is this, as Paul (1986) has also pointed out, that along with increasing education the amount of dowry is also increasing in India. In order to remove this bad custom from the society, Prevention of Dowry Act was passed in 1961, which has been twice amended in 1981 and 1986. According to this Act, both, giving and taking of dowry, in the form of cash or kind has been considered a punishable crime. This Act has been unsuccessful in achieving its goal very badly because the amount of dowry is increasing day by day. In the absence of complaint, only in very few cases the action is taken. Due to inventions of new domestic appliances and increased materialism the list of dowry is increasing continuously. For the solution to this problem, while on the one hand, awakening of social consciousness is necessary, on the other women's economic independence by increasing occupational opportunities is required. But in both the above directions no specific progress is observed. Therefore, by emphasizing implementation of law, its responsibility should be handed over to a separate administrative body whose functioning should include the involvement of social workers and intellectual members of community, then only some expected results can be seen. Alongwith boys, girls should also change their attitudes and should not marry the dowry seekers. Their courage only can get them rid of this curse.

Abortion

Unwanted conception has ill effects on the physical, mental and social life of a woman. For saving them from these difficulties, Medical Termination of Pregnancy Act was passed in 1971, according to which abortion is accepted legally and woman has right of choice for motherhood. Utilization of this Act is less for planning the family but more for getting rid of unmarried motherhood. Although such situations arise very rarely, but still this Act has increased the possibilities of improving the distorted life of such women.

Inheritance of Property

In pre-independence India, many systems of inheritance of property were in practice. In most of them status of women was of a dependant and their rights of ownership were negligible. Where they had some rights, they were regarding only maintenance of life not of full ownership. Hindu Succession Act, 1956 brought some basic changes most important change is equal rights of inheritance among male and female heirs of some category (Brother and sister, son and daughter). This Act has been applied on whole country. In this Act women's right of inheritance has been sanctioned. But alongwith 'Mitakschar Bapouti', the factor, maintaining discrimination among sons and daughters, has been kept in functioning position due to traditional resistance. According to Mitakschar system, only boys right from their birth, are considered as share holding members in the family's property. After death of father, daughter gets her share equal to son from father's self earned property as well as one share of father's ancestral property, whereas the son, along with the amount equal to daughter, gets his own independent share separately from 'Bapouti", i.e., ancestral property. This provision is prevalent in 'Mitakschar' system not in 'Dayabhag' system which is practised in a very small part of country. Removal of above mentioned inequality is required for which Bapouti system has to be finished. In new system women will have to be given equal rights of inheritance in all types of property as it is in Dayabhag system. Apart from this transfer of farming rights on landholdings which come under state laws, has been kept out of the periphery of

Succession Act, and in most of state laws in the case of ownership rights, women's ownership is placed in the last part of the list of hierarchical arrangement of heirs. In the same way, in the right of inheritance regarding residential houses also, law permits the unmarried, widow, divorced or deserted daughters to live in the house but not to the married daughter. This discrimination is also required to be finished. Otherwise also till the brothers want, sisters can not ask for division of the house. Owing to this provision the possibility has increased that brothers may never want to divide the house from the fear of sharing it with sisters. All these facts are concerned with the shortcomings and loopholes of the law. But whatever property daughters can get through law, even a part of that is not being given to them, it is the hard fact being practised all over the country. In the negligible number of houses only, father's property might be divided among brothers and sisters equally. On the name of dowry given at the time of her marriage she is deprived of her right of inheritance, and for the sake of maintaining good relations with brothers, she can not take any initiative to demand her right. The whole situation is, that, from this law, even if sisters do not get any property they can stay with their understanding brothers for at least few days rightfully.

Muslim law, although accepts women's right of inheritance but differentiates between the male and female heirs of same category, therefore share of woman is half of man's share. For Christians, in Kerala, inheritance Acts of 1916 and 1921 are applicable. In these Acts also, the woman inheriting immoveable property has the right of maintenance through it which get finished due to her remarriage or death. In cases where girl is considered a shareholder, she gets a very small share. Choudhary (1961) has also derived same conclusions on this issue.

Adoption and Guardianship of Children

Earlier in religious provision only the boys used to be adopted and women had no right to adopt the children. But in Hindu Adoption and Maintenance Act, 1956, in the condition of being unmarried, widow or divorced also, woman has been given right of adoption. In this Act in the case of both giving and taking the child for adoption, consent of wife has also been considered essential and adoption of both girl and boy is permitted married woman alone can only adopt the child when her husband has either renunciated the world or become mad. Whatever it is, this Act has improved the status of woman certainly. Now the husbandless and childless single women can experience the happiness of family and their life may be more meaningful and satisfactory. Hindu Minority and Guardianship Act, 1956 accepts the father as first natural guardian of sons and unmarried daughters and provides second place to mother. Earlier father could deprive the mother from this right by appointing some other guardian through his will but now he has no right to do so. First right of mother has been accepted only upto the protection of children below five years of age. In special circumstances even father being alive, court can give natural guardianship to mother in the interest of children. In Muslim law father's right of guardianship is very widespread. Even after father's death mother is not considered natural guardian of children. On other communities, Guardian and Ward Act, 1890 is applicable under which upto disability of father, he only remains guardian no one else can become guardian. Thus, guardianship rights differentiate between the man and woman. For the welfare of children they should be amended and provision should be made to give guardianship to any one. Later on by amendment, any one parent who is not guardian, has been given right to meet the children and children above 12 years of age are asked about their willingness to stay with any one parent and accordingly decision is taken by the court. It is a good step which helps the woman in remaining in contact with her children even after breaking relations with husband and after growing up thick relations between mother and children may develop.

Out of periphery of family, in the field of work also, some laws have been enacted to save women labourers from exploitation and injustice.

Equal Pay for Equal Work

Earlier different type of jobs were determined for women for which they were paid less and even if they were employed in same jobs they were paid less than man. The reason for this difference in wages used to be given that in comparison to men women's contribution in the work remains less due to lack of strength and work efficiency in them. Owing to their concentration in house and children they cannot work with devotion and tendencies of absenteeism and labour turnover are found more among them. Equal Wages Act, 1976 makes provisions for equal wages for equal work or jobs having equal nature, and against any sort of discrimination with women regarding employment. Clauses of Act have been applied in all types of occupations. In public establishments and large-scale private establishments this Act is being implemented properly, but in medium and small-scale private establishments efforts are made to escape from this Act and even now discrimination with women is practised regarding employment and wages.

Protection of Motherhood

In a woman's life pregnancy and delivery are such conditions when she needs enough care, rest and other facilities. It is in the interests of mother and child both. For this reason, female workers were not employed, even if they were employed, at the time of pregnancies they were released from work because they could not do the work properly and at the time of delivery and immediately after it they would require leave and remain absent quite often. There was no guarantee of getting the same job after delivery. This type of insecurity used to create many difficulties for female workers. In the Maternity Benefit Act, 1961 the provision has been made that during delivery maternity leave for 12 weeks with full wages should be given to them. In the case of abortion or miscarriage also leave with pay is to be given according to requirement. In the case of cesarean delivery, more leave should be granted but the pay will reduce along with the period of extra leave services can not be terminated on the basis of pregnancy now. In Employees State Insurance Act, 1948 provision of treatment has also been made.

Working Conditions

In Factory Act, 1948, Indian Plantation Act, 1951 and Indian Mines Act, 1952, in which many amendments have been done; provisions have been made not to employ women in the jobs requiring too much labour and involving risk. They are also forbidden to work under the ground in mines and during night time in factories. In those factories, plantations and mines where more than 50 women are working, their employers are supposed to arrange facilities of female nurses and creches near the working field. Mothers of infant children are to be given two extra 15 minutes breaks to breast feed them. During the legally approved period of absenteeism in pregnancy stage, neither they can be chucked out from the job nor deprived from the maternity benefits. For female labourers separate rest room, bath room and latrine are to be provided. All these benefits and facilities are given in a satisfactory level in the Public Sector and large-scale industries of private sector, but in medium and small-scale industries of private sector, employers try to escape from the expenditure on these facilities as much as they can. They try not to employ women or employ them in a very small number, where they have to bear the total expenditure, they try to avoid it, but in the case of insured security provisions where they have to share the expenditure, they make some efforts to provide benefits and satisfy the female workers. Women also do not like to take initiative to encounter the employers for getting their rightful dues and remain quiet. Factory inspectors are supposed to work for proper implementation of laws regarding welfare of labourers in the factory. But in their own financial interest they only try to save the industrialists from the laws. By giving false satisfactory report they help the owners to escape from fulfilling their duties. Government is required to emphasize more on implementation of the laws in order to provide their benefits to labourers in general and women labourers in particular. Along with family and working place, in social life also laws have been passed to save them from immorality and exploitation.

Suppression of Immoral Traffic Among Women

According to the Act, passed in 1956 and amended in 1986 provision has been made to hardly punish all those people who encourage or force the women to adopt prostitution by immoral flesh trading. For prostitution, adopted willingly or by force all the women involved in it are to be punished separately and simultaneously efforts are to be for their rehabilitation so that they can lead a normal life. They are kept in State homes for women and by giving them professional training, they are made economically independent. In the amended act, for those helping directly or indirectly in flesh trading provision of severe imprisonment and fine has been made. But in practice, people involved in this trade keep escaping from the clutches of law by giving bribe to the police personnel and prostitution centres keep on functioning. Even if they are captured, after getting released from jail, they again start the same occupation. Therefore, while a large number of women are involved in this profession, a very little number of them are brought to the state homes for women.

Restriction on Indecent Portrayal of Women

In 1986, an Act has been passed according to which picturization of woman's body in such a manner which is shameful or disrespectful for women has been forbidden. It bans all the advertisements, publications, books and magazines which demonstrate indecent image of women which spoil the characters of youngsters also. From this law full freedom of connected people has been restricted a little but even now usage of women for advertisements and indecent picturization of their parts of body is continuing. Implementation of this law is not being emphasized. No action is taken by police against the people putting indecent posters at the road side and even posters are not removed. Women are also not coming forward in an organized manner to protest against it, therefore they are not being benefited from this law.

Criminal Law Act, 1983

Under this Act, provision of severe punishment to the criminals of various categories of rape during the period of custody of women, has been made.

Indian Penal Code, Criminal Code Execution and Indian Proof Act, 1983

In this Act many improvements have been made in the interest of women. Provisions have been made in this Act against the atrocities of husband on wife. Within seven years of marriage if a woman dies and after examination of body or inquiry by police official or magistrate the husband is found responsible for her death, there is a provision of 3 years imprisonment and fine for him.

Family Court Act, 1984

Under this Act Government of India has established family courts in order to facilitate quick decisions on marital disputes. Facility of informal agreements between the husband and wife is also provided. But in most of the cases efforts are made that the wife agrees to accept the husbands point of view. In this situation, generally the woman is sent back to the same bad environment from which she wants to escape and then again her exploitation starts afresh. Thus, much benefit is not being achieved by women out of these laws. In spite of having sympathetic attitude of judiciary towards women, due to many wrong decisions during last few years, people are dissatisfied and annoyed with the system. Judiciary is required to work very carefully.

In this way, it can be said about the legal status of women that regarding various aspects of life of women, various Acts have been passed, through which they have been given even extra benefits, along with opportunities and facilities equal to men, and probably government has understood that status of women has risen and become equal to men. But the fact is this that implementation of these Acts is rarely observed by the concerned people and as Mehta (1987) has stated, women have to face lot of discrimination even now. Traditional values and ideals have their full influence on the thoughts and attitudes of people. Men are not prepared to accept women as equals and women are also tolerating atrocities on themselves quietly. As Sachchidananda and Sinha (1984) has stated, legal equality is a myth, the fact is this that women are being exploited to a great extent even now. Jacob (1965) has commented that, the value of these laws is not more than the paper on which they have been printed. There is no doubt that law helps in bringing about social change to some extent, but fact is that, only through enactment of laws change can not be brought in any society. As National Committee (1974) has reported, judiciary has generally remained unsuccessful in implementing the basic principles of enactment of laws and executive body has also remained unsuccessful in implementing or propagating them through means of communication, which is essential to change the public opinion.

In sum, it can be concluded as Mehta (1987) and Antony (1989) have expressed that women have not achieved equal legal status. The requirement is this as Mishra (1992) has suggested that the women have to fight their own battle. They should realize the importance of their freedom from many bonds, and along with efforts for their own liberty, they should try to liberate the whole society from unnecessary traditions. As Sachchidananda (1984) has found out women and men both to a great extent are unaware of legal provisions made for the women's interest particularly. Due to ignorance and shortcomings of laws, laws are not being implemented and women do not get their rights to safeguard their interests. Now women themselves will have to take initiatives and fight for their rights carefully.

Eleven

Political Status

Political status of women may be known through their freedom and equal opportunities of selecting representatives by voting as well as getting selected themselves as representatives and, the importance, given by society, to their contribution in determining the form of government (National Committee, 1974). In Indian Constitution, provision of political equality to women was an absolutely new step which was the result of encouragement by two main powers. Those powers were National Movement and leadership and Mahatma Gandhi.

Participation of Women in Indian Freedom Movement

During revolution of 1857, while on the one hand, Indian soldiers protested and refused to follow the orders of British officials and died; on the others Queen of Jhansi, Laxmi Bai also fought bravely with Britishers and died for achievement of freedom. After this along with establishment of Indian National Congress, a movement started for achieving independence after getting rid of the British rulership. In 1893, a foreigner woman Annie Besant, who settled down in India, and an Indian woman, Sarojini Naidu, both, influenced the mind of Indian women and they got encouraged to participate in freedom movement. In 1905, for division of Bengal, women also expressed their annoyance effectively. When the mother of martyr Khudi Ram Bose expressed her feelings of pride and honour on the death of her son, 500 women of Calcutta congratulated her. In 1907, 'Swadeshi' movements, started by revolutionary leaders, attracted the women greatly and they joined the movement. They burned the foreign clothings and sold country's cloth (Khadi). In this way, during the first decade of 20th Century, increasing number of women, were showing interest in political movement. During the First World War (1914-18) when Gandhiji provided leadership to the movement, he gave a call to women of all the sections to join the movement and the women participated in the movement in both direct and indirect forms.

As Chattopadhyaya (1983) has described and she herself has experienced, while in the direct form, women protested through participation in procession and got punished, in the indirect form, they performed the role of an assistant and motivator in the success of rebellious plans of male revolutionaries. For safeguarding their own interests, women formed powerful organizations and demanded political rights for themselves from British Government. Annie Besant established 'Home Rule League' and through its activities made the voice of protest more loud. When she was sent to prison in 1916, Indian women used to go to temples in the form of procession and pray to God for her release. In 1917, Annie Besant became the president of Congress and during her presidentship Congress accepted the principle of equality. Amongst the Home Rule League's recruited and recruiting persons, good workers were found from amongst the women only. Annie Besant had herself stated that from the women's participation, freedom movement got strengthened ten time more. In 1917 itself, when Mr. Montague, Secretary of Indian States, toured India for examining the prevailing conditions before determining the new constitutional reforms; under the leadership of Smt. Sarojini Naidu, a representative body of Indian women demanded franchise for women on the basis of equality with men. In 1919, hundreds of women died in the Jalian Wale Bag event in Amritsar and after that 200 women participated in Nagpur conference of Congress. Gandhiji organized all the sections of society and started non-cooperation movement in 1920, because due to increased political dissatisfaction after First World War, British rulership had started suppressing Indian people more. Women participated with a great enthusiasm in non-cooperation movement. In the membership of Congress the number of women increased and they demonstrated activeness and responsibility during conferences. Women were getting awakened towards their place in the society and taking part with awareness in the programme of peoples movement started by Gandhiji. The demand of freedom by Indian people became intense and sharp to the same extent as the British rulership practiced harshness and strictness. Government started beating, firing and imprisoning the revolutionaries which women also had to face and undergo along with men. It was easier for women to take part in the programmes started by Gandhiji, such as Swadeshi 'No tax on Salt' and Jansatyagraha Campaigns; breaking the ban imposed by police on demonstrations processions and meetings; closure of shops selling liquor and foreign cloth by removing the material from there, financial contribution in the form of cash and Jewellery; etc., therefore they came forward. In 1921, Gandhiji on seeing their services and contribution, recommended them for equal political rights. Women also participated in peasant, labour and women liberation movements which got flourished out of freedom movement. Women having insistence on truth (Satyagrahi) also used to be the prisoners. Annie Besant, Margarat Cousins, Sarojini Naidu, Rajkumari Amritkour, Hira Bai Tata, Kamala Devi Chhattopadhyaya, Vijay Laxmi Pandit, Rama Subhamma, Durga Bai Deshmukh, Aruna Asaf Ali, Sucheta Kriplani, Hansa Mehta, etc, performed important roles in achieving independence. Women liberation movement got enforced under the leadership of Gandhiji. Reform Act, 1921 gave franchise, for the election of State Governments, only to those housewives who were educated and financially well-off. This limited franchise was also an aspect of political equality. Till now Indian women were not given the right of candidature for elections of legislative assemblies. Foreign administrators could not believe that Indian society could ever consider women as partner equal to men. Mahatma Gandhi declared himself as the person who was not prepared for any sort of compromise on women's issues. His belief was that, in the reconstruction of society, women have to perform a definite role and acceptance to their right to equality was a compulsory step for bringing social justice. He forwarded his complete and continuous support to women's franchise also.

Participation of Women in Political Process

Along with participation of a large number of women on the freedom movement efforts of Gandhiji, had direct influence on the section of political and social elites in which their female family members were also included. In 1925, Sarojini Naidu became President of Indian National Congress and provided leadership to the women liberating movement. In 1930, in one meeting of representative women organizations, immediate acceptance of franchise without any discrimination between man and women, was demanded. In Public Disobedience Movement of 1930, women also got beating by police, walked for hours along with procession and stood on road under the sun. In 1931, they got right of candidature in elections with certain conditions of eligibility. Those conditions were: definite amount of property should be on the name of women and she should be graduate for 7 years prior to election which means that only the educated and rich women were given this right. Due to these terms and conditions almost all women got deprived of this right because in India very few, even educated women, have property on their names. Apart from this, whole middle and lower classes were out of this right because women were not getting much educated those days. Consequently only 10 lakh women got this right still this forward step was important. Due to this, is normal life, the ideal of man-woman equality came in the forefront, especially in the aspect of political life this fact was new (Desai, 1977). In 1931, itself Indian National Congress declared the provision of all types of rights to all the citizens without any discrimination.

In Indian Government Act, 1935, under the reforms right of franchise was not mentioned but due to relaxation in conditions of the eligibility for it, the number of female voters was increasing. Women organizations criticized the conditions of franchise to a great extent. In the Act of 1935, the main conditions which were determined for eligibility were: 21 years' age, some property or payment of income tax, reading and writing of the language of a very big area of the country, widow or wife of those having essential property, wife or widow of Government Official, etc. The reasons for not giving franchise to all the women were pointed out by Government as backwardness or women, unfavourable conditions and lack of united opinion of women organizations on this issue.

In 1937, elections, 8 women from common constituencies of states and 42 women from reserved constituencies got elected. Vijay Laxmi Pandit became minister for Regional Government of Uttar Pradesh. Sucheta Kriplani and Hansa Mehta also held responsible positions in other states. Experiences of last 20 years had awakened the women of big cities and made them bold. They had learnt to struggle outside homes. Many of them left richness of ornaments and costly clothings, started wearing 'Khadi' and leading simple life of renunciation. Large number of Gujarati women participated in 'Dandi Yatra' of 12 miles. They also started wearing clothes, weaved out of thread, spinned women went to jail during the fight for freedom. In Bengal, from amongst the revolutionaries while one women murdered one British officer, another one tried the murder of Governor. In 'Quit India Movement' of 1942, thousands of women participated in struggle, went to prison, got beating by police, faced tear gas shells, became victims of bullets, sent messages here and there quickly by remaining underground and hid the revolutionaries escaping from police by giving them shelter in their own houses. Kamla Devi Chattopadhyaya (1983) has written that women converted every house as the centre of breaking laws. In the last phase of political movements, activities of women got increased much more. At this time, not only getting of political freedom but to get rid of all types of social bindings, difficulties and disabilities had become the object. Women understood importance of their life, examined their capabilities realized their duty of struggling themselves to safeguard their interests, made organizations more powerful and forwarded their demands. Now they had to achieve rights equal to men in every field of life which they received in 1947 with political right at central level. Thus, the promise made by congress for political equality of women was fulfilled after independence, when constitution directed the nation to implement the principles of equality, and the state to follow the policy of respecting the prestige of a person, and declared the basic rights of women regarding political and legal equality. In the new constitution this was a great step for women's liberation. On this bases it was obvious to get equal opportunities without any discrimination of sex, in other areas also. From this women got the right of influencing the parliament not only for their own interests but they could also get changed or formed policies connected with political, economic and cultural fields, affecting the whole country. Franchise for women meant their recognition and responsibility in taking decisions regarding National life. It also meant that they are not inferior to men and if they get freedom and opportunity, they can take and properly handle the challenging jobs and responsibilities of positions like ministers, governors ambassadors, etc. Gandhiji had also approved the political rights in the form of means of achieving general equality of status and opportunities, and getting social, economic and political justice.

In order to examine the impact of equal political rights received after independence; it is necessary to know about the participation of women in political process as the voters and candidates during different elections, adoption of attitudes of political awareness, commitment and active participation, implementation of autonomy by self-decision in political procedure and behaviour and their impact on the political process, etc. Because getting only rights is not sufficient, along with that women should understand their responsibilities as citizens for which after getting educated usage of discretion power is essential.

Election figures demonstrate general tendency of increase in the number of women voters, although in comparison to men they still vote less, as Table 11.1 reveals.

The Table 11.1 clearly demonstrates that the number of male voters has also increased but among them there is a difference of about 13 per cent between 55.0 per cent in 1952 and 68.17 per cent in 1984, but in the increase of the number of female voters, there is a difference of about 22 per cent between 37.1 per cent in 1952 and 58.66 in 1984, which is as a result of their education and awareness. This is a positive aspect of improvement of their status. In the states like Orissa, Bihar, Madhya Pradesh, Rajasthan, Uttar Pradesh and Himachal Pradesh which are famous for educational and social backwardness of women generally, women voters have always used their rights very less, during elections, and in the states where literacy rate is high, women have used their rights more. In comparison to villages, women of cities use their rights more. Due to narrow-mindedness during elections while voting, women give more importance to religion, caste, and class of the candidate rather than capabilities. Most of the women do not have their own opinion and they normally support the candidate determined by the male members of their families.

TABLE 11.1
VOTING TENDENCY DURING DIFFERENT PARLIAMENTARY ELECTIONS

(Voting in Percentage)

Year	*Men*	*Women*
1952	55.0	37.1
1957	56.0	35.6
1962	62.1	46.6
1967	66.7	55.5
1971	69.7	60.0
1977	76.39	65.62
1980	62.16	51.52
1984	68.17	58.66

Source: Report of Indian Election Commission, 1984.

Regarding the candidature difference between the men and women is very much clear. In comparison to men they become candidates quite less in number and the percentage of winning the elections is also quite less. This tendency during different elections is clearly demonstrated by Table 11.2. As Majumdar (1979) has stated, in spite of a woman being Prime Minister (Indira Gandhi), very few women leaders have come in Indian politics.

Till now for parliament women have fought elections maximum for 17 per cent of total seats. In comparison to total number of candidates, the number of women have never remained more than 4 per cent. The surprising fact is this that in the less developed and backward states where number of women voters is always less, the number of candidates has remained more than the developed states. But in most of the states, stabilizing or diminishing tendency is clearly seen in their number. In some states, in many elections even one woman candidate does not come forward for which they are criticized also. This fact also reveals the apathy of various political parties along with unwillingness of women towards candidature.

TABLE 11.2
COMPARATIVE POSITION OF MALE AND FEMALE REPRESENTATIVES DURING DIFFERENT PARLIAMENTARY ELECTIONS

Year	*Percentage of men out of Total Candidates*	*Percentage of women out of total candidates*	*Number of total positions*	*Elected Number*	*No. of Elected Men*	*No. of Elected Women*	*Difference in No.*	*Difference in %age*
1952	97.27	2.73	489	489	466	23	443	90.54
1957	97.43	2.57	494	494	467	27	440	89.06
1962	96.73	3.27	494	494	460	34	426	86.23
1967	97.12	2.78	520	515	489	31	458	88.07
1971	96.94	3.06	519	519	497	21	476	88.05
1977	97.09	2.91	542	542	523	19	594	92.98
1980	96.88	3.06	542	542	499	28	471	89.37
1984	96.29	3.70	509	508	466	42	414	81.1

Source: Election Commission Report 1952-80 and Mishra, Sheela, 1989 'Women's Participation in Politics and Political Parties', Uppal Publishing House, New Delhi.

There are many reasons of quite less political activeness of women in comparison to men, as voters and candidates. The reason for increased events of leaving active politics by women coming from families showing long political tradition is their expenditure of elections, threats or fear of violence and character assassination have prevented many women from fighting the elections. The women coming from financially well-off families, rural houses and families having long political traditions can remain in politics for along period. But for young educated women of ordinary families, entrance and stability in politics, both are very difficult. Due to lack of prior political experience they totally depend upon other politicians for their own interests and get cheated. Among women of Muslim, tribal and rural communities, the number of political participants as voters and candidates, both remains quite less. Among the middle and Scheduled Castes, political participation is comparatively better. Among the educated women of upper class also political apathy is seen normally. Women of middle-class cannot take part in politics due to their heavy household responsibilities.

After winning elections also most of the female members of parliament do not get significant position as minister related to some important department. They very rarely get independent charge of a cabinet minister. Although some women become deputy or state ministers but their contribution is also not taken very seriously. Table 11.3 shows the appointment of female members of parliament at ministerial level after various elections.

TABLE 11.3
NUMBER AND STATUS OF WOMEN MINISTERS IN CENTRAL GOVERNMENT AFTER VARIOUS ELECTIONS

Year	*Women Cabinet Minister*	*Women Deputy Minister*	*Women State Minister*	*Number of Total Ministers*		
				Men	*Women*	*Total*
1952	1	1	1	31	3	34
1957	1	3	-	37	4	41
1962	1	3	3	47	7	54
1967	1	3	1	50	5	55
1971	1	2	1	50	4	54
1977	2	2	-	42	4	46
1980	1	2	1	49	5	54
1984	1	-	3	36	3	39

Source: *Times of India Directory*, 1976-77. Mishra, Sheela, (1989), 'Women's participation in politics and political parties', Uppal Publishers, New Delhi.

After independence, some experienced women of National movement, some women of rural houses and some patriot women came forward for fighting elections. Later on, while Indira Gandhi became Prime Minister, Sucheta Kriplani, Nandini Satpathy and Shashikala Kakodkar held position of Chief Ministers. This proves that women can also hold positions of great responsibilities but still they are very rarely given the positions of ministers at cabinet level, which is a frustrating situation. Due to this factor also many ambitious and capable women renounce politics.

Political awareness of women is influenced, along with education, urbanization, usage of mass media, etc, by the regional political culture, approach of political parties up to women and category of local leadership, etc, also. Among working women political awareness is found more although they do not participate much in politics. In spite of female legislators coming from families having higher socio-economic status, political awareness is found quite less among common women of this section. In comparison to men, among women, level of political information and understanding is very low because they give more importance to the problems of day-to-day life. Politicians are also unable to solve the country's problems, such as unemployment, poverty, rising prices, corruption and breach of law and order, etc. Therefore, the attitude of whatsoever becomes whosoever, it does not affect the common man's; prevails more among women. Direct problems of women also could not be solved due to lack of efforts of government for implementation of laws therefore women remain apathetic towards politics. The number of successful women candidates as well as their percentage are continuously decreasing. From the period immediately after independence, their participation has remained half. After independence the women who entered in the Government authority, used to have keen interest in the solution of women's problems, consequently they could get enacted so many laws in favour of women, but the female legislators of the new generation are paying very little attention on women's problems. As National Committee (1974) has stated in its report, that the political elites of both male and female sections are having this understanding that from the legal and administrative efforts made immediately after independence, women's problems have actually solved, therefore during the discussions and conversation in legislative boards very little attention is paid towards women's problems. At first the number of women remains quite less in legislative boards, then their position is not good in the decision taking section, therefore, the power of their voice has become weak. Under these frustrating conditions discouragement of women regarding political participation is quite natural. In this way due to lack of political ambitions lack of economic independence, obstacle in household work, maladjustment with methods of party politics, lack of experience and interference of welfare activities in politics, etc., women's participation in politics remains low.

Political Parties and Women

Election manifestoes of political parties are witnesses of this fact that they consider women as such a backward section of society for which provision of specific rights and facilities is essential, in order to bring it on a par with men.

Indian National Congress forwards the maximum women candidates in all the elections. Earlier it had determined the target of 15 per cent women candidates which could never be achieved. Late Prime Minister Rajiv Gandhi had declared reservation of 30 per cent seats for women among members of parliaments, but still, in 8th election women could not get more than 10 per cent seats in parliament. In spite of undisputed leadership of late Indira Gandhi the position of women in hierarchical arrangement in her party, is not very satisfactory. In spite of some women (05) in Executive Committee, female workers of this party have not achieved opportunities of development and demonstration of their organizing capabilities. The party has emphasized on education and occupation of women.

In Bhartiya Janata Party which was known as Bhartiya Jan Sangh earlier, 05 women in central executive and even 83 women in all-India council, occupied the seats. This party approves the progress of women and removal of their social and educational disabilities, without having any change in the traditional principles of social organization. There is a provision of taking one or more woman in various committees of party, in their constitution. The representatives of the party emphasize on maximum political participation and political awareness among women. This party is totally against the ways of usage and demonstration of women's body in advertisements or other means of propaganda.

Both the groups of Bhartiya Communist Party believe that women can achieve complete freedom only under the socialist system. They should perform their role in social revolution. Therefore, these parties oppose all types of bindings for women, less opportunities to them in comparison to men and discrimination. They claim that there is enough number of women among their members and there are female members, in National Council also. In Bhartiya Communist Party, in comparison to Marxist Bhartiya Communist Party, the position of women is better. In the former one 5 per cent, and in the latter one 1 per cent of members are women.

The Bhartiya Socialist Party believes that even now women are ignorant and apathetic towards their legal and constitutional rights. For the removal of this difficulty, social workers should work with a firm determination. The women front of the party has prepared a charter about rights of women and the party claims to make full efforts at its level, to get them achieved by women. The membership of women in the party is negligible.

As Mishra (1989) has expressed, by looking at election manifestoes of all parties and their activities afterwards, it seems as if the importance given to women, is not more than a vote catching method. There are no directives for political parties to reserve women's seats and protect their other interests specifically. During election campaign, emergency, natural calamities, etc, women are used for working and after the events they are sent back to their home. This is because as Mishra (1989) has concluded, specific socio-economic structure of Indian society is such that generally Indian women do not want to enter into politics. Even after their progress in education and economic independence their contribution in politics is negligible, and if they are in profession, then even after that they want to spend maximum time among their family members. Those who are in active politics, they are also there for name sake. There is no requirement felt to listen to them and give importance to their opinions.

Specific Women Politicians and their Contribution in Women's Upliftment

Immediately after independence out of the women who came in forefront to provide leadership, most of them were the experienced freedom fighters. They had participated in the development and welfare programmes for women, they were the advocates of women's side in representative organizations and they had performed an important role in support of social legislation, due to which immediately after independence women's legal status got changed. At that time the Government formulated the policies and chalked out the programmes for development of women in which some women also provided assistance. During freedom fighting some women got National importance and after independence most of them became members of parliament and part of Central Government. In states one new generation of women entered, who mostly belonged to the state's particular economic and political sections and were elected generally due to internal support of the party. Women belonging to the families having old political tradition and royal houses got place in state politics easily. Thus, in determining the form of Government they have played a significant role. Although very few women could get positions of higher power and prestige, but whosoever got, their administrative capabilities and efficiency of organizing their functions systematically have been recognized and appreciated. After independence many women worked in Central Government as ministers as and many became Chairpersons of both the houses of parliament. Many became the members of permanent and adhoc committees. In 1947 itself Sarojini Naidu efficiently held the responsibility of Governor of the biggest state of 'United Provinces' Rajkumari Amrit Kour became the first female cabinet minister in central government who held the department of health. The first general elections were held in 1952 in which many women became candidates for forming the Government at Central and State levels. A total of 23 women got elected for Lok Sabha and 19 women were either selected or nominated for Rajya Sabha. In 1957 elections, 27 and 23 women came in Lok Sabha and Rajya Sabha respectively. For state legislative assemblies 342 women were candidates out of whom 195 got elected. In this way 245 women were the members of different legislative boards. After that their number has not increased. The most influencing fact in the field of politics was the Prime Ministership of Smt. Indira Gandhi in 1966. Sucheta Kriplani, Nandini Satpathy and Shashikala Kakodkar have held the positions of chief ministership successfully. Vijay Laxmi Pandit was sent as Indian ambassador to Russia and for many years she carried her responsibility successfully. Madhuri Bahin Shah also performed the role of Governor of Andhra Pradesh properly. Now female wing of every important political party is functioning separately whose main object is to prepare the women politicians along with getting maximum votes of women during elections. As we have discussed earlier, old generation of women politicans protested against exploitation and social disabilities of women and prepared Government to make provisions of social legislation without any delay. These get amended from time to time according to requirement. But the situation which is existing today in the country is that, by considering the political rights as ends, satisfaction has been derived, whereas it is necessary that by considering them only the means of achieving one big target of equality in every field, social system should be changed through their implementation. For women not reservation but motivation and education is required.

Twelve

Other Aspects of Status

Freedom and Mobility

Under social status of women their freedom and mobility out of residence is considered. As Chatterjee (1988) has expressed, in the modern period, women of the middle-class in cities whose work-field was limited upto the four walls of the house, go out of the house for education and occupation. They have also got the freedom of conversation with outside males, if required. As Jha (1985) has also written, they are also getting the liberty of forming the organizations and committees, and participating actively in their activities. But all their activities are quite keenly observed by the society in general and by the family in particular. After the determined time for any outside job, they are required to come back home immediately. As Maladi (1985) has also reported, friendly relations and entertainment activities with outside males are strictly prohibited even now. Going out alone during night time is not considered desirable for women. As much as possible, their staying alone, away from the home is avoided, therefore mostly, by taking education and occupation in their home towns they stay with their family members only, while all these bindings are not applicable on men. They move out of their homes with full freedom even during night time, and entertain themselves with friends. They can go anywhere, come back at any time and live alone anywhere. All these restrictions are imposed on women on the name of their security and safety which make them further coward and weak and as Channa (1988) has expressed, project a negative self-image in their minds. Thus, lack of self-confidence and independence make them dependent on men. These restrictions are imposed on the lower class women to a lower degree because they were going out of home for earning their bread right from the beginning. Their marital bonds are also not so rigid as of middle-class. Women of upper class also remain out of house till late nights for entertainment but with their husbands or escorts, although during day time they are free to move either alone or with friends for some jobs or entertainment. In rural society, in lower class less, but in middle and upper classes more, restrictions have been imposed on their freedom of movement. Veiling custom is decreasing to a great extent in cities but in villages it is still in practice and even the conversation of women with other male family members and relatives is restricted, then association of outside males is quite a distant event. In Muslim society, as Brij Bhushan (1980) has stated, much more rigid bindings are there. In this way, we see that even today women's freedom and mobility, in comparison to men is much more restricted socially. Man can go any time anywhere without even informing the family members, whereas women are supposed to take permission and where permission is not required they should at least inform the family members before going out.

Moral Status

Under this aspect, in society in comparison to men different moral standards for women and a consequence of their violation, different provisions of punishment and its usage in practice, etc., are considered. As Mitra and Maharani (1984) have stated, double standard for behaviour of men and women exist in society. Regarding it as we observe, even today the character of woman is given more importance than the character of man. If the girl even once earns a bad name for keeping relations with one or more boys, her marriage prospects are hampered and she may be required to lead her life in hell like torturing environment and by chance if she becomes the victim of unmarried motherhood, then her severe sufferings are definite for her. Although now legally accepted medical termination of pregnancy is possible, but still it leaves its impact for the whole life. Due to this reason only security of daughters is given great importance by the parents and an effort is made to get rid of their responsibility after getting them married as soon as possible. During the married life, woman has to observe sanctity for her husband. Faithfulness towards husband has been declared as her religion and husband as her God. She has to put on some ornaments and signs showing her married status while it is not required for men. If she becomes widow then in spite of permanent absence of her husband, she has to perform her duties and observe her sanctity more strictly. By making herself more unattractive she has to remain away even from the shadow of a man. Even today her general relations and conversations with other man are given specific wrong meaning and her character is assassinated. As Mehta (1987) has expressed, although widow remarriage has got legal acceptance but it is only an exception. Her presence is forbidden during the auspicious occasions. These moral restrictions are very rigid in the middle-class whereas in lower-class more and in upper-class less relaxation is observed in them. In urban areas little relaxation is found but in rural areas they are existing in their traditional form.

Moral restrictions are not so rigidly applicable on men and for their violation, social provision of punishment is also not so severe for them, as it is in the case of women. In spite of their characterlessness, no difficulty is faced in their marriages. Although polygamy and extramarital relations are not legally accepted, but still, the wives of such husbands, having immoral relations with one or more women, cannot leave their husbands because they are not financially independent. Whereas if by chance a wife gets entangled with someone else, she is immediately deserted by her husband.

As Engineer (1987) has mentioned in Muslim community divorcing wife is much more easier. Pronouncing of the word 'Talaq' three times by husband is enough for the purpose. In the case of widower it is possible to get married immediately after his wife's death that too with a much younger girl and most of them get married also. They are not required to make themselves unattractive as widowers and their presence during auspicious occasions is also not forbidden. In the case of barrenhood or absence of son, other marriage for them is considered justified while wife cannot do so. For not having children, only the women is considered responsible, whereas medical science has proved that even man could be responsible for it. In the situation of forced lonely life the woman is supposed to be very careful and alert while remaining in contact with other men because they have to safeguard their honour. Whereas men remain careless because they do not have any such danger.

In this way we see as Antony (1989) has also noted, that legally for men and women both, same moral standards and same punishment provisions on their violation, are there. But in practice even now same traditional double standards and punishment provisions are continuing due to which conditions of differentiation towards women are still existing with very little changes. With the names of women their marital status is to be pronounced at first, whereas it is not at all required for men. They do not have to wear particular ornaments or put any signs on their bodies to demonstrate their marital status.

Religious Status

Under this dimension of status, reading and reciting of various religious books, extension and propaganda of religion, right of religious sacrifice and oblation (Yagya), right of performing various sacraments, etc., are considered. Regarding this, first of all, this fact has to be realised, that due to the impact of modernization in India, in rural areas in small amount and in urban intellectual class in large amount, the importance of religion in people's life is decreasing day by day. As Singh (1988) has found out, due to increased activities in other fields even women have become quite busy and they pay comparatively less attention towards religion. As far as equality to male and female by the state, in the field of religion is concerned, it cannot be provided specifically because after declaring itself as a secular state it can not interfere in the internal delicate issues of any religion. Therefore, in religious field, most of the taboos or negations for women are existing as they were, such as offering sacrifice and oblation to God, putting on sacred thread, continuous reciting of Gayatri Mantra (Vedic rhyme), becoming head of the institutions involved in extension and propaganda of religion such as Shankaracharya, worshipping and reciting prayers during specific festivals and occasions of rituals in others houses, delivering religious lectures in public, offering water and eatables to ancestors, performing last rites of parents, etc., are forbidden for them. Of course, daily and occasional worshipping, prayings, singing religious songs in group, reciting religious books and following religious customs during occasions of birth and marriage, etc., are observed to a great extent among women. They are more particular and active than men in observing the fasts and celebrating the festivals. It is said that due to efforts of women only more or less some religious atmosphere exists in every house and some knowledge about religion is transferred to the younger generation which is essential for the existence of religion. This is true in the case of families having very busy male adult family members of urban areas. But highly educated and working women also cannot involve themselves much in religious activities. They do not bother to achieve equality in this aspect of life, hence do not make any efforts in this direction.

Economic Status

Under this aspect, women's right on familial property, thinking about 'stridhan' (ownership of moveable property), personal income and economic independence, etc., are considered. As Desai (1977) has expressed, Indian woman is totally dependent from economic point of view. By law the right of getting a share equal to the heirs in family property, has been given to them. But as Choudhary (1961) has expressed, as far as the father's property is concerned, getting any share in it by daughters, leaving apart the share equal to sons, is out of question and it is a very common phenomenon. Of course, in the case of absence of sons, daughters get the property, in place of its distribution among other male relatives. This change has taken place. Giving share to the mother out of son's property is also not practiced. Of course, in husband's property wife gets share equal to other heirs, and in the case of minor children, till they become major, she gets full right on all the property. On *stridhan* woman has got the full ownership right, which no person can use against her wishes. But in practice it normally happens that husband forces his wife to give him or spend herself the *stridhan* at the time of some economic problem. For maintaining a normal condition at home she has to make this sacrifice. This is still better, in lower class, illiterate foolish husbands generally sell the jewellery of their wives for maintenance of their bad habits and vices. Whatever money the wives earn, husbands spend it for their own satisfaction and pleasure and if denied, they pick up a fights and beat their wives with cruelty. In lower-class even unemployed non-earning husbands ill-treat their wives and practice various atrocities on them.

As Khan (1982) has expressed, even in middle-class working women have not got full freedom of spending their income according to their desires. Generally all the expenditure is done with the consent of husband. Whatever money is given to the housewives by their husbands, to run the household, they have to give account of that money to their husbands. Whenever he wants, he expresses his annoyance on his wife for spending more money on household affairs. Thus, home conflicts on economic issues is a common phenomenon in Indian families. As Paul (1986) has written, on the cash and gifts of dowry also, daughter-in-law has no right. Her in-laws consider their full right on dowry, which they use as they want. As Rao and Rao (1985) have stated, if the daughter-in-law by considering her right asks for something brought from her parents place, she is criticised bitterly and her relationships with in-laws' family become tense which further get deteriorated in the course of time. The daughter-in-laws' bringing no dowry with her, do not get a respectable place in her in-laws family. These days in urban, educated and understanding families, some changes are coming in this situation. People normally use the dowry of their daughter-in-law in giving dowry to their own daughters. Thus, as Srinivas (1983) has expressed, on the name of common Indian woman, neither any immoveable property nor any moveable property remains. She is totally empty handed and dependent on husband. Her status is very low even today, in comparison to man. Economic independence of working woman has raised their status to some extent, but not as much as expected.

Psychological Status

Under this aspect, awareness among woman towards their own interests, and their thoughts and attitudes, towards various issues are considered. Today among the urban higher and middle-class women, awareness about their interests is existing to a great extent. Lack of detailed information about various laws is a common phenomenon but they know their rights generally. Educated and working women have more knowledge about laws. As Rao (1985) has expressed, in spite of achieving equalitarian legal status when they observe in practice, the double standards and discrimination between man and woman they are quite pained for it. As Sinha (1984) has noted, they become restless to protest against it, but then in order to keep the family united to safeguard interests of the children, from the fear of social stigma, and to escape from difficulties and problems involved in leading a lonely life in the male dominated world, experiencing lower status becomes their only option due to helplessness. In spite of their economic independence they cannot gather such courage in themselves that they can struggle with problems, therefore tolerating all the atrocities quietly is their destiny. As Reddy (1986) has expressed, in the field of occupation also regarding promotion, etc., they become victims of differentiation but cannot do anything. As Desai (1977) has also stated, women struggling with the circumstances with firm determination are very few. Housewives among women find themselves hanging between the traditionality and modernity. As Ghosh (1984) has written, in their minds image of equal status of women, does not get imprinted clearly and all the facts create poor visible scenes. They donot have any complaints against the subordination of men because he earns money outside and brings it at home for satisfaction of their needs. In rural areas and in lower class, women awareness towards their interests is found to be very little. In spite of their economic independence, they accept the subordination of man quite easily. As Paul (1987) has also stated under the shadow of their husbands, they feel quite secure.

As far as their thoughts on other issues, specially on marriage and family, are concerned, they want social change definitely. Most of the educated girls want that their consent should be taken in the case of marriages, arranged by parents, and if by chance they themselves want to marry someone, then in spite of different religion and caste, and difference in economic status, parents should permit them to marry by considering their feelings. As Desai (1977) has stated, many studies on this issue demonstrate that most of the girls were found in favour of economic independence even after marriage, 74 per cent girls wanted to choose their life partners themselves. They wanted to live in nuclear family and liked small family due to high economic standard and good rearing of children. Most of them were in favour of widow remarriage in the case of young and childless widow while some were in favour of marriage by all the widows. There were 47 per cent married women who were in favour of divorce, while 49 per cent of them did not favour it and 4 per cent were in the state of indecisive mind on the issue, while 71 per cent unmarried girls were in favour of divorce. Only very few women consider the household job as an economic contribution in the family. As Kaur (1983) has also found out, most of the women consider education as an essential condition for taking a career and consider the right age of marriage only after 20 years of age. By giving importance to individualism, they want freedom of thinking and behaviour equal to men. Most of them do not like the veiling custom and contribution of husbands in household jobs is considered proper by them.

Above mentioned facts thus demonstrate the thinking as well as preferences of women. It is clear as Kapoor (1970) has written that from thinking point of view, the women of higher and middle-class who get enough opportunities of going out of homes for education, occupation and entertainment purposes, want to experience the modernity in life as early as possible through the establishment of equalitarian values in society, in the form of social change. They want to enjoy the pleasure of status equal to man very soon as Jain (1988) has also found out. Women of lower class do not pay much attention or think about all these issues even now. They consider the inequalitarian traditional values as proper, to a great extent. Less educated, housewives of middle-class also forward this logic as Gupta (1982) has also expressed, that due to biological differences, the work which can not be done, wishing that and becoming unhappy by thinking about it is useless. But most of the women want change in their status and as wives they have got many complaints against their husbands.

Part III

Other Important Facts Regarding Status of Women in Modern Period

Thirteen

Impact of Modernization (Specially Urbanization and Technological Development) on Status of Women

As we have discussed in the earlier chapters, in traditional Indian society, Indian women have remained the victims of various social, economic, familial and political disabilities due to more importance of Brahmins, economic dependence of women, patriarchal form of family, ideal of daughter's donation, noble marriages, child marriages, joint family system, illiteracy, etc. During be medieval period their status became most pitiable. In 19th Century, during the British regime, the process of modernization (Specially urbanization and technological development) started slowly, which gathered speed gradually during 20th century, and specially after independence, influenced society to a great extent.

Modernization is a complex process in which all those changes are included which are connected with the economic, political, social, cultural, psychological and religious aspects of life. These changes are visible in the form of transformation of traditional characteristics. If the main changes out of these changes, are listed, then it can be said that; logical analysis of surrounding events, development of scientific attitudes, industrialization and urbanization, increase in social mobility, secularism, in increase political awareness, technological development, increase in per-capita income, extension of education, usage of matter-force for the benefit of human beings increasing activeness toward achieved status, increase in the means of transportation and communication, improvement in medication and health, and usage of new methods for earning livelihood, etc, are those characteristics which signify the nature and scope of modernization (Mukherjee, 1983).

Urbanization and technological development, coming under modernization, have changed the outline of the Indian society and its social structure, social system and social organization which got influenced to a great extent. Owing to the technological (Machine science) development, industrialization started and the factories were set-up for large-scale production. Lower class of people, employed in the agricultural sector and suffering from financial problems, got job opportunities in factories and they migrated from rural to urban areas in large numbers. Younger generation of upper and middle classes also come to cities for taking education as well as for services mostly in offices and educational institutions. Thus, the process of urbanization started and increased continuously. Due to this, means of transportation and communication increased, people's mobility increased, and consequently the most clearly visible impact of modernization came in the form of breaking the joint family system. Institutions of religion, caste, and marriage also got influenced. This process had its impact also on the people living in the villages which is obvious. In the field of agriculture also mechanization and commercialization were adopted and in rural areas also industrialization was encouraged.

Changes occurring due to modernization, specially urbanization and technological development, have greatly affected the life of Indian women and their status has improved. Gradually extension of education started among women also and today they are being qualified in all types of education equally to men. As Jha (1985) has stated, women also advanced towards modernization. Consequently traditional blind faiths and narrow-mindedness in women were left behind and they became increasingly aware of their interests. Today they have moved to protest against atrocities on them and they have got its benefits also. Direct or indirect information about other developed countries has helped them to become more aware of their interests and now they are active in the direction of establishing this fact that they are not inferior to men in any point of view and they can do all those jobs properly which were being considered limited only upto the jurisdiction of men.

Due to industrialization in India, numerous industries got flourished in which not only men but women also got sufficient opportunities of occupation. As Devi (1989) has stated, due to occupation women's status has risen. As a result of this, women have also started working outside homes as men and in the field of working also they have to work with men. Their economic dependence on men has lessened, inter-caste and love marriages have increased, veiling custom has decreased, and along with these, men's attitude towards women also has changed to a great extent. Growth of press and means of transportation and communication have helped the women all over the country, and world, to establish close relationships among themselves. Due to this, induction of women's movement, creation of healthy public opinion towards women's problems and extension of women's leaders views in the world, etc., have been facilitated.

Joint family is the centre of following of social traditions where old people bound with various types of blind faiths and religious beliefs are gathered who do not want to leave old thoughts and ways at any cost. Due to opposition from these older people, improvement in the status of women did not become possible. Along with it, child marriages and noble family marriages used to pose freedom and their familial status improves. Even young women are asked to express their opinions while taking any familial decision. Now she is not the slave of man but his companion. In cities a very large number of nuclear families are found, but in villages also due to increasing individualism and materialism, joint families are breaking and women are getting better status in nuclear families. Today housewife is getting variety of domestic appliances to help her, as a consequence of technological development and industrialization. Great variety of readymade eatables are available in the market, so she does not have to prepare each and every special item at home. Domestic appliances such as refrigerator, gas stove, food processor, pressure cooker, electric stove, geyser, thermos, casserolles, washing machine, vaccum cleaner, dish-washer, solar cooker, etc, have greatly helped her save time and energy both. Now she experiences less of tiredness and spends her leisure, the way she wants and she can entertain herself while sitting at home. Availability of facilities of radio, cassette player, television, V.C.R., cable T.V. specifically in cities has greatly reduced their dependence on men for entertainment purposes. Owing to the domestic appliances only, the women in cities can go outside for earning livelihood and raise the family's standard of living with her added income. Facility of quick transportation has reduced their difficulties and tiredness of going out and also dependence on men for the purpose. Quite a few of them drive their own vehicles and their movements are independent. They can spend more time on education and care of the children and enhance their social relationship going out in the evenings along with their husbands. In rural areas due to mechanization of agriculture, if their job opportunities have reduced on one side, then on the other, due to rural industrialization, they have increased also. The situation on the whole is that, their life has become more comfortable now. Due to provision of water-pumps and tap system, they are not required to go far away for fetching water from wells and carrying it on their heads. From the usage of smokeless stoves they can be saved from eye diseases. With the facility of domestic appliances, even men can work at home and possibility of their help to women has thus increased. Apart from this, by getting rid of household responsibilities for sometime, they can visit relatives and get refreshed and relaxed which is very much needed to break the boredom of monotonous life. It brings new enthusiasm and agility in their life.

In this way, we find as Ghosh (1984) has also stated, that owing to modernization (specially urbanization and technological development) in all the aspects of status of rural and urban women, such as educational, occupational, financial, marital, familial, social, and political, etc, their position has improved to a great extent. Among the upper and middle-classes of women such influences are more clearly visible, although even now in cities, a small number, and in villages a considerable number of joint families are existing where much change in the status of women is not observed. This fact is to be kept in mind that the trend has started and as the time goes on, the increasing process of modernization will accompany the improving status of women.

Fourteen

Role of Women's Organizations in Women's Movement for Improvement of Women's Status

Pre-independence Condition

Efforts made by social reformers during 19th Century, for raising the status of Indian women, influenced the women of upper castes and among them awareness towards the interests of women, got created. In the name way, the enthusiasm and force which Gandhiji provided to the National Movement, being conducted for achievement of freedom, also created a place for women to take part in public like. They participated openly in the movement while, considering their responsibility and duty towards the freedom of the Nation and it is due to this participation only, their non-familial activities and actions got legal acceptance. Later on, lower labour class women also participated in processions, etc., like the women of elite class and consequently got imprisoned. Thus, while social reform movement prepared such atmosphere which facilitated the social acceptance for higher status of women, National movement gave them opportunities to participate in non-familial, non-caste activities through which they got new strength.

In later 19th Century, various institutions were established for social reform. After 1880, under the male leadership, many organizations got established which started their work from arranging of debates on education and establishing institutions for the protection of destitute women, along with other sections; and later on, achieved their objects of opening these institutions in the society to provide facilities to them. But none of these organizations challenged various rigid customs, more so, the patrilineal system under the social system. In fact, they wanted that the roles of wife and mother should be performed more efficiently by women. In 1986, National Social Conference was also established which used to coordinate the reform work, being done in all parts of the country. Therefore, in due course of time, women felt the need of women's organizations having their own leadership and membership and in 1927 along with establishment of All India Womens' Conference, the work got started in new direction. In the form of various branches of this organization, a network of organizations was spread all over the country whose leadership came into the hands of National Movement's experienced women workers. This organization declared itself as non-political in nature and started it's work of creating social awareness for abolition of bad social customs, along with their demand for education and occupation for women. Along with maintenance of women-like characteristics and proper performance of role of a mother, emphasis was given to the participation of women in the development of self and country both. In 1930, this organization declared the equality between man and woman as an essential condition of social development. Through statements and expression of thought it brought in a revolution against the double standards between man and woman. It created courage and motivated women to boycott the behaviour of exploiting women, created favourable conditions for social legislation, forced the government and opened welfare institutions like orphanages and state homes for destitute women. Educational and occupational institutions were also opened and political rights were demanded. Women leaders of this organization established ideals for other women, specially for those who were keen to take part in outside activities. First characteristic of this organization was that although it wanted equality between the men and women but still it was not against the men. Secondly in this organization the interests of women and country both were considered as interrelated with each other. Leadership of this organization was in the hands of members of Indian National Congress who were participating in National Movement. Therefore, women's movement was not separate from the struggle of general people and due to this reason only, it became a social force having wide base. Now it has become a very big organization having 500 branches and 3.25 million membership (Kuppuswamy, 1990).

After-Independence Condition

In 1947, after independence, women have been given a status equal to men by constitution, formally. With the establishment of Central Social Welfare Board in 1953 (which provides financial assistance as well as direction to voluntary welfare organizations), many women's organizations came into existence. Due to their firm objects and their concentration on achievement of specific goals the expected devotion towards problems of women, emotional attachment and mobility could not come about as in the case of earlier organizations. In 1954, under the shelter of Leftist Political parties, Indian Women's National Organization connected with International Democratic Organization, were established. In the same way, in rural areas, as a part of community development programme, Government opened a large number of women's associations called 'Mahila Mandals'. Various studies have found that these Mandals are almost inactive and those who are little active, could not reach upto the common woman (Desai and Krishna Raj, 1987).

Till 1970, many organizations were on paper for the sake of names only. Their members had variety of activities concerned with creation of sources of income and they did not have good leadership. Kamala Devi Chhattopadhyaya (1983) has stated that most of the leaders of All India Women's Conference had got a good position and authority here and there in the power structure of centre or state. Their contact with general women was at the time of election only and they saw the problems of women in the limited perspective of implementation of welfare programme. Due to lack of good leadership, the situation of downfall creeped in after independence. Till 1970, Planning Commission also did not make any effort by thinking that welfare programmes will automatically reach to the women. This was the time when the situation of common man in the country was deteriorating. Various problems such as economic crisis, stability in progress, high cost of living, increasing landlessness, unemployment, etc., were creating general dissatisfaction in rural and urban areas both. A speciality of this time was that communist political party was quite active in opposition of Government. In spite of governments' lack of attention towards women's problems, they were involving in movements and participating in the common struggles of peasants, labourers and Scheduled Tribes, etc. Poor classes of people Naxalbadi movement influenced many women in many states. In Vardhwan district of West Bengal, 2000 women clashed with military power in which 7 women were killed. In 1972, in Maharashtra, common women struggled against landlords, while in Bihar and Madhya Pradesh, tribal women fought against landlords. Corruption, rape with tribal women by government officials, alcoholism, wife beating, etc., issues got emphasized. Women participated in the movement against the lack of essential goods and rising prices. At this time only 'Indian Women's Democratic Federation which was established in 1954 and which was affiliated with International democratic federation which is formed by the women of socialist countries, became very active. In this way, till 1975, while the mainstream of women's organizations was busy in cultural programmes, classes of various fine arts and demonstration of beauty, etc., the poor women were participating in widespread public movements, as Desai and Patel (1985) have also expressed. Leftist Political parties, by raising the issues of women's problems and providing leadership, were making the women mobile.

In 1974, in Garhwal area 'Chipko' movement was started against the cutting of trees in forests, in which women participated by coming in the forefront. For prevention of cutting of the trees, their action of embracing the trees demonstrated their courage and power of sacrifice. In 1975, important events took place. First of all, National Committee on Status of Women submitted its sensational report—'Towards Equality' whose findings regarding the inequalities shook the man and woman both in the country. The year 1975 was declared as International Women's Year, which later on got merged with the Women's decade' till 1985. During this decade not only the issues of women were discussed, but new groups of women were also developed. Thirdly, Indian Government declared the state of Emergency in 1975, due to which for atleast two years women's organizations remained inactive and could not do any work. On 8th March 1975, International Women's day was celebrated. This year only in Pune and Trivandrum, leftist political parties organized the conferences of all classes and castes.

It demonstrated women's organizing power in a new direction. Young Women's Christian Association also became active and worked for the welfare of women of all religions. During the period of women's decade many women's organizations came into existence. Now a new wave of women's movement has arisen. At present 50,000 Mahila Mandals are existing whose leadership is not only in the hands of women belonging to upper and middle-class, in their membership also, these women have the dominance.

Desai and Krishna Raj (1987) have divided the women's organizations into some categories. They are: autonomous free organizations which are working for creation of awareness and consciousness, extension and propaganda, and protest on women's issues, labour organizations connected with lower class and based on general public; organizations concentrating on giving welfare services such as facility of state home for destitute women, etc.; professional organizations of women such as women doctors' or teachers associations, female wings of various political parties; associations having membership of workers and academicians, active in collection of data and research work regarding women. Out of these organizations, the first one, i.e., free organizations of women, in which political interference is not found and which are more than 100 in number, doing very good work against discrimination, injustice and exploitation of women. They consider it proper to fight for their right, usage of strength and even sacrifice for achievement of goals. Western women's movement has influenced the Indian Women's Movement to a great extent. In the first step of struggle, womens organizations discuss the issues through conferences, seminars, workshops, meetings, conventions and representative bodies, etc., methods, later on they work for creation of awareness and consciousness in public towards the problems of women, and after that make efforts to get the justice provided to suffering women by struggling against the criminals. Joint meetings and conferences of various organizations are also organized. International conferences are also held in which the work done earlier, is evaluated and programmes for future are outlined. Even though the leadership of present women's movement is in the hands of urban women but it is related with rural areas also. Middle-class, educated and young women, having theoretical orientation and devotion, and adopting methods full of courage various methods are used to get public opinion and demonstrate the protest. Solutions of women's problems only is their target for which apart from human efforts financial resources are also needed which are generated with the help of government, public and various institutions. Saheli, Sohiyar, Multrini, Manushi, Stri Shakti, Nari Samata Manch, Vimochan, Chingari, Mahila Sangharsha Samiti, etc., are some famous womens' organizations. Educational and research work oriented organizations are given financial help by the University Grants Commission, Indian Council of Social Science, and Research, Indian Council for Science and Industrial Research, etc. In S.N.D.T. Women's University of Bombay there is one research unit of women studies. In Delhi for studies regarding development of women there is an institution of central social studies trust. Many such institutions are involved in the research work. In 1981, Indian women studies organization got established. It is the main institution of academic activities which is related with education and research, and which includes the workers and research scientists both in the discussions, conferences, seminars and workshops, etc.

In this way, we see that in order to improve the status of women, their organizations have performed an important role in women's movement, as Mathew and Nair (1986) have also reported. Behind the Governments constitutional and legal provisions, creation of awareness and consciousness in public and specially among women towards their problems, and motivation for struggling to take benefits of their rights, etc., there is a big hand of tireless efforts made by the women's organizations. Before independence their role was very significant, after that next 20 years may be called the period of apathy, although full inactivity was not there, but still no solid efforts were made to solve their problems. After 1970, women's movement again got emphasized and during the 1975-85 decade, work was done with a great enthusiasm. At this time, new organizations got established and educated, trained young women worked and continue working to safeguard the interests of women.

Fifteen

Policy and Programmes of Women's Welfare

In independent India, government earlier decided to adopt the plain path of social change, through three methods. They were : constitutional and legal reform, planned development based on mixed economy and government's assistance for social welfare activities. Through these three policies — creation of democratic, just and prosperous society was expected. All these three steps have influenced the status of women.

On 26th January 1956, the Indian Constitution promised equality between the man and woman. The Constitution provided some basic rights and freedom to the citizens in order to achieve the objects of social, economic and political justice; freedom of expression of thoughts, religious beliefs, faiths and worshipping; quality of all types of opportunities and status; and among all these, fraternity and brotherhood which maintains the honour of person as well as the unity of nation, etc. By consideration of Directive Principles of State Policy only, the Government formulates the policies and laws. These principles direct the state to make special efforts for the welfare of the weaker sections of society. Otherwise also, after declaring itself as a welfare state, the state is bound to make continuous efforts for the welfare of maximum number of people in the country. Government established the democratic republic by accepting the principle of adult franchise. By establishing the Women's Cell and Women's ministry, Government followed the directive principles of state policy. In order to bring social change and safeguard the interests of women many laws have been enacted.

Regarding the economic policy, as Desai and Patel (1985) have also written, in first five year plan, agriculture and in second five year plan, industries were given importance and preference. Government made effort to raise the National income as well as the per capita income, by emphasizing more on industrialization and by adopting a mixed economy, under which, for production of capital generating goods, mostly in the public sector, large-scale industries, requiring large capital investments, were established; and in private sector, mostly either small-scale or cottage industries were established and the task of production of consumer goods was given to them. Its consequence was an unbalanced development during the third five-year plan which created many problems. The gap between the poor and rich became more wide. Later on it was experienced gradually that right direction of development should be the mixing of large, medium and small-scale industries.

By considering this background in the mew plans suitable changes were made in policy. In the five-year plan of 1978-83 a variety of grain production and industries was extended. Now the country became self-reliant in the production of consumer goods. Still it was felt that the objects of more equalitarian society creating full employment and removing poverty, etc., could not be achieved. This encouraged the basic changes in policy such as generation of more employment, production and distribution of goods related with basic needs atleast and justice, etc. The Government which came into power after the 1985 elections, increased the large-scale industries of public sector on the one hand, on the basis of foreign capital and loans from International financial institutions; and on the other, made efforts to extend the informal private sector, exploiting the labourers. Due to monetary inflation being the basis of new policy, after budget of 1985 the rise of prices was too much. The Government who came in power after 1990, is encouraging the non-resident Indians and foreigners for more increase of large and medium-scale industries. Under the new industrial policy by paying less attention to large - scale industries, the government is encouraging people by giving extra facilities to establish small-scale industries in rural and tribal areas apart from urban area. Due to relaxation of rules and regulations and simplifying the loan related procedures and provisions, large number of small-scale industries are coming up, which is the correct way of removing unemployment by generating employment. It is very difficult to employ increasing population in the public sector.

As far as the rights of women are concerned, before the sixth five-year plan, they were thought considerable under social welfare only, and in that also they were considered along with children (Women and Child Development or Welfare). At first in the sixth plan also, like earlier plans, less attention was paid to women, but later on due to pressure exercised by violent female workers, and on adverse impact of mechanization in agriculture and industry on women's employment, in sixth plan, a separate section was kept regarding women's employment condition and reforms to be made in future. Like other countries of third world, in India also, the development process has different impacts on women of different levels of society. There is no doubt that the desire of modernization has influenced women's occupation. Mechanization of agriculture and industry has made thousands of working women unemployed. Growth of the organized sector remained limited but the unorganized sector expanded with a great speed. Most of the women got employment in the unorganized sector only. Due to emphasis on export in industries of clothing, eatables, etc., exploitation of women got encouraged. Due to rising prices in many parts of country Women's movement attained strength and momentum.

As India declared itself a welfare state there was great impact on the women's movements. In 1953, the Indian Government established the Central Social Welfare Board and State Social Welfare Boards were also established at state level. These boards provides financial assistance to the voluntary organizations for welfare work. In rural areas, establishment of 'Mahila Mandals' is also an important step. Along with financial assistance they provide direction also, and projects of welfare are also given to them. Government institutions, running development programmes for women are spread at central, state and regional levels in various departments. At central level, Planning Commission, Education and Social Welfare ministry along with its two branches, i.e., Central Social Welfare Board and National Council of Women's Education, health and family planning ministry, home ministry, labour and employment ministry, etc., generally share the responsibility of implementation of such programmes. These institutions further give the responsibility of work to various departments such as: health, education, family planning, agriculture, community development and regional government, etc. In many states separate directorates are established for women's education and welfare (there is one such directorate in Madhya Pradesh).

Planning Commission has determined three main fields under which development of women has been paid special attention, they are: education, social welfare and health. In the first five-year plan nutrition programme in schools, maternity and child health centres, and family planning were emphasized. Special attention in second plan, was on the problems of working women and in the third plan, extension of their education was emphasized. In fourth plan, education of women was taken care of and voluntary organization were permitted to run welfare programmes. In fifth plan, protection and care of needy women and occupational training for needy, poor, dependent women and working women were emphasized.

Evaluation of these plans show that in spite of investment on human resources and emphasis on welfare, investment on social services was being reduced in these plans. Declared targets and work of given task show that on education, health and welfare only direct emphasis was given and upto fourth plan no effort were made for generation and growth of employment. In fifth plan, employment was paid attention. In 1971, the Government appointed a committee to study all the aspects of status of women, which submitted its historical report entitled 'Towards Equality' in 1974, in which continuously decreasing status of women was described. It showed that change and development has adversely affected and created new imbalance. It was also reported that women's disabilities, inequalities and discrimination should be seen under the earlier reference where a very big section of population is the victim of atrocities of exploiting system. It is not possible that these inequalities should be finished only for women. Any policy or movement of protection and development of women has to be made one part of total movement for finishing inequalities in society. If whole female population is to be benefited and not only a small section among them. Later on, the Prime Minister was asked to make a detailed programme for removal of discrimination with women.

Gradually in place of making the women as target of development, efforts were made for their development so that they can participate in the development of country. Indian government prepared a National action plan for women on the basis of committee's suggestions and world action plan of United Nations. In 1976, a committee appointed under the chairmanship of Indira Gandhi approved it in order to determine proper behaviour with women. In report of National Women's Committee and United Nation's Action Plan both, suggestion of National Commission was forwarded. In 1976, in social welfare ministry, a social welfare and development bureau for women was established for the study of women's problems which got consent of the ministerial standing committee. In 1976, only special cells were established for women in labour and employment and rural development ministries. Women's cell established in labour ministry, under the schemes started by government for improving the economic status of women, is working on the problems of women labourers. Provision of facility of hostels for working women is also an important work done by government and along with it creches were also opened. For the first time in 1978 one functional group was formed by the Planning Commission which discussed the women's employment and kept its perspective in the forefront. In social welfare ministry one special minister has been appointed to take care of women's welfare. By giving importance to economic independence and welfare it has been considered an issue of priority. The education ministry also appointed one special committee for giving suggestions on adult education programme for women. Non-governmental agencies also have been working on special programmes for raising the status of women. In new organizations also, increasing awareness for women's problems has been observed. Various political parties have also opened their women wings and they provide them opportunities to advance in political life.

In this way in sixth plan, women's education, occupation, health and family planning, etc., were emphasized for development of women. In the National machinery which was made in 1975, there is a National Committee which takes advice from Central and State governments on legal and administrative issues for development of women and evaluates the programmes. Second is the Steering Committee of National Committee which selects the basic issues and determines the roles of Government, political parties and welfare organizations. Third is the interdepartmental coordination committee which analyses the bureaucratic structure from the women's development programmes implementation point of view. Fourth is women welfare and development bureau which plans the targets regarding the economic and functional aspects of National action plan. It also coordinates the programmes implemented by State Government and different departments, along with collection and analysis of data. After the election of 1883 in centre, special ministry of women and social welfare was opened. Prime Minister considered women's development as an issue of priority.

Among other efforts made by Government were: national plan of legal education and establishment of special cell in the office of police commissioner for helping the destitute and needy women. For women's welfare, provision of financial help to voluntary organizations is also there. Government is running a variety of programmes but many programmes do not reach those for whom they are prepared. Lastly, in 1990, National Women Commission got established which is totally responsible for the development of women. But in spite of many programmes they have not succeeded much in improvement of women's status. And general programmes are working to take the men one step forward while taking the women two steps backward.

Sixteen

Women Study Centres in India

In the higher education system, women studies is making its place gradually in the form of an academic field. In various subjects and courses, coordination of experiences, problems and perspectives of women, is really an encouraging step. Although such a new experiment is the subject of a serious challenge, because in this, the various issues and status of women are not only kept in courses, but they are also tested with a creation perspective. Under this, along with restructuring of courses of different subjects, usage of new methods and new teaching techniques is also needed. Regarding this, in place of old method of lectures by teacher in class, usage of informal and participative teaching and learning process, which is proper for creating thoughts and awakening emotions towards subject, is more beneficial (Desai, 1986). The requirement of keeping Women's issues, in the courses of higher education was felt more after 1960. In 1965 in America, 16 courses started and now 30,000 courses are running at different levels. In other western countries emphasis was given on this after 1970 and in Asian region during the women decade (1975-85) only attention has been paid on this issue.

Need of Women Studies in India

National Committee on Status of Women intensively studied different aspects of women's life during 1971-74 and presented its report from which many unexpected tendencies came into the forefront. Alarming facts, such as, decreasing sex ratio of women, decreasing rate of economic participation and increasing gap of death rates and life expectancy between the men and women, etc., terrified the men and women in the country both. This scene, after 30 years of independence was very painful. Leaving apart the education and services of middle-class women, in all the areas the status of women had only worsened. This report broken the illusion of people regarding the higher status of women (Desai and Krishna Raj, 1987). While some women leaders were satisfied with their roles; increasing dowry deaths, violence and prostitution, etc., were presenting a totally different picture. Firstly, in every field status of women was deteriorating fast. Second, characteristic was that even after independence, condition of women only was, the target of development programme and lower status was being given to the people taking or demanding these programmes. Different political parties including the policy determining party were almost neutral regarding women's welfare. In the sixth five-year plan (1975-80) also, issues of women were not giving much importance earlier. After great efforts it was changed and more place could be provided to women welfare. Later on, it was determined that women have to contribute in the development of the country and for that equal opportunities should be provided. This should be the approach and not that they should be made the target of their protection, safety and welfare. From this a question got created that how the learned people see the problems of women? Knowledge about it is essential. For this after examining the researches done on women, it was found, that more work was done on laws and role conflicts of women belonging to middle-class families, and on the whole, less research work was done. From 1970, political status of rural women, etc., more researches were carried out. In the field of research, the biggest shortcoming was the lack of theoretical framework for it. In western countries this facility was there but in the context of Indian culture and social system, logical and scientific thoughts were required which could be given only by academicians. Then by taking teaching, research, and field work together, if the work could be done, the objects could be fulfilled properly. For this, by establishing the women studies centres separately, in present education system, completion of this job was considered essential and different universities were given responsibility.

Development of Women Studies in India

India holds a very important place in Asia from the point of view of all its characteristics, area and population. Although women studies is not a new subject but still study of this subject in theoretical knowledge and psychological-sociological perspective, is a new fact. According to the report given by Desai and Krishna Raj (1987), the discussion of keeping the issues of discrimination, injustice and exploitation of women, in the courses of higher education, took place in 1981 in first National Conference on Women Studies, in Bombay. Organizers of the conference had asked 100 universities and 50 other institutions related with higher education, to send the reports about their condition regarding issues of women, kept in courses and research connected with women. They were also requested to send the syllabuses. Out of them, 57 responded and 23 sent the syllabuses. In 1984, the research centre on women's studies of S.N.D.T. University, Bombay, made more efforts and prepared the list of such universities where work was being done on subjects connected with women. When 43 such universities were contacted, only 30 responded. There were 26 universities which were running some programmes regarding women and only in 12 universities, subjects related with women were kept in courses and being taught. Efforts of three years gave good result. The University Grant Commission which is a responsible institution for preparing policy for higher education and providing financial assistance, accepted the requirement of including the women issues in university education and providing financial assistance. Arrangements were made to provide financial assistance for conducting seminars, workshops, conferences, summer institutes, research, etc., and in order to establish women study centres; it also helped in opening department by getting of land and constructing the building, etc. Interested people opened either study centre, unit or cell in their institutions. By considering the multipurpose functions, in 1985, in a workshop, organized by political science department of Delhi University, general objects of women studies were determined. By various research groups ways of approach to women studies in higher education, and subjects worth emphasizing, etc., were discussed. The object of women studies was determined to create interest towards women's issues in various social sciences and to coordinate there aspects, i.e., teaching, research and field work of connected subjects from their different perspectives. Thus, the subjects of sociology, psychology, history, education, political science, anthropology, etc., can contribute to the women's studies. Encouraging informal education in place of formal education was considered more helpful in fulfilment of goal. Women studies subject to keep only the women's issues in course, is not sufficient but it has to encourage people also to bring changes in their status. Its object is to increase the knowledge regarding women from the interaction of theories and field experiences. Women studies work to construct the bridge for linking the academicians and workers of lowest level. In this way in India also, women studies have started in the form of basis of knowledge enhancement in various subjects and means of women's development.

The objects of including women studies in University education are both, educational and social. Its main objective is to help women, in getting equal opportunities in economic, social, and political processes, by changing the present attitudes and values existing in the society, in participating more in National and International development, and thus changing their roles and rights. For this, creation of awareness between the men and women and for usage of full potentialities of women in development, realization by them about their social responsibility is very essential. Suppression of such institutions and powers is also necessary which want to keep the women limited only upto the reproductive role instead of productive role. Through women studies centre's procedure of functioning by being inter-disciplinary in nature, full teaching research and field work on all the aspects of all the subjects become possible.

Seventeen

Modern Women's Problems and Solutions: A Discussion

Indian women, the responsible citizens of a capitalistic, developing and democratic India, have to face a large number of problems, in spite of their hard, creative and useful functions (Paul, 1987). Indian women's section is not a homogeneous group. As Gupta (1982) has also expressed, this fact cannot be denied that like all men, all women also do not have the same social and intellectual status. Thus, women had to suffer some or the other form of problem in different degrees from time immemorial. This is true that in comparison to men, women's status has remained low, but women's status also has differed along with region, caste, class, religion, and the urban, rural and tribal differences as Srinivas (1978) has also stated. For example, lack of occupational opportunities is applicable on only middle class women. Wives of farmers were always working in the fields and the upper class women never had any desire or requirement to take up the job. Keeping the work field, limited upto only the household, was considered a symbol of higher status, which like the upper class, was adopted by an increasing part of middle-class and kept the women unemployed at home, on the name of comfortable living. And then in the situation of availability of limited resources, due to women's economic dependence on men their subordination increased continuously. After the Second World War, the conditions changed sufficiently and after independence specially planned efforts of social change started. But social change also had different influences on different groups of women, because in different groups different social norms and customs regarding the actions, increasing status, are existing. Therefore, by considering all the women's groups as one section, very limited generalization is possible regarding subjects related with them.

In modern time, mutually opposite and unequal images of women's groups get emerged and formed. As Desai (1986) has expressed, that on the one side the middle-class women of big cities have greatly improved their status and image a lot. They are seen moving here and there independently. They work for a earning money along with men on equal level and participate in other social activities also. On the other side, conditions of rural areas or small towns present a totally different picture of women where upper caste women remain busy in household work and responsibilities, and the sufferings of Scheduled Castes and Scheduled Tribes women, due to their social and economic exploitation, become a cause of concern regarding them. From industrialization middle-class women are certainly benefited but the condition of lower class women is just the same. In this way, Indian women's section presents a unique scene which cannot be understood properly. On one hand a very small part (one million) comprising of very highly educated women who have got background of higher status, earned names in different fields and achieved success, while on other hand, there are common women who are the victims of discrimination, deficiency and disabilities. National Committee (1974) has also discussed such two different worlds of women. It has commented that in spite of increasing legal changes and provisions status of common women has not changed much. They are still less educated, unemployed (due to mechanization), less visible in power structure, sick and suffering customs and norms of paternal traditions. They are neither seen much dissatisfied with their status, nor any glimpse of their efficiency and desire to make efforts to improve own status are apparent.

The state of upheaval is found in middle-class at present. As Jain (1988) has also stated, that the roles and status of women of this class are changing very fast. Awareness towards their own interests, created by education, is making the women of this class mentally upset and utterly frustrated born out of not achieving any thing much in practical form and helplessness of not being able to do anything themselves, etc., thus creating mental tension and worries, which influence their social, familial and personal life.

Right from the childhood days their struggle for equality gets started. In Indian society, at present, both, traditional values (inequalitarian) and modern values (equalitarian) are existing as Srinivas (1978) has also commented. During the last two decades, emergence of new values has clearly been seen and experienced. Adult mother of present time, since she herself has suffered due to inequalitarian values, do not want her daughters to become their victims, but at the same line she is not been able to pick up the courage to protest completely against the social system and traditions. Therefore, even after practicing equality in behaviour regarding the rearing of the son and daughter, both, inequality in their activities can easily be seen. The girls are trained in household jobs while the boys are trained in outside jobs. Daughters are not permitted to move around freely especially after sunset while the sons are completely free. The girls of modern families are seen protesting against this discrimination and to some extent are able to get rid of it also. After this arises the question of their higher education and occupation, for which their marriage poses a big obstruction. All parents of middle-class are giving education to their daughters today. Girls are also studying today at an equal level with boys due to various reasons, i.e., for getting good match, less requirement of dowry, maintaining higher standard of living, becoming independent in case of emergency, and desire of independent status in society, etc. But still due to uncertain future in the form of husband's attitudes and thoughts about her profession, facility of choosing the life of only housewife or working woman, and the acute possibility of getting married as soon as possible after becoming eligible for marriage, etc, reduce the seriousness of career orientation among common girls. Its influence is clearly visible in terms of their less efforts for making the grades in studies. Consequently they keep on lagging behind the boys in various competitions. The irony is that by giving higher education to daughters, on one hand, her marriage gets delayed and it becomes difficult to get her married in late age, and on the other, expenses are increased on higher education and in spite of this in place of any deduction in the dowry, its amount increases much more due to higher expectations. While in future for old parents it is not possible to get any help from their married daughters against the wish of their in-laws' family members. Due to all these factors daughters do not get share in the property of their parents' family, although legally, they are entitled for it. Leaving apart few exceptions of love marriages, even now, all the marriages are settled by parents, although in selection of bridegroom daughter's desire is also being given importance these days, but generally they have to compromise due to dowry and family background limitations.

Before independence, the girls who wanted to devote more time to their career, used to adopt an unmarried life and remain satisfied generally. But now owing to the changing views of men and women, the tendency of carrying out both, the profession and married life, is increasing among women. For this, they have to make many compromises. Requirement of living with husband forces them many times to leave and take services, and if they want to remain in the same profession continuously, they have to live alone and bear all the responsibilities of household by themselves or take the help of some relatives. After marriage from the birth of two or three children till their school going age, either they do not take the job or if they take it, they have to leave the children for a very long time daily with either servants or relatives. While working in the office they keep on thinking about their children and obviously cannot concentrate on their work specially if the caretakers at home are not satisfactory. Working women work in the field of their work equally to men, and after coming back from work and before going to work next day, their occupation in household affairs becomes many times more than ordinary housewives. In this way as Young (1989) has expressed, they have to keep two masters happy, inside and outside the house, simultaneously, by performance of their duties properly, and whenever they lack, they have to face the annoyance of authority. As the findings of the study of Sinha (1988: 112) are, this double burden of work has become a challenge for their work efficiency and power of tolerance. Due to high cost of living, desire of keeping the standard of living high has also forced men to accept the working wives. Rather, earning wife is now being considered as the honour of the family. But in spite of economic contribution in the house, for household affairs only the women is considered to be responsible, as Rao (1985) has stated. She does not get any help by the man in household affairs. Consequently she does not get much time for rest and gradually becomes physically and mentally tired and thus, a weary-look and fatigue sets in her more and more. Working women as Chatterjee (1988) has expressed are wandering in the market like blind people, seeking their own identity, through their personal work, without leaving their traditional role. They are moving between the two roles and trying to determine the priorities. They have to face the situation of role conflict frequently when at the same time their presence is required inside and outside the home. In such a situation it becomes difficult to decide which role they should give importance and even if they decide, after decision some times they cannot stick to it due to adverse conditions, from which mental tension and dissatisfaction are generated. It is quite obvious that if working women give more importance to their household, they will not be able to achieve special accomplishments by working with involvement, devotion and concentration in their professional work. And if they give more importance to their profession they will not be able to take care of their house, husband and children nicely by performing their roles of housewife, wife and mother properly at the traditionally expected level. An alternative course of action for them may be that by giving same importance to both the roles they should be performed at normal level, i.e., not excelling in either fields. In such a situation no role provides them much satisfaction in the real sense. On the name of compromise with circumstances in professional field whatever they get easily they accept it and whatever they do not get, they prepare themselves mentally for it, use some defence mechanism and do not become much upset. At the home front also they become used to annoyance and complaints of family members. Thus, in spite of being capable they can not do well regarding their occupation as well as traditional role' performance. In this way, married working women, have to struggle very hard from physical, mental and social point of view. Husbands of this class are expecting too much from their wives. They want them to perform all types of roles, i.e., traditional and modern, inside and outside home, and that too properly. And after this also, the irony of fate is this, that in spite of doing work many times more than men, their familial status low in comparison to men generally. They do not get appreciation and sympathy of other family members and from time to time they are accused of not performing their roles properly. Leaving apart few educated and understanding families, in common middle class families, this picture can easily be seen.

For unmarried working women it is a very big problem that how should they work together and behave with men, colleagues, friends, senior officials, etc. They have to protect their cultural background and ideals and at the same time they have to become partner of interactions and interrelations with their colleagues also. As Vohra and Sen (1985) have expressed, as long as the unmarried girls work, their parents continue to face difficulties in their marriages. Due to high ambition regarding husband they keep on rejecting normal proposals, by not realizing the facts. As they keep on climbing the stair of success in their profession on the one hand, their marriage gets more and more delayed, on the other. A time comes when in the absence of a good proposals they have to either marry an unwanted man or remain unmarried. Working women have to become the victim of jealousy of non-working women also, and due to lack of time for meeting people, they are accused of having pride of their abilities. If the working place is far away, then they have to face the difficulty of transportation and remain dependent on others. Running the household is a very challenging work for an unmarried girl in another city living without family in the absence of security provided by the man. Problems like: getting less pay in comparison to men especially in private sector, exploitation by higher officials, working more for promotion in profession, lagging behind in competition with men due to non-acceptance of immoral ways, earning bad name for low morality standard and character assassination by men, etc, are to be faced by working women.

Non-working women have no status, of their own in the society. They enjoy less or more status according to father's or husband's status. The biggest problem of non-working women is their lower status in family due to their economic dependence. Consequently they spend all the time within four walls of the house in providing services to other members of the family.

Generally economically handicapped wife has to beg for money from her husband for satisfaction of her needs. She has to spread her palm in front of her husband for the purpose and if she is not given the money, she has to take her empty hand back, which is quite insulting for an *Ardhangini* or the so-called better-half of a man. And quite often she is accused of being a spend-thrift and scolded for not saving the money. But for a very few educated and understanding families where the husbands give their earnings to their wives and do not ask for an account, the common Indian married women is given very little money in hand and all the expenses are met by men only. Thus, the main reason of familial conflicts is economic mostly.

The biggest problem in front of present girls is that, in spite of their legal rights, they do not get their share in father's property due to which custom of dowry is increasing day by day, and without that getting a good match in marriage becomes very difficult. The newly married daughter-in-law bringing less dowry or no dowry, gets ill-treatment by the in-laws family members and sometimes even gets beaten up by her husband. (Wife beating is a very common phenomenon in Indian society). They are maltreated upto the extent that sometimes after crossing the tolerance limit they commit suicide. Sometimes very greedy in-laws and even husbands chalk out and exercise the plan of killing the daughter-in-law/wife successfully. During the last few years the number of dowry deaths have increased considerably. Even after enactment of law on this issue, no special improvement is being noticed in this field. In 1990, in Uttar Pradesh maximum (1516) and after that in other states respectively, Maharashtra (858), West Bengal (420), Madhya Pradesh (397), Andhra Pradesh (344), Bihar (243), Karnataka (216), Haryana (126), Delhi (102), incidents of dowry deaths occurred (Census Report, 1991). Apart from this, owing to the increased entry of women in education and other occupation and increase in their general mobility, crimes like rape, attacks, teasing, sexual exploitation, prostitution, etc, are also increasing continuously, as Desai and Patel (1985) have stated. Thus, going out for some job alone and that too at odd times and that too on lonely places is not safe for the young and unmarried girls. This creates a serious problem in front of them and they cannot do their work with a relaxed mind. Apart from this, in dirty literature advertisements, movies and abusive language, etc, more concentration on female sex, itself demonstrates the lower status of women in society. Out of these, first three facts are related to urban society and the last fact is connected with rural environment, and in all these facts a rising tendency is being observed which puts a big question mark on the human values and relations.

From all the above mentioned facts, it can be concluded that, in front of the present women, along with the group of problems connected with their household roles, another new group of problems, connected with their educational and occupational fields, has emerged with challenge, as Subamma (1985) has also expressed. Income, expenditure and performance of roles, etc, becomes the reason of conflict in the family quite often. In the situation, if the wife gives more importance to her self-respect, the event of divorce can easily take place, thus, disorganizing the individuals and the family both.

Now the question arises that, what is the solution of these problems after all? How the status of women could be brought on a par with men? And how could they be saved from exploitation by men? According to constitutional provisions, as we know, woman has been given the status equal to man. Through various laws also full effort is being made to save her from the exploitation and give her justice. It means in the theoretical form she has got equal status completely. But from the practical point of view, the fact that, in her status little improvement has taken place. For her to achieve a status equal to man, might be possible in the professional field, but in familial field, in spite of good education and financial contribution, she has not achieved, as it was expected. Non-fulfilment of this expectation regarding improvement of women's status is becoming a serious matter of worries which forces us to think on the issue right from the beginning with a new perspective. Dur to the existing ambiguity in laws and apathy towards their enforcement, women are not being benefited by them. From the extension of education also, much difference is not being noticed. Apathy by men due to their selfishness is quite obvious which can be understood. How reasonable is the demonstration of apathy by the women towards safeguarding their own interests? This fact can not be understood easily because as Venkatrayappa (1966) has expressed, with the physical and mental points of views, both women are more powerful than men. We have seen that the women's movement has also not succeeded much and the reason of it, has been the apathy of women leaders themselves. All this is happening because the thousands years old Indian social structure, social system and culture, etc., are changing at a very slow speed.

Impacts of westernization and modernization are changing the materialistic culture of people (which includes usage of various types of things), with a great speed, consequently they are adopting the new modern lifestyle for their happiness; but they have been able to change their non-materialistic culture (which includes values, ideals, customs, traditions, etc) at a very low speed. Indian society is passing through the process of social change at present, hence it is in a state of ambiguity and upheaval. Being the characteristic of the transitional stage of a society, in India too a conflict between the old and new values is going on. Traditional ideals are not prepared to leave their place and modern ideals are becoming restless to replace them. Male and female both the sections are in a rigid grip of traditional sacrament.

Change in Attitudes

As the National Committee (1974: 37) has also stated, that the changes in the normative structure of society do not take place at the same speed, as their organizational forms or patterns change. Reforms in educational policy and laws, can not have the expected influence on the social attitudes, because the society does not remain prepared in the structural and idealistic forms, to accept their means and goals. Irrespective of the status the constitution and law has provided to the women, we see that there is a difference between their theoretical possibilities and their practice in real sense. Religion, family, and kinship roles and cultural norms limit the field of activities of women, obstruct their full and equal participation in the social life and consequently, the achievement of their full efficiencies and potentials does not become possible. In this way, the status of the present Indian woman is like a divided and hanged person *Trishanku* where on one hand, are the status and roles provided by constitutional provisions and laws, and on the other, are the status and roles imposed by social traditions. She is trying to proceed towards equality but traditions are making her feet weak due to which she is unable to walk with proper speed. If serious efforts are not made to change this situation, it can continue for a very long time, because deep-rooted traditional values and norms are working with full strength against the provision of equal status to women by obstructing the ways of achieving it. Due to this factor only, even now in society, there is exploitation of not only the women, but of low caste people villagers, tribals, poors and minorities. In Muslim community also only very few people are financially well-off and common people are very poor. When there is no equality among the men, then how can the women get status equal to men in such society. As Engineer (1987) has stated, Muslim women are suffering with various problems because as Brij Bhushan (1980) has commented, Muslim laws need reform but Muslim community is not prepared for it and not allowing the Government to do anything. As Reddy and Reddy (1987) have reported, women do not get opportunities of social participation where they can demonstrate their capabilities.

For the solution of this challenging problem, first of all, deficiencies and controversies existing in laws should be finished immediately, and along with it, serious efforts are to be made for the enforcement and implementation of these laws. Proper arrangements for searching and punishing the people, violating the laws, is very much essential.

In various subsystems, need for change in behaviour and role relationships regarding women, points out in many ways that, change in the attitudes of people is very much required. Therefore, the search of such means and ways is necessary which can change the thoughts of people, as Rao (1985) has also stated. For suppressing the impacts of double standards between the men and women, contributing to the exploitation of women, a basic change in the social system is essential. In order to achieve this, social consciousness is to be awakened and public opinion is to be created. For proper understanding and appreciation of the subjects like equal behaviour towards both sexes and social justice, etc., education of general population is compulsory. Only then will the whole society be able to become an active participant in this direction. For this:

First of all it is required that the son and daughter both should be looked after and taken care of, equally by the parents. For the same rearing pattern between offsprings of both the sexes, small number of children in the family is first condition. A great responsibility lies on the shoulders of mothers belonging to the present generation, to bring about equality among children, which they have to carry out with lot of understanding. They have to make it certain that their daughters do not suffer in their lives in such away as they themselves have suffered in their own life. Women themselves will have to come out by breaking their limited enclosure and abandon the 'Culture of Silence'. On the one hand they will have to demonstrate their capabilities and efficiencies, and on the other, they will have to fight for their rightful achievements. From this, the change in thoughts, attitudes and behaviour of men will gather speed, else the status of women will remain the same for long before any change takes place. Giving same education to the daughters as to the sons; neither for getting good match for them, nor with the object of making provision for becoming financially independent during an emergency, but to make them a fully independent person, strong enough to take independent decisions, instilling in them self-confidence and self-respect, so as to be able to counter any unforeseeable event or problem in their lives without being a burden on anybody. Thus, girls being economically independent and aware of their rights will be able to oppose their marriages to greedy dowry seekers.

Solving the Problem of Dowry

As Desai and Krishna Raj (1987) have expressed, dowry started in the form of groom's price by higher class Aryans to marry their sons with lower class Dravid Girls. Apart from this, as Srinivas (1983) has also expressed, giving of father's property's share to the daughters, equal to sons, is also very much required with this the problem of dowry will be solved automatically. Custom of dowry in India has flourished and prospered due to women's total financial dependence on men. As Tikkoo (1985) has also stated, early marriage and dowry demonstrate the wife's status of subordination to husband so much so, that even daughters want to take as much dowry as possible from their parents at the time of their marriages. The reason for this attitude first of all is that they want to raise their status in the in-laws family on its basis, secondly they want to lead a comfortable life immediately after marriage without struggling for collection of things on their own and thirdly they know that after marriage they will not be able to take away rightfully anything from the parent's house. Father's house will become another person's house for them and they will not be able to even visit that house without invitation. Therefore it is necessary that even after marriage a daughter should have full right of everything in father's house as she had before her marriage. And it will only be possible when her share in father's property is definite. National Committee (1974) has also tried to establish this fact that women on attaining economic independence will not need the enactment of law against dowry.

Achieving Financial Independence

To achieve this financial, independence before marriage, they will have to prepare themselves for getting married little late and for maintaining economic independence even after marriages, if required they will have to stay away from their husbands temporarily or permanently. For this purpose at the time of settlement of marriage itself, a verbal agreement with the boy's family should be made, so that any misunderstanding does not create conflicts later on. Right from the childhood, parents should encourage their daughters to participate in the games and do exercises for making them physically strong, swift and smart. Apart from this in order to make them self-confident and courageous they should be allowed to go alone and do all types of jobs outside the house. Development of efficiency of protecting themselves will take place only when they will be given opportunities of free mobility by taking the initial risk. When it will become a common phenomenon people will get used to it and risk factor will decrease automatically. From the less physical, psychological and economic dependence on men, the status of women will improve certainly. Such women in whether unmarried or married can maintain their careers by giving more importance to their career.

In the rearing of small children either help of willing relatives or servants can be seeked or the facility of creches (which should be available in plenty) can be availed. Here one very important point which has to be kept in mind, is that just like son, the daughter will also have to take care of the old parents as Rao (1985) has also expressed. There is no problem in keeping the parents of both the sides together in the same house, if required. For this purpose also her financial independence and share in father's property is essential. Along with, it custom of donation of daughter to the bridegroom *Kanyadaan*, at the time of marriage should also be abolished, because due to this custom parents' right on daughter gets finished and the husband gets full right over her after marriage. Otherwise also the girl is not an animal or a thing which can be passed on like this by changing the owner's possession. This custom itself demonstrates lower status of women in Indian society.

Changing the Family Structure

Then as we have seen, joint family system, is greatly responsible for the lower status of women. It becomes a problem for her to keep every one pleased. With the impact of modernity nuclear family system is emerging which means that the boy and girl after their marriage leave the houses of their parents and establish their own household separately. In India in the case of occupation in other town the joint family disintegrates but while living in the same town, joint family breaks after conflicts only. It will be an ideal state when they will be willingly allowed, rather asked to live independently immediately after their marriage, while remaining in the same town. In this case good relations can be maintained among all the nuclear families of a joint family, by taking care of mutual rights and obligations. For this change people will have to change their mentality. They will have to reduce their expectations from the children specially sons and make provisions for their old age themselves during adulthood. Until and unless total helplessness forces them, old parents should live independently which is desirable for maintaining their self-respect and dignity of age, because in any situation dependence brings subordination, and for old people it is very difficult to tolerate reversal of roles and status in the family, due to which conflicting situations arise. Hence, nuclear family system is good from both the generations freedom point of view.

Getting Rid of the Patrilineal System

As Desai and Patel (1985) have stated, patrilineal and classified Indian society has posed a big challenge for the life of women. Therefore on top of all the above mentioned facts, very serious matter which has to be thought of, is that how can we get rid of this patrilineal system which is the root cause of lower status of women and due to which sons are given more importance than daughters in the family. Daughters are considered right from childhood like other person's wealth, deposited in trust under the custody of parents, who are taken care of, by the parents temporarily till their marriages. All the offsprings get their identity in the society through their father's name and his sub-caste based surname. The mother who bears and rears them, does not come in the picture at all (although in our mythological stories we find identity of the son through mother). In the case of daughter at the time of her marriage, after *Kanyadaan*, her identity gets changed. In place of daughter of someone she becomes the wife of someone. The surname of the father is removed and husband's surname is put along with her name. After marriage she has to leave her parent's house and live in husband's house. After coming to in-laws place even her name is changed. This traditional custom which is prevalent more in rural and less in urban India even now, is the effort of practically finishing her parental identity completely. In this way, she leaves the membership of her fathers family and takes the membership of her husband's family through her marriage. Suppose, owing to modernity in the situation of divorce or widow-hood, she decides to marry again, her identity gets changed again and she will be known as the wife of new husband and her surname will again change. This process may repeat many times in the case of most modern women. In case she does not marry after being divorced she gets back her pre-marriage identity. What does it mean? It means women have no independent status in society. They derive social status through males. It also means that, the women, have no identity of their own in the society, which can be maintained throughout their life. They are either the daughter of their father or wife of husband. It is introductory to their lower status in itself. It is not so in the case of men. Although the sons get their identity through their fathers but it is maintained throughout the life and their marriages do not affect it.

Only sons carry forward the lineage through reproduction of their own sons and therefore for the peace of souls of ancestors, only sons are given the rights of performing last rites of parents and *Shradhha* worships for ancestors, so that they can achieve heaven after death and the state of salvation later on. In this way having son has been considered very important in Indian society, and for the purpose, any number of marriages were socially permitted and religiously approved. Due to this reason on ancestor's and father's property only sons have the right not the daughters and even law has made no difference regarding this. Biggest reason of discrimination between the boys and the girls is patriarchy. Therefore, abolition of patriarchal family system is necessary if women's status has to be raised. For it revolutionary steps are required to be taken up. For this purpose people will have to change their attitudes specifically men will have to cooperate shoulder to shoulder with women to bring about this change. It is only possible when they become prepared to give equal status to women by forgetting their male ego. It will be a big campaign which will take a very long time, and its success is also not certain, but it is better to do something than doing nothing in that direction. Some people will surely have to take the initiative and when other people will see its utility they will follow it in increasing numbers automatically. As Sharma, Hussain and Saharya (1984) have rightly said, man-woman equality is an ideal which can not be achieved until and unless the attitudes of people get changed.

For achieving this target, caste system which provides identity to the person, will have to be abandoned completely through enactment and enforcement of law but its consequences will not be seen unless people leave it willingly. Therefore, before making the legal provision against it creating awareness in people is essential to prepare public opinion regarding it. The awareness can be brought by making continuous efforts through the mediums of mass communication along with education. In Indian society there is a system of writing caste based surname after the name of a person. In the case of son this surname continues for the whole life but as discussed earlier, it gets changed at the time of marriage in the case of a girl. Apart from this anywhere for his identity son gives the name of his father, whereas the daughter uses the name of her father and husband respectively before and after her marriage. The ideal state should be that both, the son and daughter must write only names, and not the surnames, of both the parents after their own names, throughout their life. The parents who are responsible for their existence by giving them birth, only their names should be forwarded for identity, if required, otherwise only ones own name is sufficient to write for routine matters. On this issue serious discussions are required in conferences and seminars from point of view of its feasibility, and functionality. From this daughter will have the realization of belongingness to her parents' family throughout her life, and importance of only males will also reduce. A typical combination of all the three names of self, mother and father, will very rarely be found anywhere. Apart from this whosoever is the eldest son or daughter, or all the children together after the death of their parents can perform the sacraments regarding them and other ancestors. This will also help them in maintaining good relationships among themselves. The speed with which social change is taking place, a time will come soon, when only for last rites, children will be needed. In urban areas among the educated people, faith on performing the *shadhha* ceremony for ancestors every year, is decreasing gradually and most of them perform it due to the fear of public criticism.

As far as the property rights are concerned, sons and daughters should get equal shares out of ancestor's and the mother's as well as the father's property separately. In the case of any problems to the daughters regarding maintenance of immoveable property at parents place, it can be sold and new one can be purchased at convenient place or cash be invested in profitable schemes. For the performance of marriage without dowry and the respectful life of women their economic independence is a very important factor.

In materializing all the above mentioned arrangements some adjustment problems may arise between husband and wife in the beginning which can be solved with mutual understanding. Then, for living together happily both of them will have to compromise on some or the other issue. Accountability of everything is not possible and there should be some margin for flexibility everywhere.

Women's equal status in real sense rests on the success of the implementation of the above mentioned action plan. The important point which has to be kept in mind all the time is that for attaining a new social structure, social system and social organization, it will take a very long time, and for this purpose, very hard continuous struggle for many generations to come, will be required. But for the time being even if some educated, understanding and dedicated persons could experiment this strategy in their own life and present an ideal example as role models, in front of society. Their hopeful and happy state would motivate others to follow the same course of action.

But to achieve equal status, women will have to demonstrate their capabilities and efficiencies in very field equally to men. Along with shedding their economic, physical and mental dependence on men they will have to become completely independent while living with husband and any other male members in the family. The most crucial point to consider here is that, while doing so, men are not to be made enemies but their continuous cooperation is to be seeked in the process of achieving the target as well as in the maintenance of the new state of affairs. And it is possible only when men themselves understand the value of giving equal status to women and are willing to practice it in their life. Apart from all this, the women will be able to perform their outside roles properly only when they get help by their husbands in household affairs including the care of children. Therefore, it is required that the boys should also be trained in the household jobs right from childhood, while girls are being trained in the outside jobs as well. It may be expected from the present youngsters that they will proceed further in this direction in their life. Leaders of women's organizations and their movement will have to motivate both the men and women and set examples by following the new system in their own life. Male social workers can easily create consciousness and prepare people to change their behaviour. History is the witness of their successful efforts for improvement of women's status.

Owing to acute depth of the roots of Indian traditions overnight miraculous changes can not be expected in uprooting them but still, small jolts of culture shocks given by willing social sections, can certainly shake and make them weaker, which is sufficient for the time being. And if this process continues, the whole scenario will get changed in due course of time. To hasten the procedure Indian women should be determined to fight for their rights carefully, because taking maximum help of men. Without insulting and annoying them, is essential for the success of the programme. As Kapoor (1970) has also expressed, it should be ascertained that opposition group of men does not get created in reaction to their unnecessary criticism and attack on their male ego because as Mitra and Maharani (1984) have also commented, in the absence of their cooperation and assistance, objects of equality cannot be achieved in the real sense. In this way, women's courage and capability to solve all their problems themselves will certainly raise their status and bring it on a par with men.

Useful Suggestions to Remove Discrimination

Now we are in the situation to suggest certain measures in a nutshell, to be adopted by the Government and the society on the issue. They are:—

(i) By removing the shortcomings of laws, great emphasis is required to be given on their enforcement.

(ii) For changing the attitudes of the people, the speed of the process of change has to be fastened.

(iii) In order to remove negative impacts of caste system, extended joint family and patrilineal family tradition on the status of women, and for establishing the values of justice, liberty and equality in the society, the object of dislodging them is beneficial, which is possible through education of people.

(iv) Along with full opportunities of availing health, educational and occupational facilities, for the benefit of working women, provisions of hostels, creches and canteens in community at reasonable rates are necessary.

(v) Through various means of information and communication, awakening of people to create public opinion can easily be done, so that parents do not discriminate between the son and daughter.

(vi) Free legal education and legal assistance is required for women, to be benefited from their rights.

(vii) As it has been done in the case of polygamy, following of all the social legislations should be compulsory for government servants.

(viii) To catch hold of the criminals, police and administration have to made more swift and effective.

(ix) Severe punishment should be given to violaters of laws.

(x) Voluntary welfare organizations, working with trained social workers, and the intellectual and understanding members of community should be involved as much as possible for implementation of programmes. Participation of people is essential for the success of any scheme.

(xi) A network of family courts is necessary where quick decisions are taken on family disputes in order to provide immediate legal justice to women.

(xii) Women organizations should carry forward the women's movement in a positive manner. Women are to be motivated to leave all types of dependence on men and solve all their problems themselves. They should be convinced about the importance of independent status in society. And the most important point is that women leaders should avoid abusing men while delivering their lectures.

Apart from all these measures, the most important point is that women have to come forward and make efforts not only for their own development but to perform an active role in the development of whole society. By keeping in front the objective of establishment of equalitarian society, they have to make such efforts, so that exploitation of any section is not done by other section. When humanistic values will have an overbearing influence in the society, discrimination against women will be finished automatically. When women will participate in the development of nation by keeping the wider target of welfare of whole society and protection of weaker sections, they will also be proving their capabilities and achieving their rights with more, forceful ways. As Paul (1987) has rightly commented, in such a situation women will win certainly because there fight will not be different than the fight of common man in society.

It can be concluded that change in attitudes, thoughts, actions, behaviours, and relationships of all the people is necessary for creation of an environment where ideal principles such as social justice coexist and cooperate in such a manner that every person will be able to lead his life satisfactorily according to his desire. The efforts being made by the Government will be successful only when they will have people's especially women's participation.

Some Essays on Women Related Issues

Eighteen

Violence Against Women

Violence means the use of force against somebody. Woman and violence are the two opposite poles in the social milieu, while the woman creates human beings, the violence destructs them. And, violence against women is simply the destruction of creaters. What an Irony of Fate? (Awasthy, 1992).

Violence against women, indifferent biological and psychological forms, has remained in practice, since thousands of years in India. The root cause of this phenomenon lies in the complete subordination and dependence of women on men in the male-dominated society. In the patriarchal family system, under the Hindu Law, the husband had full right to punish his wife, if she was not behaving according to the social norms, favouring male counterparts, and even according to his own whims and fancies (Mukerjee, 1985). The act of violence, physical or verbal, was the manifestation of demonstrating and maintaining the authority, when it was challenged (Mehrotra, 1992). Woman's biological structure and less physical strength, as compared to man, have left her more vulnerable and succeptible to violence from the other male counterpart. Our social structure has in-built discrimination and oppression against women which has victimized them in exercising physical and emotional injury.

It is a matter of great concern that new forms of violence against women, are emerging and the events of different forms of violence are increasing day by day. Female foetus's abortion, girl child infanticide, rape, sexual harassment, eve-teasing, sexual exploitation and prostitution, domestic violence (wife beatings), abuse, pornography, Sati Custom, dowry deaths (murders and suicides both), all are the forms of emotional and physical violence against women. The information regarding the events of violence in our country demonstrates the seriousness of the problem. As Desai and Patel (1985) have informed in Table 18.1.

TABLE 18.1
IN 1980, PERSONS ARRESTED FOR CRIMES AGAINST WOMEN UNDER THE INDIAN PENAL CODE

Crime	*Male*	*Female*
Rape	6620	23 (abetting)
Kidnapping	15822	496
Immoral Traffic	354	214
Dowry Offence	149	181

The cases of dowry deaths reported in 1979, 1980, 1981, 1982 and 1983 were 422, 429, 452, 627 and 753 respectively (Police Research, 1985). Within the first four months of 1992, 6337 cases of rape were reported in different parts of the country, which includes kidnapping and dowry deaths also. In 1991, 25,000 cases of kidnapping and rape were registered. In this year 2,500 cases of dowry death were reported. Madhya Pradesh reported 397; 2,302; 6,300; and 1,271 cases of murder, rape, eve-teasing and kidnapping respectively in 1990. Total 10,210 cases were reported. The 1990, UP held second position in crime against women, there were total 7,509 cases which were reported which included 1,516; 1,524; 2,345, 2,124; cases for dowry murder, rape, eve-teasing and kidnapping respectively.

In Delhi, the situation regarding crimes against woman was as shown below in Table 18.2.

TABLE 18.2
CRIMES AGAINST WOMEN: DELHI (1988-91)

Year	*Dowry Murder*	*Rape*
1988	99	121
1989	108	153
1990	119	176
1991	111	182

Bhatt (1992) has reported a common practice of selling and kidnapping of women of hills. Sharma and Bhatt (1995) have reported that almost all married women are the victims of violent behaviour by their husbands in some form or the other.

The great majority, that is, 84 per cent of doctors are busy in abortions of female foetus. In 1986, a Government study had reported that, one doctor examines 270 foetus within a month on an average. And, the rate of abortion of female foetus was increasing by 20,000 every year. Growth rate was highest in Bombay, where in 1987 there were only 10 cases, in 1992, just after 5 years there were 248 case which means 24 times more cases of abortion of female foetus. According to the report of Anti-pregnancy Test Committee in 1987, there were 2400 and 13,000 such cases in Baroda and Delhi respectively. A country-wide survey has reported that out of 1000 abortions 995 are of the female foetus (Manorama Year Book 1993). In spite of recent ban on it, this practice is going on. All these astonishing figures show that, the attitude of society towards women has not changed much. They are still considered as a consumable commodity under the possession of men, like many other things at their disposal. The more painful fact is that, often the senior women get involved in the violence against young women due to some or the other reason. So much so, the severe abuses in the society are based on the sex crimes against women, which create further the violence among people.

Legal Provisions for Women: Before and After Independence

For the improvement of situation, right from the beginning of 19th century, efforts are being made to combat violence against women directly or indirectly. Awareness was brought through social reform movement and various Acts have been passed in order to protect women from violence, before and after independence both. Some of them before independence, as listed in India (1986: 479), are: Prohibition of Sati System Act, 1829; Hindu Widow Remarriage Act, 1856; Indian Divorce Act 1869; Special Marriage Act, 1872; Child Marriage Restraint Act, 1929; The Arya Marriage Validity Act, 1937; and Hindu Widow's Right on Property Act, 1937. Thus, a solid base for women, to be treated equal to men, got prepared in India, even before independence in

1947. After independence, Indian Constitution protected women against discrimination by according them equal rights with men in every respect. Consequently women started going out of the house for education and employment purposes, to lessen their dependence and subordination to men. Some of the Acts passed after independence are: Special Marriage Act, 1954; Hindu Marriage Act, 1955; Hindu Adoption and Maintenance Act, 1956; Hindu Succession Act, 1956, Suppression of Immoral Traffic in Women and Girls Act, 1956; Minority and Guardianship Act, 1956; Maternity Benefit Act, 1961; Dowry Prohibition Act, 1961; Medical Termination of Pregnancy Act, 1971; etc. (Srivastava, 1985).

Legal Provisions in Practice

But the social reality, regarding the benefits of these legal provisions to the women, presents totally a different picture. The literature dealing with women laws also demonstrates their non-implementation and consequently the continuing exploitation of women. Regarding the causes of it we find that, to some extent, the legal and administrative factors, that is, lapses and loopholes of laws, and lack of proper supervision system; and to a large extent, the psychological and sociological factors, i.e., traditional attitudes and conservative behaviour of people are considered to be responsible. Our two case studies, i.e., 'Rehabilitation of Women Prisoners' and 'Hindu Succession Act: Provision and Practice', have also confirmed these facts (Mishra, 1985 and 1986). Findings show that 22 per cent of the female married murderers were declared so, in place of their husbands and consequently sent to prison for punishment, and 87 per cent of daughters belonging to higher middle-class did not get any share in their father's property. Thus, we find that the people in general are not interested in any laws regarding equality and do not want them to be practiced actually and the discrimination continues. As explained by the theory of 'cultural lag' (Ogburn and Nimcoff as cited by Mishra, 1970), we are lagging behind in the non-materialistic part in comparison to materialistic part of social change. At present our country is passing through a transitional stage between the traditionality and modernity and the cultural changes are taking place. Due to the contacts and influences of western societies, the process of change started. Consequently, we have adopted the modern lifestyle to a great extent, started using even the aeroplane for transportation, telephones for communication and television for entertainment purposes, but our thoughts, religious beliefs, traditions, customs, etc., have not changed much. Therefore, the women going out for education and employment are further exposed to violence outside the house leaving aside the double burden of work and tension of role conflicts. Although women have to gather strength to protect themselves against violence, without cooperation of men, it can not be checked considerably. Even the severe punishment system does not produce the desired results.

Need for Attitudinal Change

For the improvement of situation, there seems to be a great need for attitudinal changes towards looking at the women. Lessening the total dependence of women on men by giving them all types of opportunities equally may work to some extent in decreasing the violent behaviour of men, but to a great extent, acceptance of women, as they are, with significance to their specific roles and capabilities, and the respect for their individuality and personality, by the menfolk, is especially required. The point is that, they should not be required to prove themselves equals although they can, in all sorts of professions in order to get equal status, because they have to fulfil their natural basic responsibility of reproducing and nurturing the human beings also. This important function of theirs can not be neglected or under estimated, until the practice of test tube babies gets wide spread in mechanical society. Even their household work is to be evaluated in terms of financial contribution, if only the monetary gain is given unnecessary importance. We find in literature that lot of importance is being given to this women issue.

Hence, it is necessary to find out the ways and means to bring about the changes in values, attitudes and perception of people. Fundamental changes in the social system are required to be made to subside the effects of established double standard for male and female which has contributed to the exploitation of women. For these achievements, social consciousness has to be stirred up and public opinion has to be created. For proper understanding and appreciation of the issues like social justice and equal treatment to both the sexes, the education of masses is needed. Thus, the whole society in general and man-folk in particular will become active participant in checking the violence against women.

Education, since it is a very strong agency of planned social change, can accelerate the process of change in attitudes and thereby in behaviour of males towards females. Formal and informal education along with the frequent messages appeals and portrayal of decent image of women through mass communication media, can play a very important role in decreasing the violence against women in society. Here one thing has to be kept in mind that our traditions are very deep-rooted, a miraculous overnight change cannot be expected, considering especially the huge population size and its higher proportion residing in the rural interiors. Therefore, it will take a very long time before the total transformation of attitudes takes place in the society, but still we can proceed towards it with a great speed by using all means of educating people both intensively and extensively. As from the education, realization and appreciation of the values of equality, liberty, social justice, etc., gets generated and then the efforts are made to bring them into practice in day to day life.

By looking at the patterns of social change in its non-materialistic aspect, especially among the educated urban people, equal opportunities given by the Government to the women, women's desire to prove their capabilities in order to get equal status, and the efforts made by Government And Non-Government agencies to create awareness and change public opinion on the issue, etc, at present. It can be predicted, the future of women in India will be quite bright in the present 21st Century. Indian society will change in this country with a great speed. The world is shrinking as the process of globalization is going on. Television, Internet and other forthcoming inventions in this field will bring the people together and the developed countries will have the impact more effectively on the developing countries. The values of equality, liberty and social justice, etc, will get well established as consequence of process of modernization at a great speed. The intelligence quotient of every young generation is always higher than older generation and every new generation has revolutionary ideas and practices in comparison to last generation. As one century witnesses atleast four generations of 'life, we can imagine very well, the totally changed scenario towards the end of the 21st Century, when women will be quite smart, courageous, strong and totally independent in all respects, and the most pleasant aspect of it is, that, they will get the support of men in becoming so. The daughters will be treated equally as sons and the wife and husband will become life partners in real sense, on equal terms. The boldness and increased physical strength of women will enhance their free and fearless mobility even in adverse situations, and alongwith it, due to the changed attitudes of men, the crimes against women will decrease considerably. The faster we move towards modernization the faster we can control the Crime against Women.

References

Awasthy, Abha, 1992: Introductory letter of Seminar on 'Violence Against Women' in Lucknow University.

Bhatt, Uma, 1992: 'Female Kidnapping: Conditions and Consequences' A Paper Presented in seminar on 'Violence Against Women' in Lucknow.

Desai, Neeva, and Patel, Vibhuti, 1985: *Indian Women-Change and Challenge in the International Women Decade, 1975-85*. Popular Prakashan, Bombay.

Desai, Neera, and Krishnaraj, Maitreyi, 1987: *Women and Society in India*.

D'souza, Victor, S. 1971: Changes in Social structure and changing Roles of older people in India' *Sociology and Research*. 55 (April, 297-304).

Department of Police Research Report, 1985, New Delhi.

India, the Year Book of 1986.

Manorama Year Book, 1993 and 98. Malayala Manorama Press, Kottayam.

Mukerjee, R.N. 1985: *Social Thought*, Ranjan Prakashan Gran., Delhi.

Mishra, K.K. 1970: *Samajik Niyantran Avam Samajik Parivartan*. Meenakshi Prakashan, Meerut.

Mishra, Saraswati. 1985: 'Rehabilitation of Female Prisoners' *Indian Journal of Criminology*. Vol. 12, No. 1, Jan. 1985.

1986, Hindu Succession Act, 1956 Protection and Practice, *Social Welfare*, Vol. XXXIII, No. 6, Sep. 1986.

Mehrotra, Nilika, 1992: Structural Bases of Violence Against Women paper Presented in Lucknow Seminar.

National Crime Record Bureau, 1995.

Sharma, Divakar and Bhatt, Sunil, Jayshree, 1995: Violence Against Women in Marital Relationship. A Paper Presented in M.P. Sociological Conference in Bhopal. 1996.

Srivastava, T.N. 1985: Women and the Law. Intellectual Publishing House, New Delhi.

Verma, Bhavana, 1998: Crime Against Women. An unpublished Ph.D. Thesis of R.D.V.V., Jabalpur.

Nineteen

Problems of Female Prisoners

By nature woman is very conscious about her security. She is god-fearing as well as peace-loving. The woman who gives life to an individual can not take the life easily, in normal circumstances. She loves her family and does not want it to be disintegrated. Our case study of lifers (Mishra, 1983) demonstrated as Dhar (1983 : 2) has also found out that, 50 per cent of the female convicts were in the age group of 25 to 30 years, 55.5 per cent belonged to the lower caste group, 89 per cent have rural background, 72.2 per cent were married, 61.11 per cent have come from joint families and 55.5 per cent have less than three children 55.5 per cent of them have murdered their near and dear ones (husband, mother-in-law, children, etc.). This fact also supports the findings of another study of female criminals (Smith, 1962 : 25): 22.2 per cent, that is near about one-fourth portion of so-called murderers have reported that their cases were false, they have been forced by the real murderers, i.e., the male members of their family to accept the charge of murder on themselves, as Ahuja (1969 : 108) has also found out in his study. Further, 50 per cent of the female convicts have their children with them in jail. In majority of the cases, i.e., 61.1 per cent, the economic condition of their families was extremely poor. Same proportion of them were working as labourers and were having very bad relations with their family members before committing the crime. This fact also supports the findings of Ahuja (1969 : 108). After being caught, the police behaviour was very bad towards them. Regarding their contacts with relatives while staying in jail, 61.1 per cent and 50 per of them did not receive any visitor and letter from their homes respectively. An overwhelming majority of those who received letters of visitors that too rarely, received them only from their parents side.

Mostly the unmarried girls have some contacts with their parents, while talking about their life in prison, most of them reported that they felt suffocated due to their living and restricted mobility within separate high-walled enclosure in jail. They got very cruel treatment from the jail authority and other employees. They were working very hard and not getting even stomach full of food. The female warders have no sympathy even towards their children who were neither the criminals themselves nor responsible for their mother's crime. Some of them reported about their sexual harassment by other inmates or female workers. They were not given proper education and vocational training. Even their children were not given education. Most of the convict-mothers remained worried about their children's future. Due to tension and anxiety, they picked up quarrels with each other frequently, for which they were punished in the form of more hard work and would get later release from the prison.

Life After Release from Prison

Regarding the after release life, most of the convicted were found to be uncertain and worried about their living arrangement but reported that certainly they would have to depend upon their ages for their livelihood. As Ahuja (1969:108) has also mentioned, an overwhelming majority (83.2 per cent) was not expecting good treatment from the people of their family and community. The data shows that in the case of 53.4 per cent of married convicts, their husbands had second wives at the time of interview whereas others were not aware of their husband's marital status due to absence of any contacts with those who mattered to them. While talking, about the general rehabilitation assistance scheme (one could get Rs. 500 to 1000 in cash and kind both, on the approval of probation officer), a great majority, that is 88.9 per cent, expressed their ignorance about it, whereas when told, 83.22 per cent of female convicts were very keen to avail this facility, but at the same time 77.2 per cent of them expressed their inability to pursue the procedure. Out of 77.22 per cent of eligible female convicts, no one was planning to get married for various reasons, i.e., child (61.5 per cent), stigma of being murderer (38.5 per cent), as obstacles, and apathy towards life after the bitter experience of imprisonment. The were 66.6 per cent of them who wanted to go back to their hometowns whereas rest of them expressed that they would prefer to live in an unknown place provided they could find jobs and a secure place to live. As far as the type of help is concerned, 72.22 per cent, 66.66 per cent, 38.88 per cent, 16.1 per cent, 11.11 per cent of them mentioned that they would like to have service, money, shop, agricultural land and knitting and sewing machine respectively. Two of them wanted Government officials to approach and persuade their family members to excuse them and accept them back as members of the family. They were very much worried about their future. (In the case of absence of family members at the time of release the female convicts are accompanied by female warder and one police constable upto the bus stand or railway station to see them off. After that what happens to them is not the responsibility of jail authority (Ahuja, 1969:118). One recent study Kushwaha (1999) has also supported the above mentioned findings. The Provision of Parole and facility of short leave at the interval of few months was also not utilized in the case of women especially which could be helpful for their rehabilitation.

On the basis of above findings we can summarize that, due to illiteracy, ignorance and dependence on males, women become victims of circumstances, conspiracy and even as scape-goats in regard to the murder cases. Once they are convicted and imprisoned family members do not care for them. In jails they are ill-treated by the authorities, leaving aside other problems like deprivation of fulfilment of various needs and boredom of life. No proper education and vocational training is given to them, no parole and leave provision is utilized and no guidance is given to seek the advantage of rehabilitation scheme. And even after release neither the family members accept them nor the after care service is given by jail authority. In a nutshell we can conclude that once the woman is convicted as murderer her life becomes hell. Although she wants to resume her family life, she can not do so. She does not get any helping hand and, she has no other option than to get lost in the darkness of sorrows forever.

Suggestions to Solve the Problems of Women Prisoners

For the solution of above mentioned problems some measures can be taken up. First of all, education of girls has to be emphasized in rural areas in order to make them knowledgeable as well as financially independent. Arrangement should be made to raise educational standard of the female convicts in jail. As Dhar (1983:2) has also emphasized, young girls should be encouraged to study as they themselves are not aware of the benefit of education. They should be given vocational training of their choice depending on their aptitude. This will give them a skill and confidence to start cottage industries with the Government's financial help. The welfare officer of jail should make them aware of the rehabilitation assistance scheme and help the deserving ones to secure it. The provision of parole and facility of short leave at the interval of few months should come into practice for all the lifers. As Sandhu (1968:123) has also advocated, through these arrangements the convicts may be enabled to re-establish their social contacts which go a long way in helping them in effective rehabilitation in society. The jail visits by the relatives of the convicts should be encouraged by jail authority The treatment of jail workers towards prisoners should be sympathetic and humanistic. The female prisoners' attention should be diverted towards religious preachings and practices. Entertainment activities should be arranged sometimes and physical exercise and yoga should be given due importance and their time should be utilized more in some productive and creative activities to keep them away from foul practices and the culprits should be further punished. Their children should be given proper attention towards their need satisfaction, especially the nutritious food and education. Prior to the release of female convicts, the probation officer should visit hometowns and study the situation for rehabilitating them. He should convince the concerned people to accept and treat them properly. The convicts willing to live in unknown place for various reasons should be provided with after care services. Counselling and guidance about various aspects of life can be given to them by government and voluntary agencies. The amount of money for rehabilitation should increased. Rescue homes, Asylums and sheltered workshops should be opened with training, boarding and lodging facilities.

Released convicts should be encouraged to form co-operative societies for production and sale of some commodities. Marriage of willing young female convicts with other handicapped males may be arranged after release. Better understanding between husband and wife in such cases may help them to lead a happy life. Police and jail authorities should be instructed for good treatment with criminals. Thus, through police and jail reforms, socially handicapped females, who get uprooted from their social environment for 14 years or so, can be made normai citizens of society to some extent atleast and consequently the chances of their committing crime again become very bleak.

References

Ahuja, Ram, 1969: *Female Offenders in India*, Meenakshi Prakashan, pp. 108, 118, Meerut.

Aiyar, R.P. 1967: *In the Crime Light*, Bombay. India Book House.

Chandra, Sushil, 1967: *Sociology of Aviation in India*, Allied Publishers, Bombay.

Dhar, Usha, 1983: The Female Offenders. Abstract of Ph.D. Thesis Lucknow University.

Jacob, K.K. 1965: *Methods and Fields of Social Work in India*, Asia Publishing House, Bombay.

Kushwaha, Laxmi, 1999: "Mahila Apradh Ke Karan Va Parinam" M. Phil, Thesis. Deptt. of Sociology, R.D.V.V., Jabalpur.

Mishra, Saraswati, 1983: Rehabilitation of Women Prisoners. *Indian Journal of Criminology*.

Nayyar, Baldeo, Raj, 1975: *Violence and Crime in India*, Macmillan Company of India, Delhi.

Rao, S. Venugopal, 1967: *Facets of Crime in India*, Allied Publishers, Bombay.

Sandhu, Harjit, S., 1968: *A Study on Prison Impact*, Ph.D. Thesis Punjab University, Chandigarh.

Smith, Ann, D. 1962: *Women in Prison*, Stevens and Sons, London.

Twenty

Legal Justice to Women: Sociological Evaluation

Social structure, cultural norms and value systems are important determinants of women's roles and their position in the society. They influence social expectations regarding behaviour of the two sexes, both as individuals and in relation to each other. Social traditions have a major role in shaping attitudes as well as behaviour patterns of human groups (National Committee's Report, 1974:37). In the matters like marriage, inheritance, religious and social obligations, etc., Hindus had been governed by Hindu laws which date back to the time of Manu (Jacob, 1965:162). In *Manusmriti* as cited by Mukerjee (1985: 424-26), we find, that in all the elaborated rules of conduct, Manu had assigned a secondary position to women. Hindu laws and customs which have been woven into the social fabric of the country, over a period of more than 3000 years, were formulated from men's point of view, and they were more liability than an asset to the Hindu women.

Enactment of Laws

During the British regime, an attempt was made to change the situation regarding the double standards between the males and females through legislation. Some instances of social legislation, as mentioned in 'India' (1986 : 479), in this field, were : Prohibition of Sati System Act, 1829; Hindu Widow Remarriage Act, 1856; Indian Divorce Act, 1869; Special Marriage Act, 1872; Child Marriage Restraint Act, 1929, The Arya Marriage Validity Act, 1937; and Hindu Widow's Right on Property Act, 1937. Thus, a solid base, for women to be treated equal to men, got prepared in India, even before independence in 1947.

After independence, India declared itself a welfare state which makes continuous efforts for the maximum satisfaction of the maximum number of people. The 'Directive Principles of State Policy' clearly instructed the state to take special welfare measures for the weaker sections of society. Consequently, Indian Constitution protected women against discrimination by according to them equal rights with men in every respect (Antony, 1989: 9-15). Without wasting much time, through legislation, efforts were made to erase the glaring defects of Hindu laws, for the betterment of Hindu women. Among various Acts : Special Marriage Act, 1955; Hindu Adoption and Maintenance Act, 1956; Hindu Succession Act, 1956; Suppression of Immoral Traffic in Women and Girls Act, 1956; Minority and Guardianship Act, 1956; Maternity Benefit Act, 1961; Dowry Prohibition Act, 1961; Medical Termination of Pregnancy Act, 1971, etc, are the important ones (Srivastava, 1985). Equality or emancipation of women has been made an important part of our general development plans. Since social legislation is considered to be the important agency of planned social change, removal of various forms of discrimination against women, has been attempted through legal provisions in our country. It is being expected that these Acts will be quite useful in enhancing the status of Hindu women.

Enforcement of Laws

But the social reality, regarding the benefits of these legal provisions to the women, presents, totally a different picture. The literature dealing with women-laws also demonstrates their non-implementation and consequently the continuing exploitation of women (Jacob, 1965; Chattopadhyaya, 1963; Kapoor, 1964; Sarkar, 1954; Choudhary, 1961; Kidwai, 1978; Minattur, 1980; Kumar, 1982; Satyasundaram, 1975; Planning Commission's Report, 1956; Gangrade, 1978; Mehta, 1987; Sachhidananda and Sinha, 1984; Gupta, 1988; Sinha, 1988; Atraya, 1988; Antony, 1989; Haksar and Singh, 1986; Yakin and Anwar, 1982; Srivastava, 1985; National Committee's Report, 1974). Regarding the causes of non-implementation of these laws we find in the literature, that, to some extent, the legal and administrative factors; that is, lapses and loopholes of laws, and lack of proper supervision system; and to a large extent, the psychological and sociological factors, i.e., traditional attitudes and conservative behaviour of people, are considered to be responsible. As cited by Yakin and Anwar (1982), our beloved Ex-Prime Minister, late Mrs. Indira Gandhi had also realized that, the general texture of our society does not permit women to get benefited actually, from the rights which are their's in theory. She has also been quoted by Srivastava (1985) expressing that, the governments action can be neither effective nor adequate, unless women themselves become more aware of their rights and the corresponding responsibilities. They are not being benefited primarily due to economic dependence and secondly due to ignorance about legal provisions.

In the Preface of Planning Commission's Report (1956), Smt. Durgabai Deshmukh stated, that it is not enough to have good laws, but to secure due obedience to the law, it must be known and approved by the public, on whose behalf it is enforced. Ex-Chief Justice of India, Mr. Y.V. Chandrachud has also expressed that law can certainly play an important role in bringing about social equality between the two sexes, but without awareness or social obligations, it can not succeed (Yakin and Anwar, 1982).

Case Studies on Obedience of Law

Our two case studies, i.e., 'Rehabilitation of Women Prisoners' (RWP) and 'Hindu Succession Act: Protection and Practice' (HSA:PP) have also confirmed these facts. Brief summaries of these studies are presented here.

Objective of Study

While the main objective of RWP study was to find out the extent to which female prisoners, are helped by the Government in their rehabilitation, after their release. The HSA : PP study was aimed at determining the extent to which women laws are implemented. Benefits to the women has been given special consideration in both the studies. In the latter one daughter's share in father's property was the main issue for study.

Methods

In the RWP study, 36 women prisoners and in the HSA : PP study, 30 married women were selected by using the purposive sampling method. In the former study, all the female murders, completed at least five years of their life imprisonment, and in the latter study, 30 married women belonging to the three socio-economic classes, were personally interviewed by the researcher. In both the studies, negative hypotheses, that is, lack of rehabilitation help and non-implementation of laws were constructed. The questions regarding the circumstances at the time of crime, present relationship with the family members and future plans, were particularly asked from the female criminals, whereas questions regarding the parental family background, dowry at the time of marriage, share in father's property and their knowledge about legal provisions, etc., were given special emphasis in the HSA : PP study. Main idea was to know about the daughter's share in father's property, but since the dowry system is very much related with it, the information about the Act regarding it, as well as the dowry in respondents' marriages, was also gathered. Data thus collected, was processed and presented in the form of tables, wherever required. Due to small number of respondents and scattered frequency distribution in the tables of both the studies, the application of any statistical method, to test the significance of differences or ascertaining the association between two variables, was not possible and only the percentage differences were worked out.

Characteristics of the Samples

In the RWP study, majority of the respondents were in the age group of 25 to 30 years, they were illiterates, belonged to the lower caste group, had rural background, were married, had come from joint families, had less than three children, were staying in the jail with atleast one child, and were having very poor economic conditions at home. Most of the respondents of our HSA: PP study, had an urban background, belonged to higher caste group, were aged between 30 to 50 years, were educated atleast upto matriculation and unemployed.

Results

Facts about crime

In the RWP study, when female prisoners were asked about the reasons of committing murders, they came out with quite a pathetic information. This knowledge was considered necessary because the women who gives life to the human beings, can not take their life easily, without any serious causes. It was quite astonishing to note, as Table 20.1 demonstrates that the cases of near about one-fourth of the female lifers (22.22 per cent), were false as Ahuja (1969: 108) has also found out. They were forced to take crime, committed by near and dear male member, on their own heads, so the family kept on functioning properly. They were also promised sincere efforts by the family members, for their quick release from jail, which were never made later on. When we looked at the main reasons of crime, we found out that, 25 per cent of convicts were forced by the violent behaviour of the family members, started basically due to lack of dowry; to commit murder of mother-in-law in quite a few cases, 19.44 per cent of respondents could not tolerate the bad character and bad habits of husbands any more and committed murder of either husband or the other woman in most of the cases, 11.11 per cent of them attacked the persons, making attempts of their rape. Where the main reason is poverty, they have killed mostly, their own children and in the case of property, they have killed either the neighbour or the member of kinship group.

This information demonstrates the intolerable conditions of the respondents under which they were leading their life. They were driven to the point when they could bear no more and under the influence of impulses, they found no option but to kill the person, most responsible for the situation. The very fact, that they were undergoing the life imprisonment, shows that, the court could not do justice with the females, trapped in false cases; as well as regarding the true cases, the circumstances which forced them to commit murder, were not given due consideration. Dowry and Bigamy banned by the laws (Dowry Prohibition Act, 1961 and Hindu Marriage Act, 1955), have emerged out to be the main reasons of crime, showing that, laws are not being implemented.

TABLE 20.1
DISTRIBUTION OF THE FEMALE PRISONERS ACCORDING TO THE REALITY OF CRIME AND MAIN REASON OF COMMITTING MURDER

	Main Reason of Committing Murder						
Reality of crime	*Not Applicable*	*Violent Behaviour of Family Members Basically Due to lack of Dowry*	*Bad character and Bad Habits of Husband*	*Rape Effort*	*Poverty Problem*	*Property Issue*	*Total*
False case	8	-	-	-	-	-	8 (22.2)
True cases	-	9	7	4	5	3	28 (77.8)
Total	8 (22.22)	9 (25.00)	7 (19.44)	4 (11.11)	5 (13.90)	3 (8.33)	36 (100.00)

(Percentages are given in parentheses).

As far as their rehabilitation is concerned, our study revealed that, their family members are not keeping any contacts with them, and most of the husbands got married again due to their absence. We also came to know that whatever are the government policies and programmes of rehabilitation of prisoners; the women are not getting much benefits through them firstly due to lack of their implementation and secondly owing to the ignorance and non-insistence on the part of women prisoners (Mishra, 1985).

Facts about Women Laws: Provision and Practice

Regarding our HSA : PP study, two Acts, i.e., Hindu Succession Act, 1956 and Prohibition of Dowry Act, 1961, were studied thoroughly in order to know their lapses and loopholes.

Shortcomings of Hindu Succession Act, 1956

Although this Act declares equal rights of succession of father's property to the daughters along with sons, deep study of the provisions of this Act, brings out some lapses and loopholes in it, which make the position of daughter disadvantageous. Due to retention of the institution of 'Mitakshara' coparcenary, the daughter gets very little share in the ancestral joint family property, in comparison to her brother. Moreover, a person's rights to renounce his share in property of coparcenary and to convert self-acquired property into coparcenary property, further creates the possibilities for daughter getting no share in father's property (Bare Act, 1983).

Another provision in the Act excludes the devolution of tenancy rights under the legislation of the states from the scopes of the Act. As different states have different land legislations, the beneficial effects of the Hindu Succession Act can be denied by resorting to this provision. Because the bulk of property in India is agricultural land, such an exemption detracts from the principles of equality and uniformity both (National Committee's Report, 1974).

Another discriminating provision in the Act is that, the female heirs are not entitled to claim partition of the dwelling house unless the male members choose to divide their shares in it. It gives them the right to reside, that too to the unmarried, widowed, separated or divorced daughters.

Further, the Act place no restriction on the power of testation through which daughters can easily be denied of their shares, in case the father believes in maintaining the traditions.

In this way we find that this Act is quite discriminating between the two sexes. But still, through this Act only, the daughters have for the first time been made entitled to succeed along with sons.

Shortcomings of the Dowry Prohibition Act, 1961

This Act failed miserably to achieve its purpose, mainly because the offence was not declared cognizable. Therefore, without complaint it could not be judicially investigated. Even after its many amendments in 1980's, it has not been made totally cognizable.

Another loophole in the Act was that, the explanation of dowry excluded any kind of gifts and presents, not made in 'consideration' of marriage. Even the amendments in the Act in which 'connection' word has been written in place of 'considerations' have not set any ceiling on the gifts to the bride, although they made it necessary to list and value them to see that, they are not beyond the capacity of presenter, and more than Rs. 500 in the case of bridegroom. On the whole, the issue of gifts presents a confused picture and encourages guise for dowry (Srivastava, 1985).

The Act also does not ban the display of dowry by the marriage parties which encourages the evil. It also does not put a ceiling on the expenditure on arrangements regarding marriage. Arrangements of returning the dowry to the bridge have been made in the amended Act, but again in the case of poor people specially, it does not serve the purpose of the Act. In this way, we find that this Act needs further amendments which are being considered now.

Practice of Women Laws

In order to know the practice of the two Acts, mentioned above, the respondents of our HSA : PP study were asked to inform about the dowry at the time of their marriages and their share in father's property which has been shown in Table 2.

TABLE 20.2
DISTRIBUTION OF THE RESPONDENTS ACCORDING TO THE DOWRY GIVEN TO THEM AND THEIR SHARE IN FATHER'S PROPERTY

	Dowry in the Form of Cash			
Share in Father's Property	*Upto Rs. 10,000*	*Rs. 11,000 to Rs. 20,000*	*Above 20,000*	*Total*
No Share	11	9	6	26 (86.68)
Unequal share	-	1	1	2 (6.66)
Equal Share	-	1	1	2 (6.66)
Total	11 (36.67)	11 (36.67)	8 (26.66)	30 (100.00)

(The percentages are given in parentheses).

As Table 20.2 demonstrates, in the case of equal proportion of the respondents, which is 36.67 per cent the parents gave dowry in the form of cash, upto Rs. 10,000 and between Rs. 11,000 to Rs. 20,000. The parents of 26.66 per cent married women gave even more than Rs. 20,000 in cash form in the dowry to their in-laws at the time of marriage. Further probing revealed that out of this amount the respondents did not get any money which is worth noting. Apart from cash, other household things were also given to them and considerable number of those things got distributed among the in-law's relatives at the time of marriage and later on. The disappointing information we got during the investigation, was that, most of our respondents, although did not like the demands of dowry from their in-laws, they cherished all the gifts and presents given to them. No one interfered and made complaint against it, as it would have spoiled the relationship between the two families.

As far as the daughter's share in father's property is concerned, as it was expected, the table shows that, a very little number, i.e., four out of 30 housewives had received some property from the parents, and the reason of getting it was not the fair distribution of property among children, in any case. Out of these four recipients of property, while one is the only issue of parents and hence, entitled for inheriting the property, the other one is the only sister of many brothers and due to love and affection the father gave her property, almost equal to brothers but in the form of cash and gold. In rest of the two cases, a piece of agricultural land and a plot was transferred to their names, just to escape from land ceiling and property tax, respectively. In the first case there is an understanding that the land will not be utilized by the daughter, while the other one is permitted to construct a house on the plot, whose price can be paid later on according to convenience. Rest of the respondents neither got any property, nor they have any hope of getting it in future. While a majority of them were found willing to accept the property if it is given to them but no one wants to take legal support for acquiring it. The main reason behind it is that they do not want to spoil their relationship with brothers (Mishra, 1986).

Most of our respondents were found to have very little knowledge about the legal provisions of these Acts.

Conclusions

Both the studies demonstrated that, on the whole, most of the women laws are not providing any benefit to the women. In almost all the Acts there are many lapses and loopholes due to which they do not protect women's rights properly, and whatever little protection they offer, even that is not practiced by the public. A large number of Acts have been enacted but there is no emphasis on their enforcement. In this way, we have found, that even today women are deprived of the legal justice and they continue to be the victims of unequal treatment and exploitation in the male dominated society.

Explanation of the Gap between the Enactment and Enforcement of Laws

In order to bring about social change through proper planning, Indian Government has passed many Acts for the protection of women, and also established the institutions, responsible for their implementation. But as we have seen, women are not getting benefitted through these legal provisions. The reason behind it is that, the people in general, are not interested in them and do not want them to be practiced actually. They still have conservative attitudes and confirm to the traditional behaviour of discriminating between the males and females. Thus, a large gap exists between the formulation and implementation of laws regarding women.

Cultural Lag

This gap can be explained with the help of the concept of 'cultural lag', forwarded by Ogburn, for establishing the 'Socio-cultural theory of Social change'. As cited by Mishra (1970 : 124-127), Ogburn, in his book *Social Change* has divided culture into two parts, i.e., materialistic culture and non-materialistic culture. Under the first part, all the man-made visible things come, whereas the latter is abstract, in which attitudes, beliefs, morality, religiosity, etc, are included. According to Ogburn's opinion, social change takes place due to the change in cultural elements. Two aspects of culture do not proceed together, the changes in the materialistic culture take place with a fast speed whereas the non-materialistic culture changes very slowly. Due to this reason the non-materialistic cultural part large behind in comparison to materialistic cultural part, and a gap generates between the two which is called cultural lag : Ogburn and Nimkoff have written in the *Hand Book of Sociology* (p. 592) as Mishra (1970) has cited, that, the strain that exists between two correlated parts of culture that change at unequal rates of speed, may be interpreted as a 'lag' in the part, that is changing at the slowest rate, for the one lags behind the other. Non-materialistic culture is related with the mcral aspect of life and there are some social ideals behind it which do not change frequently. The extension of this cultural lag, may be little or vast depending upon the constituents of culture. It may continue for a long time and during the period, the state of disequilibrium may get generated. Due to this disequilibrium the social change takes place. When no uniformity exists between the two parts of culture, the 'cultural lag' opens the avenues of social change.

Our country is passing through a transitional stage between traditionality and modernity and cultural changes are taking place. Due to the contacts and influences of western societies, the process of change started. Consequently, we have adopted the modern lifestyle to a great extent, started using the aeroplanes for transportation, telephones for communication and television for entertainment even, but our thoughts, religious beliefs, traditions, customs, etc, have not changed much and therefore we are still practicing caste and sex discrimination. In order to establish modern values of equality, liberty and social justice, Government of India has passed various Acts for the protection of Hindu women against exploitation, which have been compiled in the thick volumes of law. Our Constitution which guarantees equality in all aspects of life, is also available in the written form. Government has also established institutions like : police stations, courts, prisons, etc, for the enforcement of these laws. But as we have seen, these laws are not being implemented properly, the women are not getting any benefit out of them and their status has not changed much even after such a long time of their formulation. It is because these legal provisions are not being accepted by the general people of Hindu community. The people are not bothered even to have uptodate knowledge about these laws, as they simply love traditions.

As the National Committee has also reported (1974:37), that changes in the normative structure do not take place at the same rate, at which they take place in the organizational forms of society. Thus, we find that, reforms in educational policy and laws do not make the desired impact on social attitudes because of the normative and structural unpreparedness of the society to accept their goals and means. In respect of the status that is accorded to women by law and by the Constitution, we notice that there is a gap between the theoretical possibilities and their actual realization. Religion, family and kinship roles and cultural norms, delimiting the spheres of women's activities, obstruct their full and equal participation in the life of the society and the achievement of their full potential. Thus, social status of women can be considered as a typical example of the gap between the status and roles, provided by the constitution and laws, and the status and roles, imposed by the social traditions. The width of the 'cultural lag', i.e., the gap between the two aspects, discussed above, is quite large and therefore the state of disequilibrium between them has emerged. This state may last long because the deep-rooted traditional values and norms are posing a tough resistance to implementation of laws, creating many problems and challenges.

Discussion and Suggestions

The deeper probe regarding laws has demonstrated that, legal measures have certain inbuilt inadequacies and contradictions which need immediate efforts for correction. In many ways, the necessity of changes in role relationships and in the treatment of women in various sub-systems indicate a positive need for attitudinal changes. Hence it is necessary to find out the ways and means to bring about these changes in values, attitudes and perception of people. Fundamental changes in the Social System are required to be made to subside the effects of established double standard for male and female, which has contributed to the exploitation of women. For these achievements social consciousness has to be stirred up and public opinion has to be created. For proper understanding and appreciation of the issues like social justice and equal treatment to both the sexes, the education of masses is needed. Thus, the society as a whole, will become active participant in successful implementation of the legislation.

As our study demonstrates, dowry system seems to be the main hazard in the way of implementation of Succession Act and non-implementation of Succession Act encourages dowry in the marriages of girls. Dowry system has started and flourished in our society due to economic dependence of wives on their husbands in their married life. The solution of removing the dowry system is, to get the girls educated, not only for matrimonial and emergency purposes, which is the normal practice but to make them financially independent, self-confident and bold enough to refuse the marriage with dowry. One more fact which was observed during the study, is that the daughters themselves want their parents to spend lot of money on their marriages. One reason for this may be that they aspire to get higher status in the husband's family. Another reason may be that, they think, after their marriages, they will have no claim on any thing at their parents place. Our submission is, that the ensured share of the daughter in father's property, which sooner or later she will get, along with her financial independence before marriage, will certainly encourage marriage without dowry. National Committee's Report (1974) goes further by stating that as soon as our women get economic freedom by employment, possibly there would not be any occasion for the law against dowry, to operate. Thus, eradication of this evil by rousing social conscience is seemingly an attractive approach.

For equal upbringing of male and female offsprings, a very small number of children in the family is required. In this way, the whole process of socialization which is discriminating enough between the two sexes, needs a foundational change. For this purpose, great responsibility lies on the shoulders of mothers of the present generation. They have to make sure that, their daughters do not suffer in their lives, in the ways, they themselves have suffered in their own. The women will have to come out of their shells and deny the culture of silence. They will have to define themselves by proving their worth, on the one hand, and fight for their rightful dues, on the other. This will accelerate the process of change in the attitudes and behaviour of males, bridging the gap between the formulation and implementation of laws, consequently. Otherwise, it will take a very long time before the total transformation of the society takes place. As our traditions are very deep-rooted, a miraculous overnight change can not be expected, but the strong shake-ups by the interested section of the society, will certainly make them weaker. Therefore, the women should prepare themselves to fight their own battle, although the maximum possible help from the men folk has to be taken tactfully without offending and displeasing them to fulfill the task. It has to be ensured that the rival group of males is not generated, in the reaction of unnecessary and avoidable criticism of them, directly hurting their male ego, because without their cooperation and support the objectives can not be achieved in real sense. Thus, financial independence and boldness to tackle all sorts of problems will certainly raise women's status.

Recommendations

Now we are in a position to make certain recommendations on the issue. They are:

1. The inherent nature of many social legislations is confusing and some times contradictory. Some alterations should be made in these legislations.
2. There is a necessity to accelerate the process of change by deliberate and planned efforts to change the attitudes of people.
3. People's participation, especially of the female section of population in the form of their organized efforts, is to be encouraged for the successful implementation of laws.
4. Education for women is very essential for getting benefited. Special emphasis should be given to legal education, in order to teach them about their legal rights, even at school level.
5. Free legal aid should be provided to the women to fight for their rights.
6. Proper system of inspection to observe the implementation of laws should be evolved by the government.
7. Voluntary organizations, having trained social workers and enlightened members of the community, should be entrusted for the enforcement of social laws.
8. Following of all the social laws should be included in the Government Servant's Conduct Rules, as it has been done to prevent bigamous marriages.

9. Good network of family courts with quick settlement of the cases will be quite helpful in providing legal justice to women.
10. Police should be more vigilant and strict to adequately enforce the laws and to see that the offenders do not roam scot-free but properly punished.
11. Information and communication media can play a very important role in educating the masses, convincing them against the exploitation of women and thereby preparing them to accept the modern values of social justice, equality and liberty.

References

Antony, M.J. 1989: *Women's Rights*, pp. 9-15 Hind Pocket Books Pvt. Ltd., Delhi.

Atray, J.P. 1988: *Crimes Against Women*. Vikas Publishing House Pvt. Ltd., Delhi.

Ahuja, Ram. 1969: *Female Offenders in India*. Meenakshi Prakashan, Meerut.

Bare Act., 1983: *New Acts of Hindu Law*. Allahabad Law Agency Publications.

Chattopadhyaya, K. 1969: Women's rights and Controversy on Succession Act, *Social Welfare*, Vol. 16, No. 5, pp. 8-24.

Choudhary, Roop, L. and Firma, K.L. 1961: *Hindu Women's Right to Property*. Mukhopadhyaya, Calcutta.

Gupta, J.L. 1988: *Challenges to the Fair Sex*. Gyan Publishing House, New Delhi.

Gangrade, K.D. 1978: *Social Legislation in India*, Vol. I and II, Concept Publishing Company, Delhi.

Haksar, Nandita and Singh, Anju, 1986: *Demystification of Law for Women*. Lancer Press, New Delhi.

India, 1989: Information and Communication Ministry, Publication Department, New Delhi.

Jacob, K.K. 1965: *Methods and Fields of Social Work in India*, Asia Publishing House, Bombay.

Kidwai, Sheikh, M.H. 1978: *Women under Different Social and Religious Laws*. Light and Life Publishers, New Delhi.

Kumar, Manju, 1982: *Social Equality*, S. Chand and Company Ltd., New Delhi.

Kapoor, V.N. 1964: "Rights of the Unmarried Daughters in Father's Property. Under the Hindu Law". *AIR* (J Section) Vol. 53, pp. 63-65.

Mukerjee, R.N. 1985: *Samajik Vichardhara*, 424-26. Ranjan Prakashan Grah. New Delhi.

Mehta, Rama, 1987: *Socio-Legal Status of Women in India*. Mittal Publication, Delhi.

Mishra, K.K. 1970: *Samajik Niyantran Avam Samajik Parivartan*, Meenakshi Prakashan, Meerut.

Mishra, Saraswati, 1985: 'Rehabilitation of Female Prisoners' in *Indian Journal of Criminology*, Vol. 12, No. 1. Jan. 1985.

———, 1986: 'Hindu Succession Act, 1956: Protection and Practices, in *Social Welfare*. Vol. XXXIII, No. 6 Sep. 1986.

National Committee's Report on the Status of Women in India : Government of India Publication, 1974, New Delhi.

Nayyar, Baldev, Raj, 1975: *Violence and Crime in India*. Macmillan Company of India, Delhi.

Planning Commission: Social Legislation - Its Role in Social Welfare, 1956.

Smith, Ann. D. 1962: *Women in Prison*, Stevens and Sons., London.

Sandhu, Harjit, S. 1968: *A Study on Prison Impact*. Punjab University Publication Bureau, Chandigarh.

Satya Sundaram, I. 1975: 'The Status of Indian Women.' RHV 39, No. 6, 17-20.

Sarkar, R.N. 1954: 'Unchaste Widows' Position under Hindu Women's Right to Property Act'. *AIR* (J Section) Aug., Sep. 1954, 65-69.

Sinha, Niroj, 1988: *Women and Violence* (Ed.), Vikas Publishing House Pvt. Ltd., New Delhi.

Srivastava, T.N. 1985: *Women and the Law*. Intellectual Publishing House, New Delhi.

Sachhidanand and Sinha, R.P., 1984: *Women's Rights: Myths and Reality*, Print Well Publishers, Jaipur.

Yakin A and Anwar, B. 1982: *Protection of Women Under the Law*. Annotated Bibliography. Deep and Deep Publications, New Delhi.

Twenty One

Women Employed in Unorganized Sector

Women working in all the occupations having unorganized nature, come in this sector. The workers in this sector are outside the reach of most laws that seek to protect the security and working conditions of labour. Labour organizations are mostly absent, where they do exist, they are still in a formative stage and have had little impact on women (committee on status of women, 1974: 157).

According to an estimate by the National Commission on self-employed women (1988), 94 per cent of the women workers are engaged in the unorganized sectors of the economy, and among the women employed in unorganized sector, 80.1 per cent and 19.9 per cent are respectively employed in agricultural and non-agricultural occupations (Desai and Patel, 1990).

The women in the unorganized sector are employed in land-based occupations such as, agriculture and forestry, dairying and small animal husbandry, fisheries, sericulture, mining, tobacco and bidi industries; home-based occupations such as, handloom weaving and spinning, handicrafts garments, food processing, vending and hawking, construction, domestic work and contract work for the manufacturing industry.

Workforce participation of women is declining among certain occupations in the agrarian sector as a result of increasing pauperization leading to loss of land and insufficient growth of employment opportunities on family forms, technological displacement in agriculture, etc. There is a drastic increase in the percentage of landless women agricultural labourer from 1961 to 1991 (As per the 1991 census, 46.18 per cent of the total women workers are agricultural workers). Among the women employed in the non-agricultural sectors, there had been a serious decline in the workforce, during the seventies, in some sectors such as horticulture, livestock breeding, food-processing, dairy products (The Draft, Five Year Plan, 1978); but in the eighties this trend is reverted and we find a slight increase. In the household industry, women's employment opportunities have increased slightly (from 4.59 per cent to 4.63 per cent of the total main workers). Women were the greatest victims of the process of industrialization in the post-independence period because these household industries were the largest source of women's employment in agriculture. Many household industries like rice-pounding, tobacco, leather, hand weaving, oil-processing, etc, lost their economic viability because of factory production. In the latest census of 1991, we see women being economically active mainly in occupations such as weaving, handicraft, tailoring, forestry and sale of fish.

One of the major reasons for women's work becoming increasingly limited to the unorganized sector is that women lack the opportunity to acquire skills and training which could facilitate occupational shifts. This is related to the prevailing social relations between men and women as well as the structure of economy. Since women have to bear the major burden of domestic chores which in a poor household is time consuming and labour intensive, they do not have the time and opportunity to acquire skills and training for better jobs. Low skill attainment among women perpetuated by their unequal access to technology as a consequence relegates them to jobs which are labour intensive, time consuming and arduous.

In the unorganized sector since none of the protective labour laws such as, Maternity Benefit Act (1961), Employees State Insurance Act (1948), Factories Act (1948), Equal Remuneration Act (1976), the Shops and Establishment Act (1984), the Plantation Act (1951), the Mines Act (1951), the Child Labour (Prohibition and Regulation) Act (1976) are applicable; Women and girls are mercilessly exploited. Virtually the law of the jungle prevails. Women workers do not get equal remuneration for their back breaking work. The Minimum Wages Act is mercilessly flouted, there is no social security or worker's education programme. This section of the working class women are deprived of land and water resources, fuel, fodder, toilets, space, easy access to raw materials, market credit, licensing, identity cards, safe transport, housing, creche, ration cards, better tools, health and safety provisions. They have to work for very long hours and many times are sexually harassed by their employers and agents. There is a low productivity in this sector and there are few labour or trade union organizations to facilitate the mobilization of women workers and knit them into a conscious work-force, also due to the varied nature of occupations in this sector.

The National Commission on Self-employed Women and Women in the Informal Sector has generated exhaustive data and analysed it. While analysing the status of these groups of workers in the framework of existing macro policies and existing legislation, the National Commission has made various recommendations for their protection and empowerment (1988: 249-311). Although investment outlays in these sectors command high priority and several Government programmes exist to boost the productivity of these sectors, most endeavours are focused on men and male producer organizations. Women are viewed as indirect beneficiaries through the male members of their households and not as participants and target groups. Structural problems have risen in the rural unorganized sector as a result of the hierarchical pattern of land ownership, the nature of land relations and gender division of labour and the credit system. There is a strong class-caste relationship in the ownership of land which works to the disadvantage of the economically weaker sections and particularly against women. In urban areas, contract labourers, domestic workers and construction labourers are also exploited to a great extent, specifically.

The immediate task is that of ensuring them dignity and security at work, and regulating their work conditions through organizations and protective legislations. Simultaneously they must be provided with opportunities to seek alternative employment through skill training and education.

References

Census of India, 1991. Provisional Repot.

Desai, Neera, and Patel Vibhuti, 1990: *Critical Review of Researches in Women's Studies, 1975-88*. Research Centre for Women's Studies, S.N.D.T. Women's University.

India, 1992: A Reference Annual by Research and Reference Division. Ministry of Information and Broadcasting, Govt. of India.

Krishna Raj, Maithreyi, 1988: *Women and Development. The Indian Experience*, S.N.D.T. Women's University, Bombay.

National Perspective Plan for Women (1988-2000 A.D.). Govt. of India, New Delhi, 1978.

Shramshakti: National Commission for Self-employed women and women in the unorganized Sector, Govt. of India, New Delhi, 1987.

Towards Equality: Report of the Committee on the status of women in India. Govt. of India, 1974.

Twenty Two

Problematic Life of Urban Aged Women

The problem of old age needs due attention due to an alarming increase in the proportion of aged people in population to some extent and due to their declining roles and status in the changing Indian society (Desai and Naik, 1973: 23, D'souza, 1971 : 302). Due to advancement in medical science, the life expectancy has increased in India also, i.e., from 54 years in 1981 to 63.1 years in 1996 (Gokhale and Dave, 1996). The number of aged in population is estimated to be 75.6 million at the end of twentieth century as predicted by Bose (1995 : 25-31). According to 1991 Census, females are more than the males in older group (Rajan, 1999). In addition to increasing number of aged, the most important factor is that, due to changing social structure and cultural system, as the inevitable consequence of industrialization, urbanization and modernization in Indian society, the life of aged people is becoming more problematic, specially in urban areas. In the pre-industrial agrarian set-up, most of the aged people used to remain financially independent till they lived and even females used to perform an important role in the economic activity. Moreover, the traditional cultural and social values enabled the aged people to enjoy leadership roles and powerful positions of decision makers and advisors in joint family, Caste group and village community (Nayar, 1987; Kumar 1995; Singh, 1997). Since the wife derives her status through the status of her husband in the Indian society, the aged women also used to enjoy higher status in joint family and kinship groups, especially among the women folks. Grown-up sons were not permitted to leave their old parents alone. The mother used to have a place like Goddess and the sons used to respectfully serve her till the end of life. Now in the new industrial social order, the institutions of joint family and caste are weakening and in the community, achievements like education and wealth have become more important than the ascribed ones like age and experience (Bhatia, 1964; Singh, 1969). Practice of compulsory retirement from service has affected the males and females both. Apart from this, migration of sons outside the home-town for educational and occupation purposes, has left the aged parents alone to struggle with problems. Due to the individualistic and materialistic values, the sons want to enjoy freedom and raise their standard of living, and hence want to get rid of the care of aged parents. Consequently, while living together, the conflicts take place between two generation members of family or they get separated (Mishra, 1989; Joseph, 1988). As stated by Chadha *et.al.* (1997), Gursharan Kour (1964); Indra (1963); Sen (1996); Jamuna (1995); Prakash (1993 and 1996); Naik (1997); the situation of aged women become further deteriorated specially after widowhood, if they are resourceless. Although the legal provisions are there, but in practice they are not given any share either from their fathers' or husbands' property. In the situation, they get the 'extra-familial' status and remain no longer in position of getting respect and proper care by their sons and no longer exercise authority on their daughter-in-laws. On the other hand they are treated like maid servants and their satisfaction of even basic needs depends on their utility of carrying out the household jobs especially in the deprived class of society.

Need of the Study

Very few studies have been conducted so far on the aged women. As stated by Sharma (1999) also, most of the studies done in this field, have concentrated on the problems of rural aged women, and have not given attention to urban aged women's problems; hence it is needed. Seriousness of the problem of old age may vary from community to community depending upon the degree of their modernization and the problems of aged may also differ in different sections of community. The present study focuses on finding out the problems of all the classes of aged women living in Jabalpur city of Madhya Pradesh, which are in transitional stage tilting more on traditional side than the modern side, at present, regarding the social change. The main objective of the study is to find out that how the problem of old age is emerging gradually in Indian society. A total of 350 women above the age of 60 years have been randomly selected out of which 318 could be interviewed.

Characteristics of Aged Women

The data demonstrates that 96.25 per cent of aged women belong to Hindu religion and out of it, almost same proportion, that is one-third of Hindus, belong to general, backward and Scheduled Castes sections. Most of them are living in families having son and daughter-in-law and 61 per cent of them have 6 to 10 members in their household. A total of 72 per cent respondents are in the age group of 'young olds' having the age between 60 to 70 years and 23 per cent are in the age group of 71 to 80 years. While 57 per cent of them are married, 43 per cent are experiencing the widowhood, 76 per cent of them are illiterate, 67 per cent of aged women have led the life of housewife only 27.98 per cent were doing some manual work to earn their livelihood in past. At present 83.36 per cent of them are not engaged in any occupation while 14.15 per cent are still forced by the circumstances to do manual work for their survival, which is worth noting 66 per cent have no income of their own while 28.61 per cent have some source of income upto Rs.1000 which makes them independent. Regarding the health condition, one-fifth of them have general weakness and the same proportion have asthama. Eye trouble and pain in joints are quite common among the aged females. By considering the transitional but more in the traditional side culture of Jabalpur city, these characteristics seem quite obvious but it can certainly said that the problem of old age has started emerging in Indian society also due to which the life of aged people is becoming problematic.

Problems of Old Age

The problems of old age have been divided into four parts, i.e., financial, physical, social and psychological. The problems get generated when the obstructions are experienced by the people in the way of satisfaction of need, connected with various aspects of life. Financial problems can be described in terms of income less than requirement and lack of financial support from family members, while physical problems can be seen in terms of suffering from physical ailments and lack of physical as well as treatment support from family members. The social problem is connected with less opportunities of interaction and interrelationships with others, specially the near and dear ones, while psychological problems are related with lack of occasions for fulfilment of needs of one's respect, love and affection, significance, usefulness, belongingness, continuity, etc.

Self-perception of the Main Problem and Social Status of Aged Women

Consideration of self-perception in this regard was thought to be proper because when a continued experience is conceived by the individual as posing a serious obstacle in leading satisfactory life then only it becomes a problem for him. As a matter of fact most of the aged experience all the four types of problems to some extent atleast but the most prominent problem concerns him/her more and hence has an effect on the level of his morale. It is quite possible that different class of people may have different prominent problems. In regard to aged women, their educational level was thought to be significant for indicating their class in society. Table 22.1 shows distribution of our respondents according to these variables.

Table 22.1 demonstrates that 75.78 per cent of aged women are illiterate and according to our conviction, belong to lower class. Out of these illiterates, 70.54 per cent have reported that economic problem, i.e., lack of money is the most prominent problem for them. It means that their financial needs are being neglected by family members. As far as the middle-class having middle category of education is concerned, a considerable number, i.e., 40.54 per cent are experiencing psychological problem that is, alienation. It means that they are being ignored by the family members. A little less proportion that is, 33.77 per cent, are facing the economic problem too. Although the number of highly educated aged females is very less but all of them are facing the psychological problems. If we look at the table from another angle, we find that out of those who reported psychological problems as the prominent one, 90.91 per cent belong to the middle class whereas remaining

9.09 per cent are from the higher class. And out of those who reported the financial problem as the prominent one, 87.18 per cent are from the lower class while remaining 12.82 per cent are from the middle class. In general, we can say that although all the women are facing all types of problems, most of them are suffering from financial problems while a considerable proportion of them are suffering from psychological problems.

TABLE 22.1
PROMINENT PROBLEM/SOCIAL STATUS (EDUCATIONAL)

Prominent Problems/ Social Status	*Any Other*	*Psychological (Alienation)*	*Social (Loneliness)*	*Physical (Diseases)*	*Economic (Lack of money)*	*Total*
Illiterate	50	x	10	11	170	241
	(20.75)		(4.15)	(4.56)	(70.54)	(100.00)
(Low class)	(81.97)		(71.43)	(73.33)	(87.18)	(75.78)
Matriculation	11	30	4	4	25	74
	(14.86)	(40.54)	(5.40)	(5.40)	(33.77)	(100.00)
(Middle class)	(18.03)	(90.91)	(28.57)	(26.67)	(12.82)	(23.27)
Graduate and Postgraduate	X	3	X	X	X	3
		(100.00)				100.00
High class		(9.09)				(0.95)
Total	61	33	14	15	195	318
	(19.18)	(10.38)	(4.40)	(4.72)	(61.32)	(100.00)
	(100.00)	(100.00)	(100.00)	(100.00)	(100.00)	(100.00)

Figures in parenthesis are percentages.

When we concentrate on the characteristics of our respondents, these findings seem quite obvious and expected ones. By being mostly in the age group of 60 to 70 years and due to continuous hard work and special resistance power given to females by nature, they do not have serious physical ailments. Since most of them are living in large size families with their son, daughter-in-law and grand children, they get opportunity of social interaction and social relationship, so they do not feel lonely. For poor and illiterate people where basic need of food, essential for their survival itself, is not being fulfilled properly, psychological needs of higher family status or respect do not matter much, while the educated aged women who are economically comfortable, think about those aspects of life. The point worth noting here is that, not even a single woman reported her life, free from all the problems, i.e., the happy one completely.

On the whole we can conclude that financial problem has emerged as the major problem among the aged females living in Jabalpur City. By considering the traditional nature of city which has been called 'Sanskardhani' by Shri Vinoba Bhave, these findings are quite understandable. But at the same time we can say that the individualistic and materialistic attitudes of the youngsters might have added the seriousness to the financial problem of our respondents.

Problematic Life

When we looked at the causes and nature of problem objectively, it was found that, although an overwhelming majority of aged women are living with married children, in 75.47 per cent families, the degree of family organization is not very satisfactory and in the case of 6.29 per cent, it is in worse condition. In the case of married women, their husbands and in the case of widows, their sons are the head of family, in most of cases. Regarding decision making, in the case of married women, most of them are consulted by their husbands while in the case of widows, they are not consulted by their sons. While in the majority of cases old women's guidance is seeked by younger generation, but in the case of more than one-fourth respondents, it is not so, which is worth noting. Sometimes for formality only, the advice is taken but it is neither accepted nor practiced in action. 77.04 per cent of aged women think that sufficient income of aged is the criteria for getting respect in the family. Majority, i.e., 57.77 per cent and considerable proportion, i.e., 33.96 per cent women rarely and only sometimes get opportunity to go out along with grown-up children for entertainment respectively. In the case of an overwhelming majority, that is, 78.93 per cent, conflicts do take place in their households quite sometimes and majority, i.e., 61.24 per cent of them have conflicts due to financial reasons. Difference of opinion in the case of quite considerable number, i.e., 34.90 per cent of aged women, is also quite significant. 93.72 per cent aged women have reported that they have interaction with family members only during one-fourth of a day. And 55.98 per cent of respondents have average relationship with family members, neither good nor bad. The point worth noting is that only 1.57 per cent have reported about very good relationship with their sons. In the case of 157 respondents, the sons are living out of city and they are visiting them once in a year atleast, but in the case of 50.95 per cent old women, the relationship with sons living away, is just average. There are 23.56 and 7.66 per cent of them who have rated their relationship as bad and very bad respectively, which is worth noting. In the case of 71.69 per cent women, the youngers give only partial respect to aged. While 53.15 per cent of women reported that youngers do not feel responsibility of looking after the aged at all, 44.02 per cent said that they feel it only partially. Although most of them are enjoying good health, 52.83 per cent women have reported that their son and daughter-in-law take care of them during sickness, which indicates the fact probably that even if the youngsters do not want, they have to take care of parents due to pressure of traditional values regarding the duties of sons towards their parents. A great majority, i.e., 66.03 per cent of old women do not have their own income while 28.61 per cent have income less than required for essential expenditure. While 68.23 per cent are dependent on their husbands, 26.41 per cent are taking help from their sons exclusively. Cross tabulation of age group and prominent problem shows that, 78.60 per cent of women aged between 60 to 70 years, have mentioned financial problem as the prominent one, while a considerable number, i.e., 41.13 per cent of women aged between 70 to 80 years have mentioned death of any near and dear one, in which husbands death is quite common, under the category of any other problem. And of those aged above 80 years, 81.25 per cent have reported psychological problem as the prominent one.

Prominent Problem and Life Satisfaction

Table 22.2 demonstrates that, 50.60 per cent, 21.38 per cent and 28.02 per cent of aged women are having respectively low, medium and high level of life satisfaction. It also shows that 62.05

per cent of those having financial problem as the prominent one, have low level of life satisfaction. In the case of physical and social problems both, 100 per cent of them are having low and medium level of life satisfaction respectively. In the case of psychological problem, comparatively larger group of 39.39 per cent is having low level of satisfaction and in the case of any other problem in which the death of husband comes mainly, 50.81 per cent have low level of life satisfaction. In conclusion we can say that all the problems contribute to lower level of life satisfaction but financial problem has more impact in this regard because their various needs remain unfulfilled which pinches them and they feel that life is not worth living now.

TABLE 22.2
PROMINENT PROBLEM/LIFE SATISFACTION

Prominent Problems/ Life Satisfaction	*Any Other*	*Psychological*	*Social*	*Physical*	*Economics*	*Total*
High	14 (20.01) (22.97)	11 (15.71) (33.34)	X	X	45 (62.28) (23.08)	70 (100.00) (28.02)
Medium	16 (23.55) (26.22)	9 (13.23) (27.27)	14 (20.58) (100.00)	X	29 (42.64) (14.87)	68 (100.00) (21.38)
Low	31 (17.23) (50.81)	13 (7.22) (39.39)	X	15 (8.33) (100.00)	121 (67.22) (62.05)	180 (100.00) (50.60)
Total	61 (19.18) (100.00)	33 (10.37) (100.00)	14 (4.40) (100.00)	15 (4.73) (100.00)	195 (61.32) (100.00)	318 (100.00) (100.00)

Figures in parenthesis are percentages

Prominent Problem and Prominent Solution

After having knowledge about problems and consequently the level of life satisfaction of the aged women, it was thought proper to know whether they want help from others or they believe in self-help in order to solve the problems. For this, they were asked to give one option out of five categories as self-help, help of sons, help of society, help of society and family both, and any other. Then this variable was cross tabulated with prominent problem. Distribution of respondents according to these variables has been given in Table 22.3.

TABLE 22.3
PROMINENT PROBLEM/PROMINENT SOLUTION

	Any Other	*Psychological*	*Social*	*Physical*	*Economic*	*Total*
Any other (Govt.)	40 (14.83) (65.58)	20 (7.40) (60.61)	X	15 (5.55) (100.00)	195 (72.22) (100.00)	270 (100.00) (84.93)
Help of Society and Family Both	11 (36.68) (18.03)	5 (16.66) (15.15)	14 (46.66) (100.00)	X	X	30 (100.00) (9.43)
Help of Society	X	4 (100.00) (12.12)	X	X	X	4 (100.00) (1.25)
Help of sons	X	4 (100.00) (12.12)	X	X	X	4 (100.00) (1.25)
Self Help	10 (100.00) (16.39)	X	X	X	X	10 (100.00) (3.14)
Total	61 (19.2) (100.00)	33 (10.37) (100.00)	14 (4.40) (100.00)	15 (4.71) (100.00)	195 (61.32) (100.00)	318 (100.00) (100.00)

Figures in parenthesis are percentages.

Table 22.3 shows that, regarding the solution of problems, an overwhelming majority of aged women, i.e., 84.93 per cent want Government's help under the category of any other help, while 9.43 per cent of them mentioned that both society and family should be active to solve their problems. The point worth noting here is that, only 1.25 per cent and 3.14 per cent want help of sons and believe in self help respectively. These facts show that state of their helplessness as well as lack of expectations from family.

Cross tabulation of prominent solution with prominent problem show that, 100 per cent of those who have either physical or financial problem as the prominent one have mentioned that government should solve their problem. This response of mostly uneducated or very little educated aged women seems to be quite expected one. In the case of other problems they want society, sons, other family members and themselves to join hands for their solution.

Social Integration/Social Segregation and its Reasons

At this point it was thought proper to have knowledge whether the aged women prefer to remain socially integrated by living in the families and communities having all age group members or segregated from rest of society by living with or without their husbands in old age colonies or old age homes. For the purpose they were asked to give one option and the main reason behind it. Distribution of respondents according to these variables has been given in Table 22.4.

TABLE 22.4

SOCIAL INTEGRATION OR SOCIAL SEGREGATION/REASONS

Social Segregation Social Integration	*Want to Live in Peer Group*	*Do not want to be Burden on other*	*Unable to Manage Own Affairs*	*Family is not willing to help*	*No one is there to help*	*NA*	*Total*
Want to live among all age groups	—	—	—	—	—	—	—
Enjoyment of independent life	—	—	—	—	—	—	—
Enjoyment of family relationship's warmth	—	—	—	—	—	—	217
Enjoyment of living in place	—	—	—	—	—	—	—
Enjoyment of living among known people	—	—	—	—	—	—	84
NA	—	—	—	—	—	—	17
Total	—	—	17	—	—	301	31

Table 22.4 demonstrates that an overwhelming majority, i.e., 94.54 per cent of old women want to remain fully integrated in the network of social relationships. Among the reasons behind it, 68.23 per cent said that they want to enjoy the warmth of family relationship. Only 5.35 per cent old women want to lead a segregated life due to the reason that family members are not willing to take care of them which is quite visible by their being abused, neglected and maltreated by family members. In the city like Jabalpur this finding seems quite obvious, as traditional values are still existing here. But the point worth noting here is that even in such cities the problem of old age has started emerging. Widow dependent aged women especially of deprived class are treated so badly in families of sons that they are forced to opt for institutionalization.

Social Expectations for the Solution of Problems

In the end, the respondents were asked to express their opinions about various measures which can be taken up by society / government for solution of problems regarding various aspects of life of aged people in general. These were food, entertainment, economic, residential, health and service aspects. The data regarding their attitudes towards various measures has demonstrated that due to the difficulty in food preparation aged, 94.96 per cent and 92.18 per cent of our respondents have expressed positive attitudes towards mobile food distribution system and availability of cheap and nutritious restaurants respectively. Regarding the entertainment aspect, 59.44 per cent of aged women were in favour of day care centres while more or less proportion, i.e., 58.80 per cent were not in favour of evening club. Regarding the most important financial aspect, 74.52, 61.00, 91.19 and 73.58 per cent of aged women have positive attitudes towards measures of increase in pensionable age, opportunities for part time employment, more service pension and more old age pension respectively. By considering the fact that an overwhelming majority of aged people suffer from financial problems prominently, this finding seems to be quite expected one. Regarding the residential aspect, while 72.32 per cent expressed positive attitudes towards various facilities for owning a house, 89.01 per cent and 83.66 per cent reported negative attitudes regarding house rent and old age colonies respectively, but 81.13 per cent showed interest in old age homes for helpless aged people.

About health aspect, almost all the respondents showed positive attitudes regarding special hospital for aged, free medical aid, nursing service and free health checkups at home; and mobile medical clinic. Regarding the service aspect majority and considerable number of aged women, i.e., 63.52 and 48.08 per cent have an undecided mind on the issue of service boys for outdoor jobs and home attendants respectively; while in the case of fair price shops and home delivery of required things, 96.22 per cent and 91.22 per cent have expressed their positive attitudes. 50.31 per cent and 53 per cent of them have positive attitudes towards foster care service and old age homes or infirmaries for deserving cases respectively, whereas 50.32 per cent and 68.68 per cent do not feel the requirement of any consultancy and emergency services respectively, and 74.85 per cent do not want service of legal representative. Here while talking about majority's opinion, we should also think in terms of necessity felt by some aged due to their helplessness.

On the whole, the picture which emerges is that, at present in the cities like Jabalpur, the services like western countries are not very much required or expected rather, but basically financial and health conditions of aged should be taken care off properly so that they do not suffer much due to their dependence on others. But at the same time it is important to note that, trend of increasing problems including the social and psychological ones is quite visible in cities like Jabalpur even therefore other domiciliary supportive services will also be required in the near future.

On the basis of these findings we can assume that in the metropolitan cities of India, the problems of aged will be much more in number and complicated in nature and hence all the measures mentioned above are required to be taken up by governmental as well as voluntary organizations.

In conclusion we can say that the life of aged women has started becoming quite problematic which has the effect on their level of life satisfaction. Since quite a few of them are frustrated, unable to solve their problems either themselves or with family support, but want to remain knitted in the network of social relationships; they look towards Government or Society for the help.

References

Ara, Shabeen, 1995: Old Age Homes : The Last Resort: *Research and Development Journal of Helpage India*, Vol. 2 No. 1, 1995: 3-10.

Bali, Arun, 1995: 'Role of the family in Elderly Care': *Research and Development Journal of Helpage India*, Vol. 2, No. 4: 30-40.

Baliga, Sandhya, 1996: 'Social Security for the Aged'. *Research and Development Journal of Helpage India*, Vol. 2, No. 2: 3-8.

Bambawale, Usha, 1996: 'Abuse of the Aged', *Ageing: Indian Perspective and Global Scenario* (Ed.) Vinod Kumar, IIMS, New Delhi.

Bhatia, H.S., 1964: 'Rural Social Change and the Problem of Aged' *Social Welfare*, XI (July) : 5-6

Bose, Ashish, 1995: 'Care of the Elderly in the unorganized Sector' *Research and Development Journal of Helpage India*, Vol. 1, 16 No. 3: 25-31.

Chadha, N.K.; Agarwal, Vandana; Mangla, A.P. 1992: 'Hopelessness Alienation, and Life Satisfaction Among Aged', *Indian Journal of Gerontology*, Vol. 16 Nos 3 & 4: 82-92.

Desai, K.G. and Naik, R.D. 1973: *Problems of Retired people in Greater Bombay*, Tata Institute of Social Sciences, Bombay, Series No. 27.

D'souza, Victor S., 1971: 'Changes in the Social structure and Changing Roles of Older People in India', *Sociology and Social Research 55*, (April): 297-304.

Edwards, Allen L., 1969: *Techniques of Attitude scale Construction*, Bombay, Vakils Ferrer and Simmens.

Gokhale, S.D. and Dave, Chandra, 1996: ' Services for the Elderly' *Paper presented in Global Conference on Aging*, in Bombay and Pune on 30th August.

Gursharan Kour, 1964: *The Problems of Aged Women in Batala*. Unpublished Masters Thesis, Punjab University, Chandigarh.

Havighurst, Robert, J., 1963: 'Successful Aging' 299-320 in *Process of Aging*, Vol. I, edited by Richard H. Williams, Clark Tibbitts and Wilma Donahue. Chicago. Atherton Press.

Indra, Rajinder, 1963: *Problems of Old Women in a Village* unpublished Master's Thesis, Punjab University, Chandigarh.

Jamuna, D., 1995: Aging Women in India *Research and Development Journal of Helpage India*, Vol. 1, No. 3: 3-14.

Joseph; Joni C., 1988: 'Interaction between the old and the Young' *Social Welfare*, Vol. XXXV, No. 6, Sep. 88: 17-19.

Jai Praksh, Indir, 1997. 'Hindu World View and well Being of Aging Women'. *R. and D. Journal of Helpage India*, Vol. 3, No. 2: 43-49.

Kumar, Vinod, 1997: 'Productive Aging for the Young Old' *R & D Journal of Helpage India* Vol. 9, No. 1 Oct. 1997.

Mishra, Saraswati, 1989: *Problems and Social Adjustment in Old Age*, Gyan Publishing House, Delhi.

Nayar, P.K.B., 1987: Aging and Society, *Social Welfare*, Vol. XXXIV, No. 3: pp.28-31.

Naik, S.V., 1997: 'Income Security for Elderly in Developing Countries *R&D.J. of Helpage India*, Vol. 4, No. 1 Oct. 97.

Prakash, I.J., 1993: 'Gender Aging : Psychological Issues' *Indian Journal of Gerontology*, 7 (1 & 2), 24-29.

Prakash, I.J., 1996, Coping with Aging: Psychological Social Situation of older Indian Women in Aging: *Indian Perspective and Global Scenario* (Ed.) Vinod Kumar, AIIMS, New Delhi.

Rajan, S. Irudaya, 1999: *India's Elderly: Burden or Challenge*. Sage Publications, New Delhi.

Sen, Tulika, 1996: 'A Health and Socio-Economic Profile of the Aged Bengali Women in Aging: *Indian Perspective and Global Scenario* (Ed.) Vinod Kumar, AIIMS, New Delhi.

Sharma, K.L., 1971: 'A Survey of the Happiness and Unhappiness in Old Age' *Indian Journal of Gerontology* 3 (3&4): 76-77.

Sharma, K.L., 1969: 'Leisure Time Activities of Retired Persons' *Indian Journal of Gerontology*, 1(1), 1969.

Sharma, K.L., 1999: 'Elderly Women of Kachhi Basti, *Indian Journal of Gerontology*, Vol. 13, Nos. 1 & 2.

Singh, R.R., 1969: 'The Changing Social Structure and the Aged' *Indian Journal of Gerontology* (October): 118-124.

Singh, Yogendra 1997: 'Changing Trends in the Indian family and the Adjustment of the Aged' *R & D Journal of Helpage India*, Vol. 1, No. 1, Oct. 94: pp. 23-30.

Twenty Three

Eradication of Patriarchy; the Root Cause of Lower Status of Women: A Discussion

'Patriarch' is the person who governs his family by paternal right and 'patriarchy' is a community of related families under the authority of a patriarch under the patriarchal system. The word 'Patrilineal' refers to the male line of descent, and the family reckoned through the father or through males alone, is called the patrilineal family (Dictionaries *Readers Digest's* and *Chamber's*). In patriarchal or patrilineal joint family in India, members of many generations live together, the authority remains in the hands of the eldest male member the sons get the name of lineage of their father permanently whereas daughters join the families of their husbands after marriage and all the property is inherited by sons after the death of father (Mukherjee, 1983: 276-277). Vedic literature shows that in early Aryan Society also patriarchal family system was existing (Stowell, 1970: 256-276).'Varma' system and later on the caste system, which provides identity to a person further encouraged and helped in the maintenance of patrilineal family system in almost all the regions of India (only in very few south-west and north-east regions matrilineal family system is found). As Desai and Patel (1985) have stated that patrilineal and classified Indian society has posed a big challenge for the life of women. Due to this system, after father's death, since the son carries his name forward and helps parents in achieving salvation by performing last rites, the importance of the male children increases automatically, which results in the discrimination and further in the exploitation of women by men. The irony is that traditionally it has been religiously approved. Since thousands of years women have been tolerating it quietly.

Right from her birth, rather from the womb of mother, the girls are considered inferior species and treated differently by the family members in the average Indian society having more traditional symptoms than modern symptoms.

Various census reports show that their sex ratio per 1000 males has decreased from 972 in 1901 to 929 in 1991 as Mourya (1985) and Mitra (1974) have also reported. Due to the facility of sonographic examination of the sex of foetus before birth, termination of the female foetus through abortion is rampant nowadays. This examination being cheap as compared to the costs of rearing a girl, even poor people are taking its advantage. Educated people believing in small family norms allow birth of only one son in spite of their good economic condition (Desai and Patel, 1985). The cases of girl infanticide have been taking place in Indian backward interior areas since time immemorial. Otherwise also, after one month of birth of child, social factors start operating. The culture characterized by the male dominance and priority, forces to neglect the female infants and due to discrimination regarding the care, cleanliness, nutrition, medicine, etc, girls start dying more than the boys. Those who survive, further become the victims of discrimination and exploitation. Daughters are considered like other person's wealth, deposited in trust under the custody of parents, who are taken care of by the parents temporarily till their marriages. Therefore, they want to get rid of their liability as soon as possible. Then, girls are to be trained, as Jain (1988) had also stated, before their marriages for their future role of housewife, for which formal education is not required. They are not allowed to go out and move around freely or to do the outside jobs. Spending much money on health-care and education of girls is thought as waste of money especially keeping in view the fact that they are not supposed to earn money, keeping in mind the expenditure of their marriages including dowry. She is of no use to parents even in old age because she herself is totally dependent on others and cannot act independently. So getting them married as early as possible before puberty was religiously approved and it was considered proper from the view of her accommodation in husband's family also. The sons are trained in outside jobs, given education, allowed to choose some occupation and given full freedom to move around.

According to the patrilineal family system, all the offsprings get their identity in the society through their father's name and his sub-caste based surname, for the whole life in the case of sons and till marriage in the case of daughters. The mother who suffers a lot in bearing and rearing them, does not come in the picture at all (although in our mythological stories we find identity of the son known through mother). In the case of daughters, at the time of her marriage when she is donated to her husband by the parents, through the ritual called *Kanyadan*, along with dowry, her identity gets changed. In place of daughter of some one, she becomes the wife of some one. The surname of her father is removed and the surname of her husband is put along with her name. According to patrilocal family system the girl has to leave her parents family's residence and live in her husband's family residence. After coming to in-law's place, even her name is changed for practical purposes. This traditional system is followed even now in the middle class and lower class in urban and in all classes in rural areas. It indicates towards the hidden fact that she is made a new person by practically finishing her parental identity completely. In this way she leaves the membership of her father's family and takes the membership of her husband's family through her marriage. Even during widowhood her identity as widow of so and so is mentioned. In the case of divorce, she again gets back the pre-marital identity based on her father's name and surname. Suppose owing to modern attitudes if divorced or widowed women marries again her identity gets changed again and she will be known as the wife of the new husband and her surname will again change. This process may repeat many times in the case of most modern women. What does it mean? It means that the women have no independent status in society, as Chatterjee (1988) has also stated, they derive social status through male's status. It also means that they do not have any single identity of their own which can be maintained throughout their life. They are either the daughter of their fathers or wives of their husbands. It is introductory to their lower status in itself. It is not so in the case of men. Although the sons get their identity through their fathers, but it is maintained throughout the life and their marriages do not affect it.

Only sons carry forward the lineage through reproduction of their own sons and therefore for the peace of souls of ancestors only son's are given the rights of performing last rites of parents and *Shradhha* worships for ancestors, so that they can achieve heaven after death and the state of salvation later on. Therefore, having sons has been considered very important in Indian Society and for the purpose, any number of marriages were socially permitted and religiously approved. Due to this reason only, according to 'Mitakshara' system of inheritance of property as Choudhary (1961) has also expressed, while sons become the share holder or partner in ancestor's property at the time of their birth itself, the girls do not have right on it. According to Mitakshara system of inheritance which prevails in almost all regions of India, (only in a few south-west and north-east regions of India Dayabhaga system of inheritance is existing). Sons inherit even the position and titles of forefathers.

As National Committee on Status of Women (1974) has reported, even during the enactment of Hindu Succession Act, 1956 which provides equal share of the father's self earned property to daughters, 'Mitakshra'system of inheritance could not be abolished due to resistance shown by the conservative, Hindu society. Apart from this in spite of legal provisioning, daughters are not given any share out of their father's property if sons are there, but for exceptions. Girls also do not ask for it, leaving apart the judicial procedure through court because in doing so they will spoil the relationship with their parents family (Mishra, 1986). Just because the girls do not get any share in father's property, the dowry much more than the parents capacity to give it, is expected from the bridegrooms side at the time of marriage, as Sriniwas (1983) has also expressed. Since they do not earn themselves, all their expenses are to be met by the husbands from time to time, cash and gifts are also expected from her parents' side to her in-laws side. As Mishra (1983) has stated Dowry Prohibition Act, 1961 has made no difference. The daughter-in-laws who do not bring sufficient dowry with them and do not get much cash or gifts in between from their parents, are maltreated by the in-laws family members and sometimes even get beaten up by their husbands (wife's beating is a very common phenomenon in Indian society).They are maltreated upto the extent that after finishing the tolerance power they commit suicide. Sometimes very greedy in-laws and even husband chalkout and exercise the plan of killing the daughter-in-law successfully. As Mehta (1987) has noted, Indian women's socio-legal status is unsatisfactory. The cases of dowry deaths are increasing day by day since last few decades. As Desai and Krishna Raj (1987) have put it women are lagging far behind them men in the case of education and occupation both.

Due to patrilineal family system only the wives of sons in the family, since they have come from outside, are not readily accepted as family members in real sense by the in-laws, and every now and then, for their actions they have to listen to comments even by husband, linking them with their parents family. This is the irony of fate for women that she does not belong to any family in real sense after her marriage. Her status becomes like the cursed sage 'Trishanku' who was hanged in between the heaven and earth. This state of women is very frustrating and humiliating, but owing to her helplessness she cannot react and protest against it. In the joint family young daughter-in-law has to work like a servant round the clock and she gets very little time for rest and entertainment. The status of woman in the family as well as in the society gets enhanced along with the births of her sons. The woman having only daughters enjoys lower status and the childless woman has the lowest status. Thus, reproduction is considered to be her main function and her life gains significance on the basis of its success, in terms of providing heirs to take the lineage forward. For the sake of having children and even for sons, the husband may marry again. Although there may be some fault in the husband himself but only the wife is considered responsible for childlessness. The presence of a barren women is not desirable during the auspicious occasions. If the young women become widow unfortunately, she is blamed for the death of her husband directly or indirectly and her life becomes hell. In spite of Sati Abolition Act, 1829, earlier they were forced to become sati and burn themselves on the pyre of their husbands, and if they survived or could escape that, they had to serve like maid servants and lead a life like renunciators, by looking unattractive and by involving themselves more religious activities. Even now she cannot marry or even keep friendly relationship with other men. She has to observe 'Pativrata Dharma,' and maintain sanctity towards her late husband throughout her life. Even now sometimes we hear about some women becoming Sati, although it is rare. Confrontation or presence of widow in auspicious occasion is considered as a bad omen. But in the case of widow remarriage even after 150 years of enactment of law, i.e., Widow Remarriage Act, 1856, the improvement in this direction we find is negligible. They are only exceptions and mostly love marriages. Even the widowers and divorced persons are not prepared to marry a widow and prefer young unmarried girls. Due to bindings of traditions widows first of all do not think of remarriage and due to the fear of criticism also they do not come forward for this purpose and remain closed in their shells.

Sinha (1984) has expressed women's rights have not benefited them much. They sacrifice their life for their children who do not take care of them in later years of their life. The mother of young unmarried children gets their love and respect considerably, this is the only period of little satisfaction in her life as Venkatarayyappa (1966) has also mentioned. After the marriages of sons for few years she could exercise some authority only on her daughter-in-law but later on she has to mellow down and accept the subordination under the sons authority especially if she is widow. Earlier women never used to get any share out of husbands property but later on due to legal provisions, i.e., wife's share in husband's property Act, 1937 and Hindu Succession Act, 1956, they get equal share in it along with other heirs. But since she cannot live alone, it is snatched away by the sons. As far as her share in son's property is concerned, it is never given to mother. Thus, being economically, physically and psychologically dependent on the males throughout their life, the women remain victims of discrimination, and exploitation by males continuously till their death.

From the 19th century during the British regime efforts were made to bring about social changes through social reform movement and social legislation and later on after independence a scheme of planned social change was materialized as Subbamma (1966) and Kuppuswamy (1990) have also noted.

In place of traditional values based on inequality, the modern values based on eqalitarian ideals are being established in the society. As Kumar (1982) has also stated, Indian constitution guarantees equality to all the citizens in all respects. But in spite of social legislation and extension of education, no basic change has occurred in the caste system, although in urban areas superficial changes in the surface of the system are clearly visible. Even now negligible number of intercaste arranged marriages are performed in urban areas leaving aside the overwhelming majority of Indian population belonging to rural areas. On the contrary, casteism is emerging with a great speed in India.

As far as the patrilineal family system is concerned, it has never been touched by any authority seriously. Although the joint family system is breaking up due to impact of modernization including development of society, but the patriarchal system is still functioning traditionally.* And in spite of education and financial independence of increasing number of women in modern time they have not been able to acquire a status equal to men as it was expected earlier as expressed by Chanana (1988) also. In this way we find that the patriarchal system, which increases the importance of sons in family in particular and of males in society in general, is the root cause of lower status, of women in Indian society. This social discrimination between the two sexes is very painful on the part of women and cannot be tolerated any more. By now it has been realised that peripheral and superficial measures cannot help much in raising the women's status until and unless the fundamental changes take place. Therefore, abolition of patrilineal family system is necessary if women's status is to be really raised and brought at equal level of men's status. For this purpose revolutionary steps are required to be taken up, for which people will have to change their attitudes, specifically men will have to cooperate with women to bring about this change. It is only possible when they become prepared to give equal status to women by forgetting their male ego. It will be a big campaign which will take a very long time, and its success is also not certain,

* Although patriarchal system is prevalent in other societies also but it is not causing so much differentiation between two sexes as in India.

but it is better to do something than doing nothing in that direction. There will surely be some role models who will have to take intiative and when other people will see its utility they will follow it in increasing numbers automatically. As Sharma, Hussain and Saharya (1984) have rightly said, man-women equality is an ideal which cannot be achieved until and unless the attitudes of people get changed. Considering the severe requirement, an action plan for eradication of patriarchal family system and thereby enhancement of woman's status is being suggested. Following the small family norm may be quite helpful in providing equal treatment to son and daughter both.

But for achieving total equality target, caste system will have to be abandoned completely through enactment and enforcement of law but its consequences will not be seen till people do not leave it willingly. Therefore, before making the legal provision against it, creating awareness in people is essential to prepare public opinion regarding it. The awareness can be brought by making continuous efforts through the mediums of mass communication along with education. In Indian society there is a system of writing caste based surname after the name of a person. In the case of son this surname continues for whole life but as it has been discussed earlier, it gets changed at the time of marriage in the case of a girl. Apart from this anywhere, for his identity son gives the name of his father, whereas the daughter uses the name of her father and husband before and after her marriage respectively. The mother who has given birth does not come in picture at all.

Once the patrilineal system is eradicated from the society and the caste system also gets disappeared from the scene, the boys and girls will have equal significance in the family and society both. They will be given equal opportunities for everything possible and equal roles will bring equal status for them.

References

Chatterji, Shoma, A., 1968: *The Indian Women's Search for an Identity*, Vikas Publishing House Pvt. Ltd. New Delhi. Census of India, 1991, Provisional Population Totals.

Chanana, Karuna (ed.), 1988: *Socialization, Education and Women: Exploration* in *Gender Identity*. Orient Longman Ltd., Hyderabad.

Choudhary, Roop, L., 1961: Hindu Women's Right to Property. Firma K.C. Mukhopadhyaya, Calcutta. Dictionaries : Readers Digest's and Chamber's Dictionaries for meaning of Patriarchy.

Desai, Neera and Patel, Vibhuti, 1985: *Indian Women - Change and Challenge in the International Women Decade; 1975-85*, Popular Prakashan, Bombay.

Desai, Neera and Krishna Raj, Maithreyi, 1987: *Women and Society in India*. Ajanta Publications, New Delhi.

Jain, Shastri, 1988: *Status and Role Perception of Middle Class Women*. Puja Publishers, New Delhi.

Kuppuswamy, B., 1990: *Social Change in India*. Konark Publishers Pvt. Ltd., Delhi.

Kumar, Manju 1982: *Social Equality : The Constitutional Experiment in India*, S. Chand and Co. Ltd., New Delhi.

Kapoor, Promila, 1970: *Marriage and the Working Women in India*, Vikas Publications, Delhi.

Mishra, Saraswati, 1986: Hindu Succession Act, 1956, Protection and Practice, Social Welfare, September 1986.

Mishra, Saraswati, 1993: Legal Justice to women: *Sociological Evaluation Social Welfare*, Vol. 11-12, Feb-Mar. 11-12.

Mitra, M.S. and Maharani of Baroda, 1984: *The Position of Women in Indian Life*. Neeraj Publishing House, Delhi.

Mourya, S.D. (Ed.), 1988: *Women in India: A Demographic Profile*, Chugh Publications, Allahabad.

Mitra, Ashok, 1979: *Implications of Declining Sex Ratio in India's Population*, Allied Publishers Pvt. Ltd., New Delhi.

Mehta, Rama, 1987: *Socio-Legal Status of Women in India*. Mithal Publications, Delhi.

Mukherjee, Ravindra Nath, 1985: *Bhartiya Samajik Sansthayam*, Vivek Prakashan, Delhi.

National Committee on Status of Women, 1974: *Towards Equality*, Govt. of India Publications.

Paul, Madan, Chandra, 1986: *Dowry and Position of Women in India*. Inter India Publications, New Delhi.

Rao, N.J. Usha, 1985: *Women in a Developing Society*: Ashish Publishing House, New Delhi.

Sriniwas, M.N. 1983: *Some Reflections on Dowry*. Oxford University Press, Delhi.

Stowell, Gordon and Mason, J. Edward, 1972. *The Book of Knowledge*. Vol. 4. The Waverley Book Company Ltd., London.

Sinha, Sachchidananda, Ramesh, p. 1984: *Women's Right : Myth and Reality*, Printwell Publishers, Jaipur.

Sharma, Kumud; Hussain, Sahaba and Saharya, Archana, 1984. *Women in Focus*. Sangam Books Pvt. Ltd., Hyderabad.

Subbamma, Malladi, 1985: *Women Tradition and Culture*, Sterling Publishing Pvt. Ltd., New Delhi.

Venkatarayappa, K.N., 1966: *Feminine Roles*, Popular Prakashan, Bombay.

Twenty Four

The Role of Scientific Research Work Conducted by the Women's Study Centres in Optimising the Efforts of Welfare Agencies

Immediately after the independence in 1947, Government of India launched various development programmes to bring a planned socio-economic change in the country. Along with raising the general standard of life, special emphasis was given to the upliftment of the neglected weaker sections of the society. A very big network of administrators and workers has been laid down from top to bottom level, that is, Central Government to village and a lot of money has been spent on various development programmes. Voluntary agencies are also being encouraged. While evaluating these development programmes, they get the criticism that considering the time, money and energy spent on them, they have not produced the satisfactory results and thus the desired targets could not be achieved. The obstacles are said to be the defective basis of planning, disequilibrium between the means and objectives, bureaucratic attitudes and complexity of procedure, lack of national character, conservatism and superstitions, illiteracy, lack of healthy leadership and peoples participation in the programmes. This shows that planning as well as the implementation of various development schemes is faulty. There is an increasing awareness that planners underestimated the role of values and cultural factors in Indian life. Their estimate of the width of cultural lag, i.e., the gap between the materialistic and non-materialistic culture, was not realistic. It is being felt that the development programmes should not be only target oriented but practical and the responsibility of the implementation should be left on the local workers who are themselves interested in development, wherever possible. It is also said that these schemes may be quite successful if the requirement of these schemes is felt by the sufferers and consequently communicated to the higher levels, rather than their thrusting upon the people by the authorities (Agrawal and Pandey: 1982).

Now coming to the women's development, although right from the beginning, constitutional and legal arrangements have been made for the equality between man and woman, but considering the poor results of these arrangements, Government of India has recently become exclusively conscious and active towards the upliftment of women in the country. It has encouraged the voluntary agencies to come forward for the purpose and quite a few International agencies are also showing interest towards this objective. The efforts from 1975 onwards, that is, the beginning of women's decade, have shown promising results in certain fields but at the same time certain hidden factors are also active in neutralizing the hopes and outcomes of these efforts. Hence there seems to be the requirement of some intermediaries between the agencies and women which can help in launching effective, coordinated and integrated programmes. The women's study centres can very well act as the intermediaries for the purpose. Considering the need of it the University Grant Commission has decided to involve academicians in the process by opening the women's study centres at the University level and the women's study cells at the college level. They can play a variety of roles at the planning as well as the implementation stage of the women's development schemes especially through the scientific research work.

Development is often associated with the economic development (Aziz, Hoong and Poh: 1984), although the mental and consequently the social development is equally important. Merely technical and economistic concept and programmes often produce the effects which are an antithesis of those hoped for. Therefore great care should be taken while planning the promotion of modernization and change along the lines which are truly edifying for the society, otherwise untrammelled and misdirected changes could tear off the very fabric of the Nation. Quaranta

(1984) has observed that different societies have different absorptive capacities to pose resistance to change. The development within a cultural context is never brought about unaccompanied by problems and challenges. Therefore, creative academicians are required to engage themselves in the development through grappling with and solving many problems posed by the developing process. The study of culture, which facilitates or resists the development and change helps the fulfilment of their responsibility. They can help the nation to achieve the desired targets.

Regarding the women's development, on the basis of the findings of scientific studies of the specific needs and problems of women of different set ups, the academicians connected with the women's study centres can be advisers to the policy makers. The information about the real perspective of the women's problems, alternative situations and a broader range of alternative actions to deal with them, can be provided to the concerned authority at the Government and the private sector. Evaluation of certain programmes can be done and needed changes in the policy or its implementation can be suggested for better results. Their practical and realistic view can keep a check on the most ambitious planning. They can also clarify the social objectives to the communities and create a public opinion in order to get their cooperation and active participation. Information based on the scientific research work about the hindrances in the path of women's development and the ways of removing them, will facilitate the authority of various agencies to take immediate action with confidence, so that the severe damages done by them in future, can be checked beforehand. The scientists connected with the women's study centres can even examine the functioning of various agencies within a particular social structure and advise how they can modify their perspective and rearrange their activities, if needed. A definite course of action, based on the scientific knowledge, derived through the experimental studies, can be suggested. The scientists, thus, can work as the social technicians in the process of women's self-awareness and self identification. They can perform very important roles of clearing away the prejudices and superstitions and thus making the jobs of Government or voluntary agencies easier.

As far as the welfare of the women is concerned, we have to be extremely cautious of the cultural factors of our society. It has to be seen that the rival group of male members of the society is not generated, in the reaction of unnecessary and avoidable criticism of them. Without hurting their male ego directly, we have to take their cooperation and support without which although the economic development can be achieved but not the mental and social ones. The success of the objectives regarding women's actual development depends, to a great extent, on the degree of acceptance of the modern values of social justice, equality, liberty, etc., felt and consequently the felt requirement of the schemes by the male members of the society. For the purpose, along with the awakening of the female section the male section of the society has also to be convinced against the exploitation of women and double standard, i.e., unequality between men and women prevailing in the society. Therefore, in the scientific studies only women are not to be studied but also the men in order to find out the realities so that an appropriate approach can be adopted for the purpose.

In this way the scientific research work conducted by the women's study centres can facilitate the proper functioning and thus optimizing the efforts of various agencies working for the development, welfare and defence of women.

References

Agarwal, G.K. and Pandey, S.S. 1983: *Gramin Samaj Shastra*, pp. 511-522, Agra Book Store, Agra.

Aziz Ungku A: Hoong; Yip., Yat.; Ling, Chu. 1984: 'Introduction', pp. XI - XIV in Technology, Culture and Development Seminar proceedings, University Press of Malaya, Kualalumpur.

Quaranta, Gian Carto, 1983: 'Resistance to Technology Transfer: Remarks on Cultural Dynamics,' pp. 348-361; in 'Technology, Cultural and Development,' Seminar proceedings, University Press of Malaya, Kualalumpur.

Bibliography

Antony, M.J. 1989: *Women's Rights*. Hind Pocket Books Private Limited, Delhi.

Agrawal, J.C. 1989: *Nayi Shikchha Neeti*. Prabhat Prakashan, Delhi.

Altekar, A.S. 1962: *The Position of Women in Hindu Civilization*. Motilal Banarasidas, Delhi.

Brilliant, Fredda, 1987: *Women in Power*. Lancer International, New Delhi.

Boston, Sarah, 1980: *Women Workers and Trade Unions*. Davis Poynter Ltd. London.

Boudreau, Frances, A. Sennott, Rogers, S. and Wilson, Michele. (Eds.) 1986: *Sex Roles and Social Patterns*. Praeger Publishers, New York.

Brijbhushan, Jamila, 1980: *Muslim Women in Purdah and out of it*. Vikas Publishing House Pvt. Ltd., Delhi.

Berk, Sarah Fenstermaker (Ed.) 1980. *Women and Household Labour*. Sage Publications, California.

Bhoite, Anuradha, 1987: *Women Employees and Rural Development*. Gyan Publishing House, New Delhi.

Bharat Ka Samvidhan, 1988: Vidi aur Nyaya Mantralaya, New Delhi.

Bhattacharya, Haridas (Ed.) 1956: *The Cultural Heritage of India*. The Ramkrishna Mission Institute of Culture, Calcutta.

Chatterji, Shoma, A. 1988: *The Indian Women's Search for an Identity*. Vikas Publishing House Pvt. Ltd, New Delhi.

Chapman, Jane, Robert (Ed.), *Economic Independence for Women*. Sage Publications, Washington.

Census of India, 1991: Provisional Population Totals.

Chattopadhayay, Kamla Devi, 1983: *Indian Women's Battle for Freedom*. Abhinav Publications, New Delhi.

Channa, Karuna (Ed.) 1988: *Socialization, Education and Women: Exploration in Gender Identity*. Orient Longman Ltd., Hyderabad.

Choudhary, Roop, L. 1961: *Hindu Women's Right to Property* Firma K.C. Mukhopadhyaya, Calcutta.

Dandiya, C.K. (Ed.) 1975: *Women in Rajasthan*, Rajasthan University Press, Jaipur.

Desai, Neera 1977: *Women in Modern India*. Vohra and Company Publishers Pvt. Ltd., Bombay.

Desai and Patel, Vibhuti, 1985: *Indian Women—Change and Challenge in the International Women Decade (1975-85)*. Popular Prakashan, Bombay.

Desai, 1986: Changing Status of Women: Policies and Problems, in Gupta, Amit, Kumar (Ed.): *Women and Society: The Developmental Perspective*. Criterion Publications, New Delhi.

Desai and Krishna Raj, Maithreyi, 1987: *Women and Society in India*. Ajanta Publications, New Delhi.

Desai, A.R. 1986: *Bharat Me Shahari Parivar aur Parivar Niyojan*. Delhi Vishwavidyalaya Press, Delhi.

Dak, T.M. (Ed.) 1988: *Women and Work in Indian Society*. Discovery Publishing House, Delhi.

Devi U. Lalita, 1982: *Status and Employment of Women in India*. B.R. Publishing Corporation, Delhi.

Dahlerup, Drude (Ed.) 1986: *The New Women's Movement*, Sage Publications, New Delhi.

Engineer, Asghar, Ali (Ed.) 1987: *Status of Women in Islam*, Ajanta Publications, Delhi.

Giriappa, S. 1988: *Role of Women in Rural Development*. Daya Publishing House, Delhi.

Ghurye, G.S. 1947. *Culture and Society*. As cited by Desai (1977) referenced above.

Ghosh, S.K. 1984: *Women in a Changing Society*. Ashish Publishing House, New Delhi.

Ghadially, Rehana (Ed.) 1988: *Women in Indian Society*, Sage Publications, New Delhi.

Gupta J.J. (Ed.) 1988: *Challenges of Fair Sex - Indian Women: problems, plights and progresses*. Gyan Publishing House, Delhi.

Gupta, Amit, Kumar (Ed.) 1986: *Women and Society: The Developmental Perspective*. Criterion Publications, New Delhi.

Gupta, A.R. 1982: *Women in Hindu Society*. Jyotsana Prakashan, New Delhi.

Govt. of India 1975: *Towards Equality* (Report of the Committee on the Status of Women in India). Ministry of Education and Social Welfare, New Delhi.

Hazra, R.C. 1940: *Studies in the Puranic Records on Hindu Rites and Customs.* As cited by Desai (1977) referenced above.

Hate, A Chandrakala. 1948: *Hindu Woman and Her Future,* New Book Co. Ltd., Bombay.

Hanawerker, W. Penn. 1989: *Women's Power and Social Revolution: Fertility Transition in West Indies.* Sage Publications, New Delhi.

Indra, 1955: *The Status of Women in Ancient India.* Motilal Banarasidas, Banaras.

Jacobson, Doranne and Wadley, Susans, 1986: *Women in India: Two Perspectives.* Manohar Publications, New Delhi.

Jain, Shashi 1988: *Status and Role Perception of Middle Class Women.* Puja Publications, New Delhi.

Jha, K.N. 1985: *Women Towards Modernization.* Janaki Prakashan, Patna.

Kaur, Inderjeet, 1983: *Status of Hindu Women in India.* Chugh Publications, Allahabad.

Khan Mumtaz. Ali and Aysha, Noor, 1982: *Status of Rural Women in India.* Uppal Publishing House, New Delhi.

Kidwai, Sheikh, M.H. 1978: *Woman Under Different Social and Religious Laws.* Light and Life Publishers, New Delhi.

Kuppuswamy B. 1990: *Social Change in India.* Konark Publishers Pvt. Ltd., Delhi.

Kumar, Manju 1982: *Social Equality: The Constitutional Experiment in India.* S. Chand and Co. Ltd., New Delhi.

Kaeley, S.L. and Khanna R.N. 1983: *Indian History and Culture.* Inter University Press (P) Ltd., Delhi.

Kulish, Karpoorchandra, 1975: 'Samaj Me Nari' in *Women in Rajasthan.* Edited by Dandiya C.K. Rajasthan University Press, Jaipur.

Kundra, D.N. 1990: *History of India and Contemporary World.* Goyal Brothers Prakashan. New Delhi.

Kapadia K.M., 1947: *The Hindu Kinship.* As cited by Desai (1977) referenced above.

Kapoor, Promila, 1970: *Marriage and the Working Women in India.* Vikas Publications, Delhi

Kapoor, Promila, 1976: *Kamkaji Bhartiya Nari*. Rajpal & Sons, Delhi.

Lott, Bernice, 1981: *Becoming a Woman* (The Socialization of Gender). Charles C. Thomas, Illionois, U.S.A.

Mishra, Laxmi, 1966: *Education of Women in India*. Mac Millan & Co. Ltd., Bombay.

Mishra, Urmila, Prakash, 1987: *Prachin Bharat Me Nari*. Madhya Pradesh Hindi Granth Akadami, Bhopal.

Mishra, Saraswati, 1993: Legal Justice to Women: Sociological Evaluation. *Social Welfare,* Vol. No. 11-12. Feb-Mar. pp. 12-14.

Mitra, M.S. and Maharani of Baroda, 1984: *The Position of Women in Indian Life*. Neeraj Publishing House, Delhi.

Maurya, S.D. (Ed.) 1988: *Women in India: A Demographic Profile*. Chugh Publications, Allahabad.

Mitra, Ashok, 1979: *Implications of Declining Sex Ratio in India's Population*. Allied Publishers Pvt. Ltd., New Dehli.

Majumdar, Veena (Ed.) 1979: *Symbols of Power*. Allied Publishers Pvt. Ltd., Bombay.

Majumdar, Veena (Ed.) 1983: *Women and Rural Transformation*. Concept Publishing Co., New Delhi.

Mair, Lucille, Mathurin. 1984: *International Women's Decade: A Balance Sheet*. Oxford University Press, Delhi.

Mathew, P.M. and Nair, M.S. 1986: *Women's Organizations and Women's Interests*. Ashish Publishing House, New Delhi.

Mehta, Rama, 1987: *Socio-Legal Status of Women in India*. Mittal Publications, Delhi.

Mathew, Sarah, H. 1979: *The Social World of Old Women: Management of Self Identity*. Sage Publications, London.

Mukerjee, Ravindra, Nath, 1985: *Bharatiya Samajik Sansthayen*. Vivek Prakashan, Delhi.

Madhavananda, Swami and Majumdar, Ramesh, Chandra, 1953: (Eds.): *Great Women of India*. Advaita Ashrama, Almora.

Mukerjee, Radhakamal, 1959: *The Culture and Art of India*. George Allen and Unwin Ltd., London.

Narayan, S. 1988: *Rural Development Through Women Programmes*. Inter India Publications, New Delhi.

Oak, A.W. 1988: *Status of Women in Education*. The Indian Publications, Ambala Cantt.

Pal, B.K. 1987: *Problems and Concerns of Indian Women,* ABC Publishing House, New Delhi.

Paul, Madan, Chandra, 1986: *Dowry and Position of Women in India*. Inter India Publications, New Delhi.

Pannikar, K.M. 1966: *Hindu Society at Cross Roads*. Asia Publishing House, Delhi.

Prasad, Ishwari, 1968: *History of Medieval India*, Indian Press Publication Pvt. Ltd., Allahabad.

Rao, N.J. Usha, 1985: *Women in a Developing Society*. Ashish Publishing House, New Delhi.

Reddy, Raghunath, 1986: *Changing Status of Educated Working Women*. B.R. Publishing Corporation, Delhi.

Reddy, G. Narayana and Reddy, Suma Narayana, 1987: *Women and Child Development (Some Contemporary Issues)*. Chugh Publications, Allahabad.

Rao, Prakash, V.V. and Rao V. Nandini, 1985: *Marriage, the Family and Women in India*. Heritage Publishers, New Delhi.

Rashtriya, Samiti, 1975: *Bharat Me Mahilaon Ki Sthiti*, Allied Publishers Pvt. Ltd., Bombay.

Raj, Krishna, Maithreyi, 1986: *Women's Studies in India: Some Perspectives*. Popular Prakashan Pvt. Ltd., Bombay.

Sri-Niwas, M.N., 1978: *Changing Status of Indian Women*. Oxford University Press, London.

Sri-Niwas, M.N. 1983: *Some Reflections on Dowry*, Oxford University Press, Delhi.

Scanzoni, John and Szinovacz, Maximiliane, 1984: *Family Decision Making: A Developmental Sex Role Model*, Vol. III, Sage Publications, London.

Savara, Meera, 1986: *Changing Trends in Women's Employment*. Himalaya Publishing House, Bombay.

Sinha, Pushpa, 1988: *Role conflict among the working women*. Janaki Prakashan, Patna.

Sharma, Premlata, 1988: *Rural Women is Education: A Study of Under- achievement*. Sterling Publishers Pvt. Ltd., New Delhi.

Sethi, Raj, Mohini, 1976: *Modernization of Working Women in Developing Countries*. National Publishing House, Delhi.

Shakeshaft, Charol, 1986: *Women in Educational Administration*. Sage Publications, California.

Shukla, Ramchandra, *Hindi Sahitya Ka Itihasa*, 1964: Nagari Pracharini Sabha, Kashi.

Stowell, Gordon and Mason, J. Edward, 1970: *The Book of Knowledge*, Vol. 4. The Waverley Book Company Ltd., London.

Sahay, S.N. 1985: *Women in Changing Society (Bibliographic Study)*. Mittal Publications, Delhi.

Singh, Rama, 1988: *Shikshit Mahilayen Avam Dharam. Aek Samajshastriya Vishlashan*. B.R. Publishing Corporation, Delhi.

Sinha, Sachchidananda, Ramesh, P. 1984: *Women's Rights: Myth and Reality*. Print Well Publishers, Jaipur.

Sharma, Kumud, Hussain, Sahba and Saharya, Archana, 1984: *Women in Focus*. Sangam Books Pvt. Ltd., Hyderabad.

Subbamma, Malladi, 1985: *Women: Tradition and Culture*, Sterling Publishing Pvt. Ltd., New Delhi.

Stead, Bette, Ann, 1985: *Women in Management*. Prentice Hall Inc. New Jersey.

Sharma, Suresh Chandra and Upadhyay, Rajendra (Eds.) 1987: *Bharat: Varshik Sandarbh Granth.* ' Suchana Va Prasaran Mantralaya Prakashan Vibhag, Delhi.

Tikoo, Prithvi Nath, 1985: *Indian Women*. B.R. Publishing Corporation, Delhi.

Vohra, Roopa and Sen, Arun, K. 1985: *Status, Education and Problems of Indian Women*. Akshat Publications, Delhi.

Venkatarayappa, K.N. 1966: *Feminine Roles*. Popular Prakashan, Bombay.

Young, Kate (Ed.) 1989: *Serving Two Masters: Third World Women in Development*. Allied Publishers Limited, New Delhi.

Yadav, Santosh, 1987: *Unniswi Va Bisawi Shatabdi Me Striyon Ki Sthiti*. Print Well Publishers, Jaipur.

Index